Brief Table of Contents

ETHICAL DECISION MAKING

IN SOCIAL WORK AND COUNSELLING

Pamela Miller   University of Calgary

ETHICAL DECISION MAKING

IN SOCIAL WORK AND COUNSELLING

A Problem/Inquiry-Based Approach

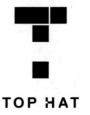

TOP HAT   **NELSON**

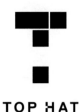

TOP HAT

Ethical Decision Making in Social Work and Counselling,

by Pamela Miller

Associate Vice President, Editorial Director:
Evelyn Veitch

Executive Editor:
Anne Williams

Marketing Manager:
Kevin Smulan

Developmental Editor:
Sandra Green

Senior Production Editor:
Bob Kohlmeier

Copy Editor:
James Leahy

Proofreader:
Sandra Braun

Indexer:
Dennis A. Mills

Production Coordinator:
Ferial Suleman

Design Director:
Ken Phipps

Interior-Design Modifications:
Katherine Strain

Cover Design:
Sasha Moroz

Cover Image:
Randy Olsen/National Geographic/Getty Images

Compositor:
Interactive Composition Corporation

Library and Archives Canada Cataloguing in Publication

Miller, Pamela, 1946–
Ethical decision making in social work and counselling : a problem/inquiry-based approach / Pamela Miller.

Includes bibliographical references and index.
ISBN 0-17-641527-0

1. Social service—Moral and ethical aspects. 2. Social workers—Professional ethics. 3. Counselors—Professional ethics. I. Title.

HV10.5.M54 2006   174'.9362
C2005-905423-9

Extended Table of Contents

Preface

The focus of this text on ethical decision making reflects the reality of practice in human services, where we are increasingly faced with complex and contentious issues that do not lend themselves to simple solutions. Part of the complexity arises from the deepening seriousness of questions, concerns, and problems service users present to us. We are also called on to play multiple roles as we engage in inter-professional practice with colleagues from a variety of allied professions. This all occurs within a context of conflicting directives from codes of ethics, legal requirements, often inadequate or limited organizational resources, and complex service user needs and expectations. To assist in learning how to respond in an ethically thoughtful manner in these circumstances, this text provides decision-making models, core concepts related to ethical practice, value clarification exercises, practice situations with inquiry questions and tasks to assist the reader to think through and become engaged with the ethical dimensions of the situations. We have also provided in the appendices the professional codes of ethics from Canadian and U.S. contexts for social work and counselling that are referred to in the text. These codes reflect the increasingly international and inter-professional context within which we practise as Canadians.

The practice situations and decision-making resources provided in this text are largely the result of work undergraduate and graduate students completed in my social work ethics courses over the past six years. I owe them much gratitude for sharing their practice experiences with the class and working with the concepts and decision models described in this text. The students provided a testing ground to try out and develop class material and teaching and learning processes to support learners in identifying and thinking through ethical dimensions of practice. Students have repeatedly told me that they thought they knew and understood professional codes of ethics, but after working with practice situations using an inquiry approach to ethical decision making they realized there was much more to ethical practice than simple application of directives in codes of ethics.

For the instructor who is examining this text as a possible foundation or guide in their teaching, I encourage you to think about it as a resource. Use it and adapt it to fit the context of your teaching by, for example, replacing or supplementing the practice situations in this text with ones that fit the communities and practice contexts your students are or will typically be engaged with. The text is structured so that questions and tasks that require the reader to search, apply, compare, and reflect are provided in an integrated manner throughout each of the chapters. This type of active learning is based on constructivist learning theory, which assumes that active engagement with concepts in relevant contexts is critical if the learner is to attain a deeper understanding of the meaning of concepts through application and reflection. At the same time, readers are called on to critically evaluate their values, priorities, and professional positions. After working through the active-learning, inquiry process in this text, readers should experience an increased level of confidence in their ability to both recognize and respond in a thoughtful and professional manner to the ethical dimensions of practice, especially in situations where the meaning of ethical practice is not transparent.

Whether you are an undergraduate or graduate student, a beginning or seasoned practitioner, I invite you to use this text in a way that is helpful to you in your professional development. The inquiry approach to learning used in this text calls on you to spend significant time performing a variety of learning tasks such as searching the Internet for specific types of information, reviewing professional codes of ethics, applying decision models, reflecting on your values and priorities, taking positions, and defending them. By taking the time to engage in these tasks, you will maximize the opportunity to learn and grow as a professional in your ability to engage in ethical decision making as an ongoing, dynamic dimension of your professional practice. I welcome your comments, as well as those of instructors, about how this text can be improved for future learners.

Acknowledgments

I owe a debt of gratitude to the students whose work helped shape this text, to my colleagues in the Faculty of Social Work, and to my partner, BJ Eib.

Thank you as well to the manuscript reviewers who took the time to give me feedback for improving initial drafts: Linda Fehr at the University of Calgary; Norm Garlie at Memorial University; Estelle Hopmeyer at McGill University; Terri McDade at St. Lawrence College; Andre McNamara at George Brown College; Sharon Mayne at the University of Guelph; and Lisa Shaw-Verhoek at Algonquin College.

Sandra Green, the developmental editor from Thomson Nelson, was consistently supportive and respectful as we worked on preparing this text for publication. I owe much to the quality of her work and direction.

Because a text is always a work in progress, I welcome your comments and suggestions for use in future editions.

About the Author

Pam Miller has an M.S.W. and two Ph.D.s, one in social work with a focus on organizational theory and higher education from Ohio State University, and the other in philosophy with a specialization in ethics from Indiana University. She has taught ethics at the University of Calgary's Faculty of Social Work since 1999 and is director of eLearning and distance education for the Faculty. She was elected president of the Alberta College of Social Workers for the 2005–2007 term.

Inquiry and Ethical Practice

ETHICAL PRACTICE

What is "ethical practice"? What does it mean to act "ethically" as a professional in a human service profession, such as social work or counselling psychology? Some reply that to act ethically means to practise according to the values of the profession, to act in a respectful manner toward the client, or to adhere to a profession's code of ethics. Others may mention an ethical obligation to follow legislation as it pertains to your practice. For example, if you are a professional practising in a child welfare context you are expected to keep current on child welfare legislation and report child abuse in accordance with the requirements of the legislation. While all of these replies at least partially define what it means to practise ethically, sometimes values clash or principles and standards in codes of ethics give vague or contradictory directives or they conflict with the law; in these cases, the professional must engage in a reflective process to reach a decision about how he or she "ought" to proceed. In practice situations such as these, where it is unclear what we "ought" to do, the professional must be able to deliberate about actions that go beyond adhering to a set of values, following directives and standards in a code of ethics, or even obeying the law. It is the ability to identify and think through these conflicts, issues, and concerns and come to a judgment based on sound reasoning, grounded in the ethical dimensions of the situation, that sets the professional apart as an "ethical practitioner." We are not minimizing the importance for ethical practice of knowing and following professional codes of ethics and relevant legislation when what "should" be done in practice is clear according to standards and guidelines and relevant legislation.

"HABIT OF MIND"

The focus of this book, however, is on the "habit of mind" that reflective practitioners require to both identify and grapple with practice situations that require ethical decision making—that is, situations in which the "right" course of action is not clearly apparent because ethical dilemmas are present or there are conflicts between principles and standards given in codes of ethics or between values, codes of ethics, and/or laws and organizational regulations. "Habits of mind" provide the "lens" through which we "look at the world" and interpret and develop responses to our experiences (Bruner, 1987).

While professional social work practitioners in Canada are the primary target audience for this book, given the impact of globalization, internationalization, and inter-professional contexts on professional practice, social work colleagues in other countries, as well as those in related professions, such as counselling and community development, will find the approach taken in this book helpful in their work in professional ethics. The book is designed to assist the reader in developing his or her own "lens" or habit of mind to recognize and respond effectively to the ethical dimensions of professional practice. To this end the reader is asked to reflect on and articulate his or her own personal values and principles. The reader is also asked to apply principles and standards from professional codes of ethics and use models of ethical decision making to come to a conclusion and give sound reasons for his or her choice in ethically contentious practice situations.

Although the Canadian Association of Social Workers' (CASW) *Code of Ethics* (2005a), along with its companion document, *Guidelines for Ethical Practice* (2005b), is the primary code of ethics used in this text, the U.S. National Association of Social Workers' (NASW) *Code of Ethics* (1999) is also referenced to demonstrate the commonalities and differences within the profession of social work in both countries. The two codes are in fact closely related: the acknowledgment section for the CASW *Code of Ethics* thanks the NASW "for permission to use sections of the copyrighted NASW 1999 *Code of Ethics* in the development of the CASW 2005 *Code of Ethics* and CASW 2005 Guidelines for Ethical practice." Although the unique multicultural context of Canada accounts for differences between the Canadian and U.S. codes of ethics, the core values of each are similar. Given the reality of globalization, readers are invited to include in their reflections professional codes of ethics from other countries, including the Australian Association of Social Workers *Code of Ethics,* which is also identified in the CASW acknowledgment section.

Given the inter-professional nature of service delivery in human services, the reader is also invited to examine codes of ethics of other professions. Within this context of inter-professional practice, the American Counseling Association's *Code of Ethics* (1995) will be referenced to provide an example of the similarities and differences in core values and principles between social work and another human service profession in North America.

Finally, the reader is also encouraged to compare professional codes of ethics, including alternative social work codes, such as feminist and Aboriginal social worker codes of ethics, to identify those with which they are comfortable as a way to come to a greater awareness of their own values and related principles as well as a deeper understanding of the Canadian Association of Social Work's *Code of Ethics.*

INQUIRY-BASED LEARNING

Inquiry-based learning is the dominant approach we use to help you be sensitive to and work effectively in ethically contentious practice situations. "Inquiry" is often defined as "a seeking for truth, information, or knowledge through questioning" (Barell, 1999). It is based on the assumption that the skills experts use in generating knowledge are similar to the ones that students must use to make sense of it. Both must form patterns in order to structure information so that it is most useful, accessible, transferable, and applicable to a variety of situations.

As professionals we are frequently called on to resolve "ill-formed" problems; that is, problems that have either too little or too much information. In the practice situations in this text you may determine that there is "too much" information or "too little," or that it is not of the quality or type you need. In addition to questions about quantity, quality, and type of information for decision making, we often have a relatively short time line in which to formulate the problem in meaningful terms; develop alternative approaches to addressing it while considering as many factors as possible, including ethical considerations; choose an approach or combination of approaches; implement the approach(es); evaluate and learn from the implementation; make any necessary modifications; and continue the work. This ability to make decisions in the face of uncertainty requires the "habit of mind" or lens that has the conceptual tools, skills, and attitudes that inquiry learning fosters—that is, involvement of the learner in her own education to acquire skills and attitudes that permit her to solve problems and resolve issues (Gardner, 1999).

The traditional approach to learning is primarily focused on the mastery of content, with less emphasis on the development of skills and practice of inquiry that would promote the development of meaningful questions and effective strategies for addressing them. Assessment is for the most part focused on the importance of identifying the "right answer." The inquiry approach we are using fits the ethically contentious and uncertain nature of the problematic practice situations we are asking you to work with. These require being able to come to an informed, reasoned judgment. Therefore the approach used in this text is focused more on working with content as a means to develop information-processing and problem-solving skills. Consequently, assessment in the approach to inquiry we are using should be focused more on determining how you have progressed in skills development, in addition to content understanding, with a particular emphasis on assessing application in authentic practice situations (Joyce, Weil, & Calhoun, 2000).

We have organized the work in this book to give you many opportunities to reflect on authentic practice situations; formulate questions; search for information; apply relevant concepts and decision models; analyze applications of concepts and formulations of problems and questions; identify when information is needed; search for relevant information; evaluate applications of concepts, models, and information; modify approaches; and start the process over, given what you have learned. You should become increasingly more responsible for generating meaningful questions and taking responsibility for your learning as we move through the chapters.

THE ROLE OF PRACTICE SITUATIONS

In this chapter we introduce the process of thinking through the ethical dimensions of a practice situation. In the following chapter we discuss core concepts that are helpful to have in your conceptual "toolkit" when considering ethical issues. Each chapter contains at least one practice situation for you to work with; some have two or more. The situations provide enough background so that you can determine the relevance of the information for decision making—that is, you decide whether you have enough, not enough, or too much information and assess the quality of the information provided for decision making.

After completing this chapter's practice situation, you will develop your own practice situation to either exchange with another student or work on your own.

The following practice situation concerns a boy who is reaching out to a school social worker who does not have organizational support to work with him without putting him through a formal assessment and diagnostic process. At the conclusion of this practice situation you will respond to questions put to you as if you were the professional working with the boy in this school.

Practice Situation: **Dan**

Dan is a thirteen-year-old grade 8 student attending Oakmont Junior High School. Dan has recently initiated voluntary, minimal contact with the school social worker. This contact began with Dan dropping by the worker's office when it was convenient or stopping to talk when he saw the worker in the hallway. The worker's contact with Dan has increased. Dan often comes to the social worker to discuss difficulties that he is experiencing at home and with his peers. Although contact has been minimal up to this point, Dan has started to develop trust and rapport with the social worker.

The social worker is employed by the school system to provide support and service to children who have been diagnosed with emotional or behavioural disorders, such as conduct disorders. Consequently, the social worker's mandate in this school setting does not support her contact with Dan because he has not been diagnosed with a disorder. Dan's teacher is unaware of Dan's contact with the social worker. Mr. Smith has requested several times that Dan be tested and assessed for behavioural disorders due to his disruptions in class and low academic achievement. The principal has asked for the social worker's assistance and professional opinion. The principal and teacher support a formal assessment for Dan. If a diagnosis is reached based on this assessment, and Dan is labelled with a disorder, the school receives additional funding for special needs and the social worker has formal sanction to meet and work with Dan. However, the worker is aware that labelling may have negative effects and the child may be put on medication. The worker believes that in certain situations, medication can be more for the benefit of the teacher than the child. The worker is also aware that there are additional environmental effects, such as conflicts at home, that may be influencing Dan's disruptive behaviour in class.

ETHICAL CONTEXT FOR DAN'S SITUATION

Dan's situation reveals several practice questions such as the impact of diagnosing Dan given the trust and rapport he currently enjoys with the social worker, along with practice considerations related to organizational policies and the funding context. When the professional takes into account the ethical dimensions of Dan's situation, the following ethical issue contributes to the complex set of factors the social worker needs to consider in arriving at a course of action:

> Potential conflict between professional obligation to focus on the needs of the individual and professional responsibility to follow organizational policies and objectives and budget concerns.

This is often a major source of conflict for school social workers as well as for social workers and related professionals in other settings. In Dan's situation, it would appear obvious that the worker is obligated to put the child's needs first as required by social work professional values and codes of ethics, but upon reflection the complexity of the issue becomes more apparent. In considering ethical dimensions of a practice situation, we need to consider the organizational context; relevant practice knowledge and research along with pertinent ethical principles; and, depending on the decision model we use, the consequences for those involved directly and indirectly in the situation.

Background Information

Employer/Organizational and Funding Context in Dan's Situation

Social workers in school settings potentially can provide a variety of services including crucial support services to students, which can be explored on this link: http://www23.hrdc-drhc.gc.ca/2001/e/groups/4152.shtml. However, limited budgets or financial decisions often undermine the ability of school social workers to provide these support services, which frequently are in high demand.

For example, although social workers perhaps should have the organizational sanction to work with every student in a school who requests services, a number of school social workers have a restricted sanction to provide services only to those students who have been diagnosed with emotional and behavioural disorders. A number of these schools have a policy that social workers only work with students who have a diagnosis for which the school receives provincial funding. In part this reflects budget constraints that limit the ability of schools to hire enough social workers to provide service to students who are not diagnosed. However, the restriction of services to students who have been identified as having "special needs" often creates a conflict for a school social worker due to the large number of students who request services but are not diagnosed and therefore not eligible to receive support services.

When schools are faced with budget constraints the response is frequently to prioritize programs so that some receive more funding than others. In addition to these budget constraints, provincial funding to schools for special-needs children frequently requires children to meet specific criteria before the funding is granted. If a child meets the criteria, she is categorically labelled and additional funding is granted for the school. An example of a clear process for funding services to special-needs students based on criteria can be found in Alberta and is clearly outlined in "Standards for Special Education, Amended June 2004," which can be accessed through this link: http://www.learning.gov.ab.ca/k_12/specialneeds/.

The potential negative consequences of diagnosing children in order to be able to provide services creates an ethical dilemma for many professionals. The dilemma arises out of the conflict between the necessity of testing, assessing, and labelling, and the potentially negative effects of this process on the child.

Example of Relevant Knowledge and Theory in Dan's Situation

As you work on practice situations such as Dan's, you will be called on to refer to and incorporate relevant research and theory to assist you in thinking through possible scenarios to arrive at a recommendation for a course of action. To use Dan's situation as an example, at least one area of research to include in our deliberations is the impact of labelling on self-concept and behaviour. There is a history of research that describes both the positive and negative consequences of labelling. Nadira Persaud (2000) found that before students were labelled they were eager and conformist, but after the labelling, their behavioural and educational achievement deteriorated. Gallagher (1976) provides a summary of both negative and positive findings about labelling and is referenced in an article by Riddick (2000), who examines the relationship between labelling and stigmatization, especially with regard to dyslexia and special-needs children. Two of the conclusions Riddick draws from the research on labelling and stereotyping is that we need a "careful deconstruction of the role of labeling" and that the "disabled" or special-needs children need "ownership" of the labelling process so that there is a "move towards self-definition with personal understanding and control" (p. 665). Thus the labelling/diagnostic process could have potential benefits depending on the social context.

Another related area of research we should examine when reflecting on Dan's situation is the reliability and validity of testing used to determine a diagnosis. Researchers have identified important questions and issues regarding the reliability and validity of many test results. In an interesting study on the identification and treatment of dyslexia, Reason and colleagues (1999) report that mistakes have been made by taking too narrow an approach to "diagnosing" dyslexia and argue for a multidisciplinary method that considers a range of factors influencing a child's performance in school. At the time of testing, for example, a child could simply be experiencing a range of issues which then affect her performance on a test. A misdiagnosis or mislabelling may have lasting effects throughout her educational experience. As a child continues her education, the results of the testing often follow her from one school to another. Teachers often know which children have a file and what their test results and diagnosis are. Even if the behaviours are alleviated and there are no existing areas of concern, the test results and diagnosis often stay in the child's education records.

Relevant Sections in Professional Codes of Ethics

Dan is making contact with the social worker and possibly seeking help to deal with the issues he is having at home and with peers. These issues may be a result or cause of some of the problems he is having in the classroom. However, as some of the literature on labelling states, labelling Dan could result in negative consequences and could lead to further disruptions in the classroom as well as further issues regarding his emotional well-being. As stated in the Canadian Association of Social Workers' (CASW) *Guidelines for Ethical Practice* (2005b): "Social workers maintain the best interests of clients as a priority, with due regard to the respective interests of others" (sec. 1.1.1). If the effects of labelling are going to cause more harm to Dan, is it in his best interests to proceed with testing that could result in a label and, perhaps worse, an incorrect label?

On the other hand, the social worker must also look at her responsibility to the school. As stated in the U.S. National Association of Social Workers (NASW) *Code of Ethics* (1999), "Social workers generally should adhere to commitments made to employers and employing organizations. Social workers should work to improve employing agencies' policies and procedures and the efficiency and effectiveness of their services" (sec. 3.09). Following these directives, the social worker could inform Dan of the limitations regarding her ability to provide appropriate and acceptable services. If the social worker, however, were to refer Dan to another professional or agency because of her inability to provide support, Dan may not access the new resource. He may feel disregarded and disheartened, which could result in further disruptions in the classroom. The social worker, following the same directives, could also feel ethically justified in voicing her concerns that requiring a recognized diagnosis for Dan before she is sanctioned to meet with him decreases her professional effectiveness and may decide to advocate for a change in policy. The CASW *Guidelines for Ethical Practice* (2005b) states that the social worker is obligated to advocate for workplace conditions that are in accord with ethical practice: "Social workers take all reasonable steps to ensure that employers are aware of their professional ethical obligations and advocate for conditions and policies that reflect ethical professional practice" (sec. 4.1.6). It is not always clear what it would mean to be "consistent with ethical practice" given the multiple responsibilities the social worker has in many situations, including Dan's, where the social worker has responsibilities to Dan, the school, and other professionals in the school.

For example, Dan's teacher may want testing done, not only to help him with the classroom disruptions, but also for the benefit of other students. The effects of integrating both streams of students, low- and high-achieving, can hinder the latter's success. In this case, if the teacher constantly stops the teaching process to reprimand Dan about his behaviour, the other students in the classroom may suffer academically from the disruptions.

The social worker then must take into consideration the well-being of the other students in the classroom. As stated in the CASW *Code of Ethics* (2005a), a core principle of social work practice related to the value of pursing social justice is that "social workers advocate for fair and equitable access to public services and benefits" (Value 2). One interpretation of this directive is that the social worker must take into account that a formal assessment and diagnosis of Dan may be beneficial not only to his fellow students, but also to Dan, as he may then receive services within the school. Another way to interpret the directive is that it supports the social worker in advocating for Dan to have access to services without a formal diagnosis.

INQUIRY PROJECT

Summary of Situation

The funding mandate from the province stipulates that a child must meet the criteria for special-needs children, and this requires that the child undergo testing and receive a diagnosis. If a child is not diagnosed as having a behavioural problem, learning deficit, or related issue that falls in one of the special-needs categories, the worker is directed not to enter into a professional relationship with the child but instead to focus on the children who are diagnosed as having special needs and for whom the school receives funding for professional services.

Further Information and Questions

Given what we have briefly described within the context of our beginning discussion of relevant literature and ethical issues, place yourself in this practice situation and take on the role of Dan's social worker. As the social worker, respond to the following:

Information-Related Tasks

- Identify further information, if any, you would want to review to inform your thinking about Dan's situation.
- Identify potential sources of the information.
- Think about how the information you access would affect your thinking about the ethical dimensions of this situation.

Related Ethical Questions

- What, at this point, are the primary ethical issues in this situation that for you would be particularly compelling, and which ones would be less compelling?
- What influenced you to arrive at this list of issues and your separation of them into more and less compelling?

CORE CONCEPTS

As we reflect on Dan's situation and the decisions the professional in this situation must grapple with, we have used practice-related concepts that are particular to this situation, such as labelling, diagnosis, and special needs. As we reflect on the ethical dimensions of the situation we need to have in our conceptual toolkit core ethical concepts that we can draw on in reflecting on ethical dilemmas, conflicts, and concerns in the decision process. Such a toolkit includes concepts such as professional and personal values, self-determination, confidentiality, dignity, and justice, among others. For the remainder of the chapter we will discuss in an introductory manner the concept of value so that we can begin to build a toolkit that will be important in our work of identifying and reflecting on ethical dimensions of contentious practice situations.

PROFESSIONAL VALUES AND PROFESSIONAL ETHICS

What do we mean by "values" when we talk about professional values and how do values relate to ethics, specifically professional ethics? It is not unusual to find confusion about the relation between values and ethics. Are those who can articulate their values and claim that values are important to them ethical? Values are apparent in our preferences as they are at the core of the criteria we use in making choices in friendships, employment opportunities, life partners, distribution of our resources, and so forth. Knowing and understanding your own values and the values of the professional association you are a member of or strive to be a member of is a critical step in developing a framework for thinking about practice from an ethical perspective. While this understanding is necessary, it is not sufficient for the sensitivity and thought processes required for thinking through the ethical dimensions of practice situations.

REFLECTION QUESTIONS—IDENTIFY AND REFLECT ON PERSONAL VALUES

Take a few minutes and use the following questions to reflect on what is important for you:

- Can you think of two or three people in your life who display values you think are important?
- Why do you think those values are important?
- Would others view these people as highly as you do? Why or why not?

Continue to reflect on your personal values as we work on core concepts, codes of ethics, and decision-making models. You will find further opportunities to examine your values using tools we give you in the book. We will also ask you to find or create meaningful ways to continue to be self-reflective beyond your work in this book.

When we examine the value base of a profession such as social work, it is helpful to conceptualize it so that we can reflect on how professional values influence both the choices we make and our behaviour. Mullaly (1997) invites us to conceptualize professional values as residing on two levels: fundamental values, which relate to ideals or goals, and instrumental values, which relate to the means for achieving the first-level values.

In examining Dan's situation we have referenced both the NASW *Code of Ethics* (1999) and the CASW *Code of Ethics* (2005a) in part to show indirectly the agreement between the two social work associations in terms of core values, ethical principles, and standards as they apply to the ethical issues faced by the school social worker. Both the CASW and NASW codes advocate humanism and egalitarianism, which are themes present throughout the description of principles and standards in the codes.

INQUIRY QUESTIONS

- What do the concepts humanism and egalitarianism mean?
- How are they present in the two codes?

The CASW and NASW codes also share common instrumental or secondary values for practising in a humanistic and egalitarian manner. An example of a core instrumental value that is central in both codes is the obligation to practise in a manner that respects client self-determination and shows acceptance of the client.

INQUIRY QUESTIONS

- In what sections is the instrumental value of client self-determination to be found in each code?
- Is it discussed in similar ways in both codes or are there significant differences between the codes? If the latter, what are these differences?
- Are there any other instrumental values in the codes that are similar or different? What are they and why are they important?

It is important to note that while the two North American social work professional associations have a common core of fundamental and instrumental values, there are differences between the codes. When comparing them, notice that they differ in how they are structured and in the degree of development and detail in how they describe values, principles, and standards. The CASW *Guidelines for Ethical Practice* (2005b), for example, contains eight statements that apply the values and principles in the CASW *Code of Ethics* (2005a) to common areas of social work practice. The responsibilities are not "intended to be exhaustive or entirely prescriptive," and the extent to which they are "enforceable" is left to the judgment of the individual social worker and to the provincial/territorial regulatory body or professional association within which the social worker practises. The core responsibilities are to: clients, professional relationships, colleagues, workplace, private practice, research, profession, and society.

The NASW *Code of Ethics* (1999) is organized into six standards covering the areas of social workers' ethical responsibilities to clients, to colleagues, in practice settings, as professionals, to the profession, and to broader society.

INQUIRY QUESTIONS

- Compare the two codes (CASW and NASW) and identify the one with which you feel most comfortable.
- Why have you chosen that code?
- Is there any other code of ethics beside CASW or NASW that you identify with? What is it?
- Do you notice any omissions in the code you identified above? If yes, what are the omissions and how would you have written the code differently?
- Search the Internet for other professional or interest-group codes of ethics. Choose one that is meaningful to you and reflect on how it is similar to or different from CASW or NASW.

There are two major criticisms of professional codes of ethics. One is that they are too abstract, which it is claimed diminishes their usefulness as guides for action (Reamer, 1998). The other criticism is that the categories in codes tend to overlap and do not match well with the ethical issues with which professionals are faced (Freud & Krug, 2002). Keep these criticisms in mind as we work on practice situations in the book and take note of whether you think the criticisms are justified.

Practice Situation: **Your Story**

Using Dan's case study, think of a practice situation you have experienced that was particularly engaging: you may have been a service user, professional, volunteer, or practicum student. If you have not experienced a practice situation or at least one that has engaged you, then think of one you have read about or create one that includes issues about delivery of services about which you are genuinely concerned. The practice situation you describe should involve some complexity in terms of the issues, problems, and access to human services faced by the service users as well as difficult choices and conflicts for the professional(s) involved.

INQUIRY PROJECT

- Describe your practice situation in some detail, including the context, the people involved, and their roles—for example, service users, professionals, relatives, or neighbours. Your description should be at least one typed page, double-spaced.
- Describe what you think were important issues, questions, conflicts, or difficult choices faced by the participants. This can be integrated with the previous description of context or provided after that description. It should be at least one-half page, typed, and double-spaced. The final overall

description including context, participants, human-service needs, with issues, conflicts, and so on should be at least one and a half pages, double-spaced.

Exchange your story with another student in the class and place yourself in the position of a professional in the practice situation described by the other student. If you cannot exchange your story with another student then place yourself in your story as a professional. (If you are already in the story as a professional then proceed to describe either what you actually did or what you would have done now that you are looking back at the situation.) Write down your responses to the following for your practice situation (story) or that of another student:

Information Tasks

- As a professional in the situation, identify what core issues you would face, if they were different from or in addition to what has already been identified. Describe the professional role you are taking in the situation.
- Consider how you would think through the issues given your professional role.
- What further information would you need to come to a decision? From what sources would you obtain this information?
- How do you think this information would affect your decision process?

Questions Related to Ethical Issues

- Identify the core ethical issues and reflect on how you would prioritize them.
- Refer to a professional code of ethics that you identify with, such as the CASW *Code of Ethics,* and find at least three clauses in the code or accompanying guidelines for practice that relate to the issues you have identified.
- Are the code and/or guidelines helpful in giving you direction?
- Do you find conflicts in the directions you are given in the code?

CONCLUSION

In this chapter we have provided an overview of an inquiry approach to learning. We have chosen this approach, within a context of examining practice situations, to assist you in your development as an ethical practitioner. We argue that a "habit of mind" is useful in situations where professional judgment is required. Core aspects of this habit of mind include: developing inquiry skills and attitudes for identifying ethical issues in practice, framing meaningful questions, developing a strategy to address those questions, and implementing the strategy. In our discussion of the CASW *Code of Ethics* we have highlighted the multicultural context of Canadian society as well as the reality of globalization and internationalism and, finally, the inter-professional context of social work practice.

Work on values is central to an understanding of ethical practice. For that reason we began our discussion of values and ethics with a discussion of the relation of personal values and professional values. The focus on values is continued in Chapter 2 and is particularly emphasized in Chapter 3, where both individual and group-based value clarification exercises are provided. In addition to the ongoing focus on values and professional codes of ethics, Chapter 2 describes the relation of ethics to law in order to deepen awareness about the nature and role of professional ethics in practice. In particular, it focuses on models of ethical decision making that provide conceptual frameworks for thinking through and responding to the type of questions about ethical issues introduced in this chapter. As you work through the inquiry questions in these chapters you are challenged to delve deeper into the meaning of ethical practice.

NOTES

NOTES

NOTES

NOTES

NOTES

_____

_____

_____

_____

_____

_____

_____

_____

_____

_____

_____

_____

_____

_____

_____

NOTES

_____

_____

_____

_____

_____

_____

_____

_____

_____

_____

_____

_____

_____

_____

_____

REFERENCES

Calgary Rocky View Child and Family Services. (2003). *Alberta response model.* Retrieved November 2, 2003, from http://www.child.gov.ab.ca/whatwedo/albertaresponse/pdf/factsheet1.pdf

American Counseling Association. (1995). *Code of ethics and standards of practice.* Alexandria, VA: author.

Ausubel, D.P. (1968). *Educational psychology: A cognitive view.* New York: Holt, Rinehart, and Winston.

Barell, John. (1999). *PBL: An inquiry approach.* Arlington Heights, IL: Skylight Training and Publishing.

Bloom, Lynn Z., & White, Edward M. (Eds.). (1993). *Inquiry: A cross-curriculum reader.* Englewood Cliffs, NJ: Prentice-Hall.

Bransford, John, Brown, Ann, & Cocking, Rodney (Eds.). (1999). *How people learn.* National Research Council, Washington, DC: National Academy Press.

Bruner, Jerome. (1987). *Actual minds, possible words.* Cambridge, MA: Harvard University Press.

Canadian Association of Social Workers. (2005a). *Code of ethics.* Ottawa: Author.

Canadian Association of Social Workers. (2005b). *Guidelines for ethical practice.* Ottawa: Author.

Christensen, Carole P. (2003). Canadian society: Social policy and ethno-racial diversity. In Alean Al-Krenawi & J. Graham (Eds.), *Multicultural social work in Canada: Working with diverse ethno-racial communities* (pp. 251–282). Don Mills, ON: Oxford University Press.

Freud, Sophie, & Krug, Stefan. (2002). Beyond the code of ethics, Part I: Complexities of ethical decision making in social work practice. *Families in Society, 83,* 474–482.

Freud, Sophie, & Krug, Stefan. (2002). Beyond the code of ethics, Part II: Relationships revisited. *Families in Society, 83,* 483–492.

Gallagher, J.J. (1976). The sacred and profane uses of labels. *Exceptional Children, 45,* 3–7.

Gardner, Howard. (1983). *Frames of mind: The theory of multiple intelligences.* New York: Basic Books.

Gardner, Howard. (1999). *The disciplined mind.* New York: Simon and Schuster.

Hurdle, D.E. (2002). Native Hawaiian traditional healing: Culturally based interventions for social work practice. *Social Work 47*(2), 183–192.

Joyce, Bruce, & Weil, Marsha, with Emily Calhoun. (2000). *Models of teaching.* Needham Heights, MA: Allyn & Bacon.

Lecca, P.J., Quervalu, I., Nunes, J.V., & Gonzales, H.F. (1998). *Cultural competency in health, social, and human services: Directions for the twenty-first century.* New York: Garland Publishing.

Mullaly, R. (1997). *Structural social work: Ideology, theory and practice* (2nd ed.). Oxford: Oxford University Press.

National Association of Social Workers. (1999). *National Association of Social Workers code of ethics.* Washington, DC: Author.

Persaud, Nadira. (2000). Labeling: Its effects on labeled students. Paper presented at International Special Education Conference, University of Manchester, July. Retrieved March 2004 from http://www.isec2000.org.uk/abstracts/papers_p/persaud_1.htm

Reamer, F.G. (1998). *Ethical standards in social work: A review of the NASW code of ethics.* Washington, DC: NASW Press.

Reason, R,. Frederickson, N., Heffernan, M., Martin, C., & Woods, K. (1999). Dyslexia, literacy and psychological assessment. *Report by a working party of the division of educational and child psychology of the British Psychological Society.* Leicester: The British Psychological Society.

Riddick, Barbara. (2000). An examination of the relationship between labelling and stigmatisation with special reference to dyslexia. *Disability and Society, 15,* 653–667 http://www.ingentaconnect.com/content/routledge/cdso/2000/00000015/00000004/art00007

chapter

Law, Ethics, and Tools for Rational Decision Making

In Chapter 1 we began to examine some critical concepts in ethics by discussing the notion of values, specifically professional values. In this chapter we will extend our discussion of the relation of values to ethics and examine how law is related to ethical codes. We will conclude the chapter by presenting frameworks for thinking through ethical issues to assist you in arriving at sound judgments.

ETHICS AND VALUES

"What is the right action in this situation?" "What does this situation require of me given the value base of my profession?" These are the types of questions we raise when we are concerned with ethical issues in a practice situation. They differ from questions about effective ways to proceed or questions typically focused on practice issues. It is frequently difficult to separate ethical from practice issues. For example, if a couple with three children refuses to relate to a worker in a family service program who recommends family therapy, this may be identified as an issue of "resistance." On the other hand, it may also be viewed as an ethical issue involving client or service user self-determination and professional respect for diversity versus the worker's view of "best interest" for the family. Suppose the worker and his supervisor step back from the situation and determine that while the worker, based on his work with other families, believes that it is in the "best interest" of the family to participate in therapy together as a unit; the parents, on the other hand, disagree based on cultural reasons. The couple's refusal to relate to the worker can now be viewed as a more complex issue involving ethical considerations rather than solely as a problem of "resistance" on their part. Examining the disagreement through the lens of who defines "best interest," we see that client self-determination and respect for diversity introduce ethical dimensions of practice into the decision process.

Professional codes of ethics provide guides for dealing with questions about "right" and "wrong" conduct and such issues as who decides "best interest" and how conflicts between client self-determination and best interest should be resolved. However, as we started to discuss in Chapter 1, though codes of ethics reflect agreement among some members of a profession as to what behaviour is right and wrong in terms of agreed-on, normative values, they fall short in providing enough detail to be able to prescribe the behaviour of members in all situations.

Practice Situation: **Diab**

Keep the following questions in mind the as you read Diab's situation.

- If you were the professional working with Diab, what further information/research would you want to pursue and why would you need this information?
- Are there questions that have not been raised in the description of the situation that you think should be asked? Why do you think these questions are important?
- Do you agree with the decision the professional arrived at in working with Diab or would you have acted differently? Think about how you would justify your decision.

Diab, age six, is involved in a children's recreational program at a local family resource centre. The program is offered through the summer months to provide opportunities for children to have fun in a safe and creative environment. The program was also developed to provide respite care for parents and is offered free of charge to families receiving social assistance. A social work student, who is supervised by the community centre director, runs the program.

One morning when the group is preparing to go on an outing, Diab and his mother arrive visibly upset. After his mother leaves, Diab announces to the worker that his father slapped him because he was dawdling and goes on to say that this happens "a lot." Diab asks the worker to talk to his mother but not to "tell anyone else." The resource centre also offers services to families such as a stay-and-play program, individual and family counselling, and a mentoring program for teens. The worker has had considerable contact with Diab's family as his mother and younger sister have participated in the stay-and-play program. The worker has on occasion provided the mother with resources, information, and referrals for services but has not had contact with the father.

BACKGROUND INFORMATION

As we noted in Dan's situation in Chapter 1, when working on a practice situation for which the direction is not clear, you should research background information pertinent to the situation and read applicable sections of your professional code of ethics. It is also important to include culturally relevant information that affects how you interpret both relevant practice and ethical issues. In Diab's situation, his parents immigrated from Iran two years ago and his father has found it difficult to find a job in his area of expertise, which is engineering, as his education credentials are not recognized in Canada. He drives a cab during the day and is starting as a part-time university student to work toward a degree.

The worker in Diab's case examined information about child abuse and also read about professional obligations related to protection of confidential information. For the cultural content the worker relied on advice from colleagues who she felt were knowledgeable about Iranian society and culture.

CHILD ABUSE

Child abuse is a prevalent social issue in Canada. According to Alberta Child and Family Services (2002), physical abuse is defined as

> the intentional use of force on any part of a child's body that results in serious injuries. It may be a single incident, a series or pattern of incidents. The Criminal Code states that physical force cannot be used on children unless the force used is "reasonable" and has been used for "corrective purposes" by a parent or someone acting in the role of parent.

The literature clearly states that it is important for professionals to respect their obligation to report child abuse and that there are both legal and professional sanctions for failing to report. According to Beauchamp and Childress's (2001) principle of beneficence, it is not sufficient to simply do no harm—there is an additional ethical obligation to actively pursue the welfare of others. The authors feel that, while it is important to adhere to legal and ethical standards, it is equally important to recognize the intrinsic value, worth, and uniqueness of all individuals. Through this lens, the professional sees the importance of weighing all known factors in any given situation as a means to honour the needs of clients while operating within the guidelines of a profession's code of ethics.

Questions about Child Abuse

Find the literature that clarifies for you the professional obligation to report child abuse and locate the relevant child welfare legislation that defines child abuse and reporting obligations for your province. Does the fact that Diab and his family are recent immigrants affect your inquiry? If yes, explain and describe the information you would be interested in. Also indicate from what sources you would locate this information.

Confidentiality

In the area of confidentiality, the Canadian Association of Social Workers (CASW) *Code of Ethics* (2005a) states that

> a cornerstone of professional social work relationships is confidentiality with respect to all matters associated with professional services to clients. Social workers demonstrate respect for the trust and confidence placed in them by clients, communities and other professionals by protecting the privacy of client information and respecting the client's right to control when or whether this information will be shared with third parties. (Value 5)

The CASW *Code of Ethics* companion document, *Guidelines for Ethical Practice* (2005b), makes it clear that the worker is obligated to look after the "best interests" of the client: "Social workers maintain the best interests of clients as a priority, with due regard to the respective interests of others" (sec. 1.1.1).

One of the questions the worker in Diab's situation poses is: "What does 'best interests' mean for Diab in this situation?" Since every set of circumstances is unique, the worker realizes that she needs to carefully consider her decision and its impact on Diab, his mother, their relationship, and her relationship with the father.

In reviewing the literature, the professional notes that ethical issues about reporting abuse and confidentiality are complex. Schultz (1990) reports that "most therapists, whatever their discipline, agree that breaking confidentiality creates significant problems." He continues by saying, "the ethical codes of the various helping professions are intentionally vague, general and elastic to cover all types of situations, but all take confidentiality very seriously."

The Professional's Decision

After thinking about the definition of child abuse, the relevant sections in the CASW *Code of Ethics,* her professional obligations, and the ethical issues related to abuse and reporting, the professional decides to assure Diab that she wants to help him and his family but that, in order to do this, she needs to get help from others.

She then decides to meet with Diab's mother and explain that as a social worker and in light of her conversation with Diab, she is obligated to contact Child and Family Services. The worker, because of her prolonged contact with the family, feels she has a good rapport with Diab's mother. She knows that Diab's mother has been forthcoming in the past about her need for assistance in dealing with financial stress as well as behavioural and emotional issues she has faced with Diab. The worker hopes that while talking with Diab's mother she can provide information about the function of Child and Family Services and highlight the positive support they may be able to provide. The worker wants to continue to support the whole family through the provision of services and feels that while the situation is awkward, she needs to be honest with Diab's mother. By using this approach the worker feels she is also honouring Diab's request to speak with his mother and at the same time will be fulfilling her obligation to report suspected child abuse. In regard to disclosure, the CASW *Guidelines for Ethical Practice* (2005b) states:

> Social workers discuss with clients the nature of confidentiality and limitations of clients' right to confidentiality at the earliest opportunity in their relationship. Social workers review with clients when disclosure of confidential information may be legally or ethically required. Further discussion of confidentiality may be needed throughout the course of the relationship. (sec. 1.5.1)

 INQUIRY QUESTIONS REVISITED

Take a moment to respond to the inquiry questions posed at the beginning of the discussion about Diab's situation. What do your responses at this point tell you about professional practice and the role of information, culture, values, and ethics in practice? Now consider the questions posed at the beginning of this practice situation:

- If you were the professional working with Diab, what further information/research would you want to pursue and why would you need this information?
- Are there questions that have not been raised in the description of the situation that you think should be asked? Why do you think these questions are important?
- Do you agree with the decision the professional arrived at in working with Diab or would you have acted differently? Think about how you would justify your decision.

LAW AND ETHICS

Laws, which include legislation, court decisions, and regulations, have, according to Dickson (1998), had an increasing impact on professional practice in human services. Bergantino (1996) claims that the greater presence of law in human services has created a climate in which practitioners are concerned more about personal liability than client welfare (p. 31). Whether this is in fact the case, it is important for the professional to include in deliberations about issues in practice situations an inquiry about relevant directives in laws. Generally, laws support ethical practice, but adhering to the law does not always result in ethical practice.

As we saw in Diab's situation, legal mandates to perform certain functions, such as reporting child abuse, have significant influences on practice decisions. Professionals who are sensitive to cultural variations among client groups may be caught in a dilemma when faced with laws that do not take into account differences in cultural practices and professional codes of ethics that call on the professional to respect cultural practices and advocate for the best interests of their clients. When our notion of what is ethical does not agree with laws and regulations it becomes even more important for the practitioner to be clear about the laws involved and the consequences of not following the law. Although codes of ethics provide guidelines for practice decisions, unlike laws, they are not binding unless they are incorporated into law. Professionals can be sanctioned by their professional associations for not adhering to the association's code of ethics, the consequences of which range in severity from reprimands, fines, and suspension, to being denied the right to practise. These professional sanctions, however, do not necessarily lead to legal action. Laws that regulate professional behaviour are often based on professional codes, and the development of laws regulating professional behaviour has encouraged professions to revisit their ethical codes to increase clarity and specificity.

Informed consent, privileged communication, and confidentiality are examples of practice issues discussed in professional codes of ethics and also found in legal documents defining the rights of clients and practitioners along with the rights and responsibilities of professionals.

The landmark legal decision in the *Tarasoff v. Regents of the University of California* (1976) court case caused many human service professions to specify in their codes of ethics the professional obligations to potential victims of dangerous clients. The courts decided in that case that there is a duty to warn and protect an identifiable and foreseeable victim. The case focused on Posenjit Poddar, the defendant charged with the 1969 killing of Tatiana Tarasoff. Two months prior to the murder, Poddar confided his intention to kill Tatiana to a psychologist employed by the University of California at Berkeley. Although the psychologist had Poddar detained by the campus police, Poddar was later released. Neither the psychologist nor the campus police warned Tatiana of the potential danger to her life. The courts concluded that

> public policy favoring protection of the confidential character of [client], psychotherapist communication must yield to the extent to which disclosure is essential to avert dangers to others. The protective privilege ends where the public peril begins. (*Tarasoff,* 131 Cal.Rptr.at27)

Although there is a clear and direct relation between the directives in laws and ethical practice, they are not synonymous, and in fact on occasion they can be in conflict. A practitioner's decisions can be unethical but not illegal. Treating people in a wrongful manner is not ethically right even when required or sanctioned by law. Failure to inform a client of the limits of confidentiality or how confidential information might be used may not be unlawful but it is unethical according to most professional codes of ethics in human services. The reverse is also possible: a practitioner's actions may be unlawful but ethical in terms of a profession's codes of ethics. For example, the ethical duty to disclose information to protect a third party may lead the practitioner to disclose a client's HIV-positive status to his or her partner, even though it is illegal to disclose such information in some jurisdictions. A third possible conflict is for the practitioner to decide for ethical reasons not to perform as required by legal regulations. For example, suppose the worker in Dan's situation in Chapter 1 decides not to put Dan through a diagnostic process and to continue meeting with him without telling her supervisor, which is in violation of the province's funding requirements for the school. The worker in this case comes to this decision after determining that the "best interests" of the client take precedence over the funding regulations set by the province and the employer's regulation concerning which students she is to work with. Another worker may come to a different decision based on his own decision process. Both positions may be supported by sound ethical reasoning.

It is important therefore to know the relevant law in your area of practice, but it is just as important to know how to think through situations where legal requirements, codes of ethics, your own values and principles, and perhaps the client's values and cultural practices are in conflict. The next section will provide an outline of major approaches for thinking through ethical issues.

ETHICAL DECISION MAKING

The automatic application of arbitrary rules is not ethical decision making. To be involved in authentic decision making means deliberating about a number of options in a contentious practice situation, each option having both negative and positive elements. In these contexts, the professional enters into a process of assessing and weighing conflicting principles, values and interests, and, depending on his or her ethical framework, consequences.

Many practitioners are not fully aware of the criteria or reasons for the choices they make, but the extent to which we become aware of the basis of our decisions enables us to improve our ability to provide sound rationales and evaluations of our professional judgments. To this end we need to continually reflect on the values and interests we bring to our work as professionals and use an inquiry approach to asking questions and seeking relevant information to inform our process of choosing a course of action.

CORE ELEMENTS OF ETHICAL DECISION MAKING FOR CHOOSING A COURSE OF ACTION

As you review the models of ethical decision making provided in this section, note that the core elements of any framework for choosing a course of action include

- having "real" options that are in contention, one or more of which the professional must choose;
- identifying goals, values, and interests;
- developing key questions to direct information gathering;
- devising an information-gathering strategy (Where will you get the information? How? When? In what form?);
- gathering and assessing information;
- developing criteria to decide on a course of action;
- assessing each option and selecting an option(s);
- implementing the course of action;
- evaluating the implementation; and
- using what has been learned about implementation to adjust actions and decision making.

When elements such as these are listed in "problem-solving" or "decision-making" models we often think of the professional as progressing through them in a sequential manner. Practice, however, is a dynamic process that requires flexibility in terms of information available, time constraints, resources, policy directives, staffing changes, and client issues. In order to be effective, we must minimize irrational, impulsive, and unplanned choices but at the same time allow for creative application of the core elements of decision making. In this way we are able to take a reflective, rational approach to our decision making and respond to new developments that might be beneficial to our deliberations.

Before you start to review ethical decision-making models, it is important to note that how we use decision models in part depends on what options we perceive are available to us, and that is often affected by our values, creativity, energy, and determination. For example, if the worker in Dan's situation perceives she does not have the option of working with Dan without a formal assessment and diagnostic process, then this is not an option in her deliberations. If, however, she embarks on a fact-finding effort to determine if the policies in question give her more flexibility than what appeared at first, she has not closed off the possibility that she could still work with Dan without a prior assessment. If she decides that, regardless of policy, she should consider working with Dan without a formal assessment and diagnosis, then this becomes an option that will influence questions she develops for information-gathering about the consequences, for her and her clients, of going against policy.

MODELS OF ETHICAL DECISION MAKING

Each of the approaches to ethical decision making that we will now examine explicitly or implicitly includes the core elements of decision making. They differ in terms of what primary ethical consideration is the focus in the decision process. This in part reflects the ethical theory underlying the approach. Two general categories of ethical theories that are relevant to professional practice are ethical absolutism and ethical relativism. Ethical absolutism argues that "good" or "right" is determined by principles or moral rules that prescribe which actions are ethically justified, apart from any consideration of consequences. The validation or authority for moral rules or principles may be religious texts, social contracts, natural laws, duties, legislation, professional bodies, and so on.

Ethical relativism, by contrast, claims that "good" or "right" depends on context. A professional is justified in choosing an option by the results that will ensue versus the results that will come from choosing another option or set of options. Teleological or consequentialist theories fall under the ethical relativist category and are based on some form of utilitarianism, which considers the "greatest good for the greatest number" or the calculation of a cost and benefit ratio as justification for choices. Using these broad categories to classify examples of ethical decision-making models in social work, we come up with the frameworks for comparing the two main approaches, presented in Figure 2.1.

Figure 2.1 ▼ Comparing Frameworks

Ethical Absolutist Frameworks	Ethical Relativist Frameworks
Ethical Principles Screen	ETHIC Model
Hierarchy of Duties and Rights	Tracking Harms Model
Bioethics Principle and Rules Model	Ethical Problem-Solving Model

Ethical Principles Screen Framework

The decision framework developed by Dolgoff, Loewenberg, and Harrington (2005) is a two-step process. The first step involves assessing the situation through an "ethical rules screen (ERS)," which consists of examining relevant professional codes of ethics to determine if any of the principles, standards, or rules in the codes apply; if they do, they take precedence over the professional's preferences if there is a conflict between them. The professional is directed to follow the directives of the principles, standards, or rules in the relevant code of ethics, thus concluding the decision process. If no directives in the codes apply or if the directives provide conflicting guidance, the professional is directed to move to the second step and use the "ethical principles screen (EPS)" (see Figure 2.2) which is a rank ordering of

Figure 2.2 ▼ The Ethical Principles Screen (EPS)

Ethical Principle 1	Principle of the protection of life
Ethical Principle 2	Principle of equality and inequality
Ethical Principle 3	Principle of autonomy and freedom
Ethical Principle 4	Principle of least harm
Ethical Principle 5	Principle of quality of life
Ethical Principle 6	Principle of privacy and confidentiality
Ethical Principle 7	Principle of truthfulness and full disclosure

The professional is directed to choose according to the operating principle that the satisfaction of the higher-order principle takes precedence over the satisfaction of the lower-order principle. Protection of life, for example, takes precedence over least harm and least harm takes precedence over privacy and confidentiality.

seven ethical principles developed by Dolgoff and colleagues on the basis of their perceptions of what could be a consensus among social workers (p. 65).

**Reflection
Questions ?** ## REFLECTION QUESTIONS

- Do you see any benefit in using the ethical principles screen framework in any of the situations we have examined at this point?
- For which of the situations (Dan, Diab, your practice situation) would you use this framework and how would you use it?
- If you would not use this framework, what are your reasons for not using it?

Hierarchy of Ethical Duties and Rights

Gewirth's (1978) hierarchy of duties and rights, as adopted by Frederic Reamer (1999), is similar to EPS in that it provides a rank ordering of duties and rights comparable to the process of determining principles for decision making. A major difference between the two is Gewirth's focus on the fundamental rights of all persons to freedom and well-being and his identification of the "core goods" that enable or enhance these rights. The core goods include *basic goods,* necessary to well-being, such as food and shelter; "*nonsubstractive goods,*" such as honesty and fidelity in relationships, the loss of which would compromise fundamental rights; and "*additive goods,*" such as education and material wealth, which increase or enhance well-being.

Gewirth ranks the duties and rights (see Figure 2.3) according to their importance in the distribution of core goods. Underlying Gewirth's rank order of duties and rights is his "principle of generic consistency," in which action is fundamental to ethics and entails at least the ability to act or the freedom to make choices and act accordingly. The rank ordering of

Figure 2.3 ▼ Rank Order of Duties and Rights

1. Rules against basic harms to the necessary preconditions of action (the basic goods—food, health, shelter, and so forth) take precedence over rules against harms such as lying or revealing confidential information (nonsubstractive goods), or threats to additive goods such as education, recreation, and wealth.
2. An individual's right to basic well-being (core goods) takes precedence over another individual's right to freedom.
3. An individual's right to freedom takes precedence over his or her own right to basic well-being.
4. The obligation to obey laws, rules, and regulations to which one has voluntarily and freely consented ordinarily overrides one's right to engage voluntarily in a manner that conflicts with these laws, rules, and regulations.
5. An individual's right to well-being may override laws, rules, regulations, and arrangements of voluntarily associations in cases of conflict.
6. The obligation to prevent basic harms such as starvation and to promote basic public goods such as housing, education, and public assistance overrides the right to retain one's own property.

duties is related to what is required for individuals to be able to act, that is, to be purposeful and free in their choices. For example, an individual's right to basic goods takes precedence over another's right to freedom as basic goods can be viewed as a precondition of action and this takes precedence over another's right to freedom. An individual's right to freedom, however, may take precedence over his or her own right to basic well-being. If there is a conflict between those rights—for example, when we are faced with a person who wants to die—the person's ability to choose death may take precedence over his or her well-being.

REFLECTION QUESTIONS

- What are the advantages of using Gewirth's approach to ethical decision making for social work practice?
- What are the impediments to using this model in practice?
- Can you see any benefit to using this model as a practitioner? If yes, would you modify it, and if so, how?

Bioethics Principles and Rules Model

The bioethics principle model developed by Beauchamp and Childress (2001) applies not only to medical settings but also to the range of settings within which human service professionals, particularly social workers and counsellors, practise. The model applies four principles and a set of rules derived from the principles to guide action (see Figure 2.4).

Figure 2.4 ▼ The Bioethics Principle Model

Principle 1	Respect for autonomy or the right to make independent decisions concerning one's own life and well-being
Principle 2	Nonmaleficence, or the obligation to do no harm
Principle 3	Beneficence, or the obligation to actively pursue the welfare of others
Principle 4	Justice or fairness in the distribution of resources and opportunities

The rules drawn from these principles include veracity or truth telling, protection of client's privacy, upholding confidentiality agreements, and being faithful to one's promises and commitments to clients.

REFLECTION QUESTIONS

- Do you agree with the rank order of the principles in Beauchamp and Childress's model?
- If you agree, what is the basis of your agreement, and if you disagree, how would you rank the principles?
- Would you add any principles that are not present? If yes, what would they be and where would you place them in the rank order?

CONCERNS ABOUT A PRINCIPLE- OR RULE-BASED APPROACH TO ETHICAL DECISION MAKING

Theorists have identified major concerns about applying absolutist approaches to ethical decision making. Some believe that the absolute nature of principles leaves little leeway for modification and makes it difficult to apply when there are conflicting considerations. When two obligations conflict, as happens in practice, the practitioner may become immobilized. Another related issue is that the principle- or rule-based approach to ethical decision making in any of the models we have looked at assumes consensus on both the principles and the rank ordering of the principles. This assumption may be problematic, as evidenced in the findings of a study conducted by Osmo and Landau (2003). They compiled a list of twelve ethical principles from social work codes of ethics and ethical decision-making models, including two of the models we have just outlined (see Figure 2.5).

Figure 2.5 ▼ Twelve Core Ethical Principles in Social Work Codes of Ethics and Relevant Literature

> 1. Equality and inequality (equity)
> 2. Basic justice
> 3. Privacy and confidentiality
> 4. Protection of life
> 5. The good or interest of the individual
> 6. Truthfulness and full disclosure
> 7. Autonomy and personal freedom
> 8. Quality of life
> 9. Provision of basic human needs
> 10. The public good
> 11. Least harm
> 12. Obligation to obey laws and regulations

The authors asked social work practitioners to rank the principles and apply them to two cases. They found that there was a lack of agreement and consistency in the ranking and application of the principles across the cases: "The ethical hierarchies of social workers (in this study) are not constant, with the importance attached to ethical principles changing with change in context" (p. 46). The findings show that for the practitioners in the study interpretations and application of ethical principles vary, and that rather than possessing a universal professional ethical hierarchy of principles, practitioners adhere to an internal personal hierarchy (p. 47). This leads to a discussion of virtue ethics as an important foundation for professional ethical decision making, and we will discuss this after briefly examining the frameworks we have identified under the relativist category of ethical decision-making frameworks.

ETHICAL RELATIVIST FRAMEWORKS

For an absolutist an act is "right" because behaving in a certain manner is in accordance with principles, duties, or rights that are inherently correct, such as the principle that we should always keep client information confidential. For the relativist frameworks we will now survey—actions are justified by future consequences—breaking confidentiality may be justified because of the negative consequences of not doing so.

The ETHIC Model

The ETHIC model developed by Elaine Congress (1999) consists of five decision steps which incorporate considerations of relevant values and professional codes with a focus on consequences of alternative courses of action within a benefit/cost calculation that benefits those who are most vulnerable (see Figure 2.6).

Figure 2.6 ▼ The ETHIC Model

Step 1	**E**xamine relevant personal, societal, agency, client, and professional values.
Step 2	**T**hink about what ethical standard of the NASW (Professional) *Code of Ethics* applies to the situation, as well as about relevant laws and case decisions.
Step 3	**H**ypothesize about possible consequences of different decisions.
Step 4	**I**dentify who will benefit and who will be harmed in view of social work's commitment to the most vulnerable.
Step 5	**C**onsult with supervisor and colleagues about the most ethical choice.

The Tracking Harms Model

Robison and Reeser's (2000) tracking harms model of decision making also has five steps (see Figure 2.7). The focus in this model, however, is primarily on the goals and motivations of the participants. It takes into account participants' goals and strategies for achieving those goals as well as their possible motivations. For each option, potential obstacles to achieving goals are calculated within this context of goals and strategies with the ultimate objective of choosing options that minimize harm.

Figure 2.7 ▼ Tracking Harms Model of Decision Making

Step 1	Construct arguments that justify the acts or omissions of participants to try to understand their motivation for their actions.
Step 2	Determine the actual goals of the participants and the means by which they thought they would achieve those goals. Determine what their goals ought to be and what means would be best for achieving those goals.
Step 3	Identify the harm of alternative courses of action and identify to whom the harm would occur, as well as the kind and degree of harm.
Step 4	Make a judgment about what is the best outcome and what will minimize harm.
Step 5	Determine how the outcome should be achieved in a way that will produce more good than harm.

THE ETHICAL PROBLEM-SOLVING MODEL

The final relativist decision framework we will outline is the ethical problem-solving model advanced by Corey, Corey, and Callahan (1998). The model uses six "fundamental principles" for evaluating consequences of options for action and combines aspects of the absolutist use of principles and the relativist emphasis on context and deliberation about consequences of actions (see Figure 2.8). The authors clearly state that the steps in their model are not necessarily meant to be followed in a sequential manner but are for "stimulating self-reflection" and encouraging discussion with clients and colleagues (p. 17).

Figure 2.8 ▼ The Ethical Problem-Solving Model

Step 1	Identify the problem or dilemma during information gathering and consultation about the nature of the problem.
Step 2	Identify potential issues involved in the problem in terms of rights, responsibilities, and welfare of all involved.
Step 3	Review relevant codes of ethics to see if and how they apply.
Step 4	Review applicable laws and regulations.
Step 5	Consult to get other perspectives about the problem.
Step 6	Consider courses of action.
Step 7	Enumerate consequences of various courses of action using the principle framework (autonomy, nonmaleficence, beneficence, justice, fidelity, and veracity).
Step 8	Decide on the best course of action.

Reflection Questions

REFLECTION QUESTIONS

- Which of the relativist approaches to decision making do you feel most comfortable with? Explain your reasons.
- Apply the model you are comfortable with to one of the practice situations we have discussed. What would you recommend to the professional in that situation?
- If you are not comfortable with applying any of the relativist decision models to the practice situations, what makes you uncomfortable about them and which of the absolutist models would you use instead?
- If you choose not to use a decision-making model from the relativist framework, apply the absolutist model of decision making you are comfortable with to one of the situations and describe what you would recommend to the professional in the situation.
- What do your choices tell you at this point about your values and preferences in ethical decision making?

CONCERNS ABOUT RELATIVIST APPROACHES TO DECISION MAKING

As with absolutist approaches, theorists have outlined several drawbacks to relativist approaches to decision making. A major concern with a consequentialist approach, which many of the authors who are relativists use, is that in weighing costs or harms and benefits it is difficult to anticipate consequences of alternatives, and accurate measures of outcomes are not easy to develop given the limited knowledge and time we have in practice. We often need to rely on short-range consequences to justify actions given our limited ability to anticipate long-range outcomes. Given the unanticipated consequences of planned action, which makes accurate prediction of consequences untenable, Popper (1966) questions the rationale of justifying decisions based on calculating benefits and costs.

SUMMARY OF CONCERNS ABOUT USING ETHICAL DECISION-MAKING MODELS

Both the relativist and absolutist approaches to ethical decision making have drawbacks when we attempt to apply them to particular cases. Both, however, provide conceptual tools that are helpful to draw on as we face the complexity of ethical issues in practice. The more conceptual tools we bring to the process of coming to a judgment, the more informed and thoughtful that judgment can be in arriving at a course of action. We owe no less to our clients, colleagues, and profession. Relativist approaches to decision making provide conceptual frameworks that yield a range of options with calculated choices that can be revised given new information. The absolutist framework directs the professional to consider ethical principles, rights, and duties to guide decision making within the fluid context opened up through the relativist considerations of options. As Nulman (1983) states, however, it is ultimately the nature of the relationship between the professional and client and, I would add, community, profession, and service system, that forms the basis of ethical activity, and it is the professional who is accountable for his or her decisions and subsequent activity.

VIRTUE ETHICS AND CONTEMPORARY APPROACHES TO THINKING ABOUT ETHICS

The importance of professional judgment is not emphasized in either relativist or absolutist approaches to decision making to the degree it is in virtue ethics and contemporary (for example, feminist and Aboriginal) approaches to thinking about ethical behavior. Virtue ethics, which has been developed by several contemporary theorists, was first articulated by Aristotle in *Nicomachean Ethics*. For Aristotle virtue refers to the excellence of something and the effective performance of its function. Thus, a good person is one who performs the function of a person well. Aristotle goes on to describe what it means to function well as a person and relates functioning well to good reasoning. Contemporary virtue ethics focuses on subjective qualities, traits, and habits that lead to choices and actions that in the end address questions about the kind of person we want to be. Instead of attempting to develop a strategy to decide what actions are "right" based on sound ethical reasoning, virtue ethics attempts to avoid using pre-established rules or principles or examining consequences as the determinant of what one should do but instead assumes that a person becomes the agent of the acts he performs and self-understanding is necessary for determining the right action. This leads to a distinction between "doing" what is good and "being" a good person; thus the goodness of an act is determined not by its consequences or adherence to established rules but primarily by the qualities of the agent performing the act. Doing a "good" act, therefore, is not necessarily ethical if it is not done from good motives.

Teehan (1995) summarizes the major characteristics of contemporary virtue ethics as follows:

- It is for the most part an alternative to the limitations of the two major categories of ethical theories (absolutist and relativist) in not capturing our experience of what it means to be a good person.
- The focus is shifted from assessments of acts to assessment of the actor.
- It provides both an account of virtues and a discussion of the virtues of the actor. (pp. 859–862)

Virtue is defined in general as a disposition to act, desire, and feel that involves an exercise of judgment and leads to excellence or to the "human flourishing" Aristotle referred to when examining the character of the actor rather than the acts as the focus of ethics. Osmo and Landau (2003), in their discussion of the problems they found in ranking principles in social work, concluded that the best guidance for choice is probably "What kind of person do I want to be?" They also concluded that ethical issues we face often focus on the nature of our relationships to others. The differences they found in the interpretation and ranking of ethical principles, they concluded, reflected judgments by individuals who retain personal integrity and commitment to what they believe is universally just or what a just person would do. They recommend the following for developing self-knowledge and making sound ethical judgments:

- Develop awareness of your own belief system.
- Be explicit about the principles that guide your ethical decisions.
- Develop a personal sense of accountability and personal responsibility.
- Provide explicit justification of your judgments and subject reasoning to careful scrutiny and evaluation. (p. 48)

This model for self-knowledge potentially combines conceptual tools from both the absolutist (principles) and relativist (context and consequences) approaches. Personal qualities (awareness of one's own belief system, accountability, and personal responsibility) are developed in a deliberative, thoughtful process (explicit justification and subjection of reasoning to careful scrutiny and evaluation) that accords with our experience of being ethical.

INQUIRY PROJECT

At the beginning of the section on virtue ethics, we referred to feminist and Aboriginal approaches to ethics. What do Aboriginal and feminist approaches to ethics consist of and how do they differ from the approaches described in this chapter? To respond to these questions, try the following activities:

1. Conduct an Internet search to find at least one example of Aboriginal and feminist ethics. If you have time, locate more than one example so you can

compare descriptions to develop as accurate a depiction of each ethic as possible. For each ethic, develop a half-page to one-page, double-spaced summary of what you think are the core characteristics of the ethic. (You can copy from documents; just make sure you provide citations.)

2. After completing the summary descriptions for each ethic, choose either the Aboriginal ethic or feminist ethic and respond to the following (you may do both but you are not required to do so):

- Describe any similarities between the ethic you have chosen and any of the decision models described previously. If there are no similarities, outline the major differences.
- Compare the ethic you have chosen with the CASW *Code of Ethics,* or a code of ethics from another human service profession, by looking over the general themes and structure of each ethic. Are there significant differences in emphasis, themes, and structure between the two, and if so, what are they? Which of the codes do you feel more comfortable with and why?

CONCLUSION

We have covered a lot of ground in this chapter, and you will be coming back to the concepts and frameworks discussed in this chapter to assist you with your work throughout the rest of this text. The distinctions between ethics and values and ethics and law are essential ones to keep before you as you work with the decision models presented in this chapter. Finally, also keep in mind the alternative ethic you examined for the concluding inquiry part of this chapter so that you can continue to compare the ethic you chose with the CASW (2005) *Code of Ethics* as you work with practice situations.

The next chapter picks up on the discussion of values in Chapter 1 and in this chapter to examine values in the context of the multicultural Canadian context. It concludes with a focus on clarifying personal values and provides examples of both individual and group-based value-clarification exercises.

NOTES

NOTES

_____

_____

_____

_____

_____

_____

_____

_____

_____

_____

_____

_____

_____

_____

NOTES

NOTES

NOTES

NOTES

REFERENCES

Alberta Child and Family Services. (2002). *What is child abuse?* Retrieved November 5, 2003, from http://www.child.gov.ab.ca/whatwedo/childwelfare/page.cfm?pg=What%20is%20Child%20Abuse

Aristotle. (1987). *The Nicomachean ethics* (J.E.C. Welldon, Trans.). Amherst, NY: Prometheus Books.

Beauchamp, T.L., & Childress, J.F. (2001). *Principles of biomedical ethics* (5th ed.). New York: Oxford University Press.

Bergantino, L. (1996). For the defense: Psychotherapy and law. *Voices 3,* 29–33.

Canadian Association of Social Workers. (2005a). *Code of ethics.* Ottawa, ON: Author.

Canadian Association of Social Workers. (2005b). *Guidelines for ethical practice.* Ottawa, ON: Author.

Congress, Elaine P. (1999). *Social work values and ethics: Identifying and resolving professional dilemmas.* Chicago: Nelson-Hall.

Corey, G, Corey, M.S., & Callahan, P. (1998). *Issues and ethics in the helping professions.* Pacific Grove, CA: Brooks/Cole.

Dickson, D. (1998). *Confidentiality and privacy in social work: A guide to the law for practitioners and students.* New York: Free Press.

Dolgoff, R., Loewenberg, F.M, & Harrington, Donna. (2005*). Ethical decisions for social work practice* (7th ed.). Belmont, CA: Brooks/Cole.

Gewirth, A. (1978). *Reason and morality.* Chicago: University of Chicago Press.

Nulman, E. (1983). *Morality, law, and ECT.* Hastings Center Report 13(3).

Osmo R., & Landau, R. (2003). Professional and personal hierarchies of ethical principles. *International Social Welfare 12,* 42–49.

Popper, K. (1966). *The open society and its enemies* (5th ed.). London: Routledge and Kegan Paul.

Reamer, F.G. (1999) *Social work values and ethics* (2nd ed.). New York: Columbia University Press.

Robison, W., & Reeser, L.C. (2000). *Ethical decision making in social work.* Neeham Heights, MA: Allyn and Bacon.

Schultz, L.G. (1990). *Confidentiality, privilege, and child abuse reporting.* Retrieved November 5, 2003, from http://www.ipt-forensics.com/journal/volume2/j2_4_5.htm

Tarasoff v. Regents of the University of California, 13 Cal 3d 177, 529 P. 2d 553 (1974), vacated, 17 Cal. 3d 425, 552 p. 2d 334 (1976).

Teehan, J. (1995). Character, integrity and Dewey's virtue ethics. *Translations of the Charles S. Peirce Society, 31,* 841–863.

c h a p t e r **3**

Values and Professional Ethics

In the two preceding chapters, we have touched on the relation of values to ethics and distinguished ethics from law. Given the centrality of values to ethics, in this chapter we will focus on values as the heart of a professional relationship, with the social work profession as an example of a profession identified by its core values. Within the context of the core social work values of respect for the inherent dignity of persons and the pursuit of social justice, this chapter will highlight the importance of being aware of personal values and acknowledging the difficulty of applying these values in practice.

The Canadian value of respecting diverse cultures will be used to point out the difference between morality and professional ethics as well as the difficulty of determining what it means to practise ethically in a multicultural society such as Canada, with its multiple moralities. The chapter concludes with value-clarification exercises at the individual and group level to provide tools for self-assessment and reflection.

School Social Worker Situation: **Conflicting Professional Responsibilities**

Read the following situation with a critical eye to the values that are represented by the social worker. Keep these questions before you while reading the situation:

- As a social worker, what do you think your professional responsibility would be in this situation? Given your response, identify what you think this reflects about your values and identify the core values represented in your response. Examples of core values are showing respect for individual differences and promoting social justice.
- Would the social worker be justified in locating alternative funding for the resource centre despite the hesitation of the school board and school? What would be the basis of the justification for moving ahead or not moving ahead with alternative funding?

Samira has been hired as a school social worker in what she considers to be a socially conservative junior high school. She is a recent B.S.W. graduate who is committed to social change and social justice. Samira has decided to look for funding from the school board in order to develop a resource centre to address issues of diversity in the school setting. She has noticed problems with racism, lack of religious tolerance, homophobia/ heterosexism, discrimination against individuals with disabilities, and what she has identified as overly conservative views and teachings concerning sex education. Samira's proposed resource centre would attempt to address these issues through educational seminars and support programs that would be accessible by students, staff, and parents.

Samira's proposals have been turned down, time after time. The board does not believe that problems caused by negative reactions to diverse groups in the school are significant enough to fund a resource centre. Samira feels she is faced with

> the ethical responsibility to adhere to the core values of recognizing the inherent dignity and worth of persons, pursuing social justice, and respecting diversity and the right of individuals to have access to resources while honouring her professional responsibility to respect and follow the policies of the workplace.

POTENTIAL RESPONSES TO SAMIRA'S SITUATION

Consider the following responses given by students in an undergraduate social work ethics class to Samira's dilemma. Identify the response or combination of responses that you think best represent the position you would take. Think about what values are represented in your position and outline the argument you would give to justify your position to a professional who argues for a different response.

Student Response 1: Pursue Alternative Funding

I feel that my professional responsibility as a social worker would be to abide by the *Code of Ethics* of the Canadian Association of Social Workers (2005a) concerning social justice and equitable distribution of resources. It states: "Social workers believe in the obligation of people, individually and collectively, to provide resources, services and opportunities for the overall benefit of humanity and to afford them protection from harm. Social workers promote social fairness and equitable distribution of resources, and act to reduce barriers and expand choice for all persons, with special regard for those who are marginalized, disadvantaged, vulnerable, and/or have exceptional needs" (Value 2). My actions to carry out "social justice" in this situation would likely include creating a resource centre to increase students' respect for other students, especially those who are different from themselves. If the worker considers the student body as her client she must work toward their best interests. In this case the students' best interests as a whole would be to respect each other and thus increase acceptance of diversity in the student body. The worker's view of the best interests of the students conflicts with the school board's priorities for school funding.

A section of the CASW *Guidelines for Ethical Practice* (2005b) supports an argument that it is a professional responsibility to continue pursuing the resource centre even in the face of lack of school board support: "Social workers take all reasonable steps to uphold their ethical values, principles and responsibilities even though employers' policies or official orders may not be compatible with its provisions" (sec. 4.1.7). To put this simply, I would definitely pursue the goal of increasing respect and acceptance of diversity among the students through a resource centre as I view this as my professional responsibility supported by the code. It would be important to inform the school administrators and the board that the worker is pursuing alternative funding. The social worker is taking action in the interests of her client, the student body, and thus is justified in locating alternative funding.

Student Response 2: Pursue Alternative Methods to Address Issues

As a social worker, I think the professional responsibility in this situation would be to respect the employee (school) and find other approaches to address the issues related to diversity in the school. CASW *Guidelines for Ethical Practice* (2005b) states that the social worker is accountable and responsible to the employer to "carry out the stated aims and objectives of their employing organization, agency or service contractor" (sec. 4.1). I interpret this statement as supporting the argument that the worker should abide by the school board's decision as best she can. I think that the social worker is also bound by the responsibility to society in general because her work with the students will affect the larger society. In working with individual students in the school community, she will be offering equal opportunities for all and working for an even distribution of resources.

As mentioned in the case, the worker has noticed problems with racism, and, given directives in the "Responsibilities to Society" area of the CASW *Guidelines for Ethical Practice* (2005b), she would be responsible for taking reasonable actions to prevent and eliminate discrimination. "Social Workers strive to identify, document and advocate for the prevention and elimination of domination or exploitation of, and discrimination against, any person, group, or class on the basis of age, abilities, ethnic background, gender, language, marital status, national ancestry, political affiliation, race, religion, sexual orientation or socio-economic status" (sec. 8.2.1).

I think that the worker could perhaps facilitate group meetings or programs that introduce cultural awareness and address other issues that she has noticed. This response would not be as visible and influential as a resource centre. My argument is that if she is successful in getting students and teachers aware of issues related to lack of acceptance and respect for diversity in the student body, eventually the school board will pay attention to these issues and change their funding priorities to address the need to change the climate in the school.

Student Response 3: Work with Board's Decision or Change Employment

Since I have just been hired and turned down time after time by the school board for funding for a resource centre, it would be in my best interests to respect the board's decision. I am obligated as a professional social worker to continue to work to improve school practices that I think are not in accord with professional values, but in an "appropriate" manner, which in this case means thinking of alternative ways to address discrimination in the school. The CASW *Guidelines for Ethical Practice* (2005b) states that the social worker will "appropriately challenge, and work to improve, policies, procedures, practices and service provisions" that are "not in the best interests of clients, are inequitable, are in any way oppressive, disempowering or culturally inappropriate and demonstrate discrimination" (sec. 4.1.4).

My professional responsibility would be to assess resources available to me and attempt to minimize discrimination using the resources at my disposal.

If the social worker feels her employment at the school is no longer tolerable without a resource centre, then I would suggest finding work elsewhere, where her values can be supported.

INQUIRY QUESTIONS

- What core or priority personal values are represented in the response or combination of responses that you have chosen?
- Can you identify core professional values from a professional code of ethics, such as the CASW code, that are represented in the response or combination of responses you have chosen? If yes, what are they and how do they relate to the personal values you identified in your reply to the first question?
- What is your argument for your position? Develop your argument, keeping in mind any opposing positions.

CORE PROFESSIONAL VALUES

A profession's core values are typically identified in the preamble or introduction to its code of ethics. Codes of ethics for social work vary, with each variation reflecting the uniqueness of the particular jurisdiction—for example, the CASW *Code of Ethics* (2005a) is slightly different from the code of ethics for social workers in Australia or the United States. However, there is agreement about the core values described at the beginning of each of these codes. The core values they all have identified as key for social work are

- respect for the inherent dignity and worth of persons;
- pursuit of social justice;
- service to humanity;

- integrity of professional practice; and
- competence in professional practice.

How is a core value such as "respect for the inherent dignity and worth of persons" implemented in practice? How are core values related to professional ethics? By examining a professional code of ethics, you will see an example of how values are linked to ethics. The principles, commentary, or guidelines prescribe certain behaviours (ethical conduct) in order to actualize the value in question, in this case, "respect for inherent dignity and worth of persons." For example, in the CASW *Code of Ethics* (2005a) the value of respect for the inherent dignity and worth of persons is followed by a list of practice principles that include working with clients to ensure the client's right to self-determination and right to choice based on voluntary, informed consent. Examples of other principles in this list are the professional's obligation to respect diversity among individuals in Canadian society, including their beliefs and ways of life as long as these do not interfere with the rights of others (Value 1).

The commentary section of the Alberta College of Social Workers' *Code of Ethics* (1983) offers a "more detailed statement of the reasonable standard of practice expected from the social worker's commitment" to core values and related principles (p. 1). The commentary for the statement "respect the intrinsic worth of persons I serve" includes a paragraph that provides an expanded discussion of what voluntary mutual agreements between the social worker and client mean in relation to both voluntary and involuntary clients (p. 1). In the CASW *Guidelines for Ethical Practice* (2005b), the section with guidelines for "practical application" of the value of "respect for inherent dignity and worth of persons" is approximately seven pages in length and includes the areas of priority of clients' interests, cultural awareness and sensitivity, client self-determination and informed consent, involuntary clients and those not capable of consent, privacy and confidentiality, vulnerable members of society, client records, and termination or interruption of services (secs. 1.1–1.8).

The core value we started with is respecting the intrinsic worth of persons. By examining principles, commentary, or guidelines in codes of ethics related to this value we can begin to understand, although in general terms, what this commits us to in terms of our practice with service users (clients), employers, and other professionals.

Inquiry Questions

INQUIRY QUESTION

Think back to Samira's situation and the position you developed in response to the dilemma she identified in working with students and the school board.

- Do you see any application of principles related to the values of "respect for intrinsic worth of persons and respect for diversity" with relevant commentary or guidelines in professional ethical codes to support your position?

In the CASW *Code of Ethics* (2005a), the description of the core value "pursuit of social justice" includes, among others principles, directing social workers to "advocate for fair and equitable access to public services and benefits" along with advocating for "equal treatment and protection under the law and challeng[ing] injustices, especially injustices that affect the vulnerable and disadvantaged" (p. 1). In the CASW *Guidelines for Ethical Practice* (2005b), under "Ethical Responsibilities to Society," the directive to "advocate for fair and equitable access" is further elaborated:

> Social workers advocate for change in the best interests of clients and for the overall benefit of society, the environment and the global community. In performing their responsibilities to society, social workers frequently must balance individual rights to self-determination with protection of vulnerable members of society from harm. (sec. 8.0)

It is clear that directives in commentaries or guidelines such as these are "general" in the sense that decisions about how to enact them in specific contexts and circumstances are left to the professional. "Fair and equitable access" will be interpreted differently depending on the service user group or individual client and the position of the social worker in an organization or his ability to leverage relevant resources. Although the principles, commentary, and guidelines in codes give us more direction in terms of practice behaviour than core values alone provide, they are general enough to allow for a range of interpretations all of which may be viewed as acceptable. This generality provides for flexibility in interpreting values to provide room for the professional to apply core values in ways that are meaningful for himself, for the service users, for the employing organization, for other professionals, and for the community. Given this generality, it should be even clearer at this point why the development of decision-making skills, access to decision-making models, self-awareness, and critical consciousness are important in order for a professional to apply professional codes of ethics in a thoughtful and ethically sound manner.

INQUIRY QUESTIONS

Respond to the following questions within the context of your solution to the integration of respect for individuals and diversity in Samira's work with students and the school board:

- Can you apply social justice principles and commentary or guidelines about social justice from professional codes of ethics, such as CASW, in your position for how Samira should proceed with the students and school board? How does this relate to your integration of the values of respect for individuals and diversity in your position? Identify the code of ethics you are using and the particular sections of the code or companion document (guidelines or commentary) that apply.
- Although this is not a requirement, we encourage you to apply any of the contemporary or alternative codes you examined in Chapter 2 (Aboriginal and/or feminist codes of ethics) to the question of how Samira should proceed.

MORALITY AND MULTIPLE MORALITIES IN CANADA

One of the complexities faced by professionals in Canada is the multiplicity of moralities service users present to professionals in Canada's increasingly multicultural environment. Morality is similar to ethics in that it helps define the parameters of appropriate behaviour for members of a community. "Mores" are the rules or principles of a morality for a group or community. For example, Canadian citizens who are members of religious organizations may have a sense of what is "right" or "moral" based partially on their adherence to the moral code of their religion and on their identification with Canadian society. When a country such as Canada values and promotes multiculturalism, the difficulty of defining "appropriate" behaviour in terms of community mores becomes complex given the many groups and communities that constitute Canadian society. I may, for example, be a Canadian citizen who has recently immigrated and I may be torn between the moral code of my country of origin and what I perceive to be accepted practices in Canada. To further complicate matters, I may also identify with a religious community that has its own moral code. I am, consequently, a member of multiple communities some of whose mores may conflict.

Practice Situation: **June Ying**

As you read the following situation think about the primary group or groups you identify with and reflect on how that identification impacts your sense of "right" and "wrong." Next think about how this sense of "morality" has or will affect your work as a professional.

The Catholic Church's definition of what it means to be "moral" for its members includes positive responsibilities such as treating others with dignity and respect. It also includes prohibitions against engaging in certain behaviours, such as abortion. June Ying, a social worker, in addition to being a member of the Catholic Church, is also a member of secular society: she is a Canadian citizen. June Ying is also active in an Asian cultural group that is promoting awareness of the group's cultural practices in a certain region in Canada.

Each group of which June Ying is a member—Catholic, Canadian, and Asian—has its own sense of morality, which potentially may cause conflict for June Ying. For example, in Canadian society having an abortion is viewed as the right of each person to decide, but the Catholic Church prohibits abortion, as do some Asian cultures.

A social work professional such as June Ying, who is Catholic, Asian, and a Canadian citizen, may experience further conflicts because her profession's code of ethics core value of respect for the dignity and worth of the individual leads to ethical principles that support a person's right to choose an abortion. Therefore, the profession's core values and code of ethics conflict with the mores of the groups June Ying is a member of, as well as the mores of services users and other professionals June Ying may work with.

INQUIRY PROJECT

When there is a conflict between the directives given by two or more "moralities," the professional code of ethics takes precedence over the mores of other groups the professional is a member of. Develop an argument to support or argue against this position using statements from a professional code of ethics to support your argument.

In some Canadian jurisdictions certain types of corporal punishment for children are clearly identified as unacceptable parenting behaviour and may result in intervention by children's services agencies. In some cultures corporal punishment is viewed as not only appropriate but morally justified parenting behaviour. For social workers involved with parents and children from such cultures, it may not be clear what is ethically the best direction to take: to respect the culture of the family or to uphold the mores and laws of Canadian society. There are also questions that need to be addressed about who the primary service user is: the parents or the children.

Inquiry Questions

INQUIRY QUESTIONS

- When there is a conflict between the larger society's mores and those of the service user, in this case Canada, with the mores of one or more groups a service user is a member of, such as a religious group or an ethnic group, which one is the professional ethically obligated to support?
- Now take the opposite side and develop an opposing argument to the one you gave in the question above in opposition to the response you support.

Think about the following situation, which involves an international adoption. What would you do if you were the social worker involved with Kayleigh? What values are important to you and how do they impact your response? Is multiculturalism a factor in this story? Explain why or why not.

Practice Situation: **Kayleigh**

Kayleigh was born in Guatemala. She is the biological daughter of a Mayan mother and Mexican father and was adopted by a culturally diverse family in Canada when she was five months old. Her adopted family is composed of a father from India, a mother from France, an adopted sister from Korea, and two brothers who are her adopted parents' biological children.

She always knew that she was adopted, but when she turned ten years old, her adoption became a stigma for her. It altered her emotional development and she became obsessed with her adoption circumstances. As time went on, she began to question her adoption and wondered why she had even been born. Kayleigh's parents attributed this change of attitude to the onset of puberty, but the reality for her was that she felt alone. She had no feeling of personal history or roots to connect her with a larger social group.

When she was twelve, the family decided that she and her mother would visit Guatemala. The goal was to spend a week with the foster family with whom she spent the first five months of her life. Kayleigh had kept in contact with the foster family and wanted to meet them. She did not, however, want to search for her birth mother.

In the tourist village of Panajachel, populated mainly by Mayans dressed in traditional costumes, Kayleigh could easily pass for a resident. The young men who encountered her, trying to sell her merchandise, quickly understood that she did not speak the local language. The Guatemalan women, particularly the Mayans, were intrigued at the sight of this young girl who visibly appeared to be Guatemalan but who was not dressed appropriately and was accompanied by a large Canadian woman with knotted hair.

"The girl is Guatemalan, where is her mother?" asked one woman in the street where Kayleigh had gone to have her hair done. Her mother answered the lady by saying "Here I am, I am her mother."

"No, you are not her mother. Her mother is Guatemalan," came the reply.

Kayleigh noticed that many of the streets were strewn with garbage and beggars were seen on the major roads. Children between the ages of five and six walked the streets from morning to night selling anything or waxing shoes.

Upon returning to Canada, Kayleigh reflected that the people were very poor, and that if she had not been adopted, she would be among them. At the same time, she wondered why *she* had been adopted and not one of the other children. This feeling of guilt is often shared by many other internationally adopted children who return to the country of their birth.

BACKGROUND INFORMATION

Ethical Directives Focused on International Adoption

The International Social Services–International Resource Centre's (ISS–IRC) ethical principles for international adoption practices stresses that children should be allowed to be raised in their own family. Governments and civil society must do their best to ensure that families of origin have the possibility, and are encouraged, to care for their children (1999). The ethical guidelines promote and uphold women's rights, the reduction of world economic imbalances, and other policies that deal with the issue of human equity. Additionally, they dictate that poverty alone should not be a criterion for severing a child's bonds with his or her family.

For practitioners who subscribe to the ISS–IRC's principles, awareness is paramount because of the possibility of removing children from families in developing countries and placing them in wealthier North American families. Practitioners must be aware of the circumstances and policies surrounding the relinquishment of children in their country of origin. Practitioners should ensure that all efforts to promote adoption in the child's country of origin have been exhausted and should not assume that the most suitable parents are always North American. Practitioners also need to be aware of illegal baby-trafficking in countries such as Guatemala, Russia, China, and South Korea in order to ensure that North American families are not adopting children under these circumstances, which often occur in unregistered international adoption agencies.

PRACTICE ISSUES

With the increased availability of abortion and reliable birth control and the greater acceptance of single-mother-led families in "Western" nations, the number of domestically available adoptable children has declined dramatically in the last several decades (Groening, 2003). The "demand" for healthy babies to adopt has not decreased; if anything, it has increased. This has led couples who want to adopt to look to other nations to provide a healthy baby of their own. The large numbers of homeless or orphaned children in countries affected by war, famine, and poverty have met this demand.

Problems arise when the desperation of the adoptive parents and the motivations of the people who commit to helping them work in concert to allow the development of an illegal traffic in children. In some countries, this has led to practices such as outright theft of babies, coercion of mothers to give them up for adoption, and payments to women to get pregnant for the sole purpose of selling their babies.

As these types of practices have come to light over the past decade, there have been initiatives to stop them. One of the most important was the signing in 1995 of the Hague Convention on protection of children and cooperation with respect to international adoption (Hague Convention, 1995). As of 1999, twenty-one countries have ratified the Convention (including Canada) and four others have acceded to it. The Convention bans any "improper financial or other gain" and "the abduction, the sale of, or traffic in children" and obliges all who have signed to safeguard against it.

IMPLICATIONS OF ETHICAL DIRECTIVES FOR PRACTICE IN A MULTICULTURAL CONTEXT

The Canadian Association of Social Workers *Code of Ethics* (2005a), with regard to "integrity in professional practice," stipulates that professionals must "demonstrate and promote the qualities of honesty, reliability, impartiality and diligence in their professional practice" (Value 4). For practitioners involved in some manner with international adoptions, diligence translates into seeking out information about the circumstances surrounding the child's adoption in his or her country of origin as well as requesting the credentials of the organizations and individuals involved with the adoption process.

The practitioner also needs to keep in mind that the CASW code, in its opening statement on the value of "respect for the inherent dignity and worth of persons," emphasizes the importance of recognizing and respecting "the diversity of Canadian society, taking into account the breadth of differences that exist among individuals, families, groups and communities." It goes on to declare that "social Workers uphold the human rights of individuals and groups as expressed in the *Canadian Charter of Rights and Freedoms* (1982) and the *United Nations Universal Declaration of Human Rights* (1948)" (Value 1).

INQUIRY QUESTIONS

- What core ethical concerns would you need to be sensitive to if you were a professional involved with international adoptions? In working on this question think about the core values of a profession and the principles related to these values as a way to identify ethical concerns in this context. How has the context of international adoptions shaped the ethical concerns you have identified?
- If you were a professional involved with the adoption of Kayleigh, what ethical issues might you be concerned about? Can you think of any that might arise?

PERSONAL AND PROFESSIONAL VALUES

Given the work you have completed in the practice situations and inquiry questions in this and previous chapters, you have a good foundation to reflect on and describe your personal values and those of your chosen profession as they relate or at times conflict with one another.

In this text values are the criteria that predispose us to choose among courses of action and often reflect the beliefs of the families we were raised in and the groups and communities we identify with, such as church communities, ethnic and racial groups, political parties, and countries. When we make a conscious choice, as you have been doing in the inquiry questions, you provide an insight into what you value by weighing alternatives and deciding what is "right" or "best." Values often change over time in response to changing life experiences. Value-clarification work, described in the exercises below, provides tools to assist you in recognizing your present values and monitoring their changes over time. The work you do in value clarification does not tell you what your values should be; it simply provides the means to discover what your values are.

When you are assessing the range of values you identify with, it will be helpful to keep in mind the concept of "full value" developed by Raths, Harmin, and Simon (1966). For a value to be a "full value" it must meet the following three criteria:

"Full-Value" Criteria

1. It should be *chosen* freely from alternatives after thoughtful consideration of the consequences of each alternative.
2. It should be *prized*—cherishing, being happy with the choice; willing to affirm the choice publicly.
3. It should be *acted on*—doing something with the choice; doing something repeatedly, in a consistent manner. (p. 16)

Use the following value-clarification exercises to apply these criteria to values that are key for you and your work:

- Have you chosen those values as "most important" after carefully considering the other values in your list?
- Have you affirmed those values in a public way, such as by stating to others what you think is important, right, or best?
- Do your past or present actions reflect the values you have identified as most important?

INDIVIDUAL WORK ON VALUE CLARIFICATION

Given what you have demonstrated thus far about your preferences or values, complete the following exercise and share your thoughts with others in your class.

Exercise 1: People of Value Exercise

One way to identify values that are important to you is by describing people you know who embody those values. Return to the exercise you completed in Chapter 1, entitled "Reflection Questions—Identify and Reflect on Personal Values." Examine your responses to the three questions (repeated below) in that exercise and either keep your previous responses or modify them to reflect your current thinking and then respond to the Reflection Question that follows.

1. Identify three people whom you hold in esteem or look up to.
2. For each of these individuals describe the two or three core values they model for you.
3. Would others view these people as highly as you do? Why or why not?

Reflection Questions

REFLECTION QUESTION

- Take a few moments and jot down what your responses tell you about your core values. What do these core values tell you about who you are?

Exercise 2: Personal Core Values

In addition to identifying people in your life who are important to you, the following process of ranking values will also assist you in the process of assessing your core values or preferences.

Rank each of the following as high, medium, or low in importance and then choose the ten that are most important and rank them from 1 to 10, with 1 being the most important and 10 being the least important. You may add values to the list.

Personal Values	High/Medium/Low	Rank (1–10)
Achievement (accomplishment)		
Advancement		
Adventure		
Affection (love and caring)		
Competitiveness		

Cooperation
Creativity
Economic security
Fame
Family happiness
Freedom (independence)
Friendship
Health
Helpfulness (assisting others)
Inner harmony
Integrity
Involvement (belonging)
Loyalty
Order
Personal development
Pleasure
Power (control, influence over others)
Recognition
Religion
Responsibility
Self-respect
Wealth
Wisdom (understanding life)
Other(s)

REFLECTION QUESTIONS

- What are your top ten, and of those which ones are the top five?
- How do the values that have been identified through this process relate to the values you identified through the "People of Value" exercise?
- What do these exercises say about who you are at this time in your life?
- How does this relate to your earlier responses to the inquiry questions for the situations we have been working with?
- Is there agreement between what your earlier responses said about your preferences and what you found from completing these exercises? If there are differences, what accounts for those differences?

At the end of this chapter you will find three exercises in value-clarification work that you can do with groups of peers.

PROFESSIONAL VALUES AND YOUR CORE VALUES

The core values of the social work profession are also found in related professions such as counselling and nursing. Each profession has its own unique focus, but in the helping professions of social work and counselling there is a common set of values that emphasizes the following: service, respect and dignity for service users, professional integrity, and professional competence. We all have a number of personal and professional values. In certain situations, it may become apparent that some of these values are in conflict. For example, a professional may value life. He or she may also value the alleviation of pain. As a rule, these are not conflicting values. However, when working with a terminally ill patient a worker may experience conflict. For example, when a family decides to provide intravenous fluids to a terminally ill family member, the patient's life is prolonged but so too is the pain.

When values conflict, we often find it necessary to re-examine them. Through this process we often come to acknowledge that, under certain circumstances, we can hold values that are inconsistent. For example, health care professionals are unlikely to believe that because valuing life and valuing pain relief are in conflict, they should stop valuing either of them.

In other circumstances, however, challenging professional practice situations may arise that will lead us to conclude that our values have changed. Early in our careers, we may value life and do everything humanly possible to support the decision by health care professionals to prolong a person's life. Over time, however, our experiences may lead to a change in our values. Let's suppose that we begin to value the quality of life and begin to question the absolute value of life as existence—there may be a change in our interactions with and feelings toward terminally ill patients. We may no longer experience the emotional struggle we once had when a decision is made to terminate life support for a terminally ill patient.

When personal and professional values are inconsistent with each other, carrying out our professional role may become very difficult. This often leads to feelings of discomfort or frustration with our professional role if we cannot work out a solution that allows us to choose one value over another. Let's suppose that our religious beliefs conflict with our professional ethical obligations. To return to an earlier example, some churches believe that abortion is morally wrong. If we are a member of a church that has that belief it may be difficult to discuss abortion options with a woman who is considering alternatives to a pregnancy. One option for us is to refer the service user to a professional who can discuss abortion with her. Choosing the option of not working with the woman indicates that for us adherence to the "morality" of our church is a higher value in our personal hierarchy than the professional value of the patient's right to self-determination. In a sense we have carried out our professional obligation to respect the patient's right to choose an abortion (self-determination), but we have done so indirectly by referring her rather than working directly with her.

CONGRUITY BETWEEN PROFESSIONAL AND PERSONAL VALUES

Respond to the following questions, keeping in mind that becoming a member of a profession entails a commitment to abide by the profession's core values and related ethical principles and standards of practice.

Process

For the following list of professional values think about how the personal values you have identified through the previous exercises and in your responses to inquiry questions support or conflict with each core professional value. A woman's right to choose abortion is often given as an example of a potential conflict. Another source of value conflict surrounds the belief that parents have a right to discipline their children according to the practices of their culture even when the larger community views such methods as inappropriate and harmful. Think of at least two other potential sources of value conflict that may arise in professional practice before you map out the relation of your core personal values to professional values.

You probably will need to refer to professional codes of ethics commentaries and standards of practice to clarify what the following professional values mean in terms of practice behaviours (ethical behaviour). For example, respect for the inherent dignity and worth of persons includes, as we discussed earlier, practising in a manner that shows support for client autonomy (self-determination).

Under "Rank Professional Values," rank each value in terms of its importance to you as a professional. Label the value that is highest as "1." If there are professional values that you feel are missing, list them and include them in your ranking. Explain why you included them.

In the column "Personal Values," match your core values with the professional values (e.g., the personal value of upholding life may support the professional value of "respect for the inherent dignity and worth of persons" but it may also conflict with it, depending on the meaning of the personal value for you in the context.

Rank Professional Values (ranked)	Personal Values (support or conflict with a professional value?)
Respect for the inherent dignity and worth of persons	
Pursuit of social justice	
Service to humanity	
Integrity of professional practice	
Competence in professional practice	
Confidentiality	
Other professional values not listed	

Reflection

Take a moment and share your thoughts about congruency or conflicts between your personal values and professional values with others in your class.

CONCLUSION

As we continue to work on practice situations it is important to examine how values predispose us to choose certain courses of action and how they reflect our beliefs about what is "right" and "best." We can change our beliefs and thus our values to the extent that we are open to evaluating ourselves and seeing ourselves through the eyes of others. Some would say we are obligated as professionals to continually hold our beliefs up to scrutiny.

The next chapter focuses on what are considered by most helping professions as the essential professional duties and obligations to clients. The chapter also revisits the ethical decision-making models presented in Chapter 2 through inquiry questions that require application of one or more of the models to practice situations.

NOTES

NOTES

NOTES

_____

_____

_____

_____

_____

_____

_____

_____

_____

_____

_____

_____

_____

NOTES

_____

_____

_____

_____

_____

_____

_____

_____

_____

_____

_____

_____

_____

_____

_____

NOTES

NOTES

REFERENCES

Adopting a child from another country. (2003). Retrieved October 29, 2003, from http://www.child.gov.ab.ca/whatwedo/adoption

Alberta College of Social Workers. (1983). *Code of ethics.* Retrieved March 29, 2003, from http://www.acsw.ab.ca/regulation/code/index_html/view

Callahan, J. (Ed.). (1997). *Ethical issues in professional life.* New York: Oxford University Press.

Canadian Association of Social Workers. (2005). *Code of ethics.* Ottawa, ON: Author.

Canadian Association of Social Workers. (2005). *Guidelines for ethical practice.* Ottawa, ON: Author.

Ethics on the World Wide Web (2004). Retrieved March 1, 2004, from http://commfaculty.fullerton.edu/lester/ethics/books.html

Groening, M (2003). The complexity of adoption ethics. Retrieved October 28, 2003, from http://www.bcadoption.com/articles.asp?pageid=38

Hague Convention on protection of children and co-operation in respect of international adoption. (1995). Retrieved October 29, 2003, from http://www.hcch.net/index_en.php?act=conventions.text&cid=69

Professional ethics. (2004). Retrieved April 10, 2004, from http://www.ethicsweb.ca/books/professional.htm

Raths, L.E., Harmin, M., & Simon, S. (1966). *Values and teaching: Working with values in the classroom.* Columbus, OH: Charles E. Merrill.

International Social Services. (1999). The rights of the child in internal and intercountry adoption: Ethics and principles, guidelines for practice. Retrieved October 25, 2003, from http://www.iss-ssi.org/Publications/publications.html

Simon, S.B. (1993). *In search of values: 31 strategies for finding out what really matters most to you.* New York: Warner Books.

Simon, S.B., et al. (1992). *Values clarification: A handbook of practical strategies for teachers and students.* New York: Warner Books.

Simon, S.B., Howe, L.W., & Kirschenbaum, H. (1995). *Values clarification.* New York: Warner Books.

Smith, H.W., and Blanchard, K. (2000). *What matters most: The power of living your values.* New York: Simon and Schuster.

Values at work questionnaire (2004): Retrieved March 20, 2004, from http://www.maccoby.com/Surveys/VAWIntro.html

Van Hook, M., Hugen, B., & Aguilar, M. (2001). *Spirituality within religious traditions in social work practice.* Pacific Grove, CA: Brooks/Cole.

Appendix: Value-Clarification Exercises for Groups

EXERCISE 1: NEEDS AUCTION

This group exercise is designed to indicate the importance of certain needs for each person in the group to help you clarify your values in the context of needs.

Process

1. The group should generate a list of ten or twelve needs. The needs can range from basic needs (food, water, sleep), to recreational (hiking, reading), or be a combination. Set a spending limit for each person's auction account, e.g., $100, $1000.
2. Each group member should prepare a budget showing how much he or she is willing to spend for each need.
3. Auction off each need, allowing bidders (group members) to spend their budget.

REFLECTION QUESTIONS

- Did you spend more or less on an item than you had budgeted?
- Where and why did you spend more or less?
- What happened if you overspent and still had needs left?
- How did you evaluate what is important?

EXERCISE 2: FREE TIME

In this exercise group members plan the use of twenty-four hours of free time. This period without responsibilities, obligations, or demands begins at the start of the group work. The work you do in this exercise should help you understand what is important to each member of the group.

Process

1. The group should brainstorm how to spend the free time with each member participating in the brainstorming session. Limit the time you spend on this activity and make sure you structure the brainstorming session so each person participates.

2. Next, each participant should write a plan for the twenty-four hours, listing activities, mapping out blocks of time for each activity, and perhaps explaining the reasons for the choices.
3. At the conclusion, each member should share his plan and what it tells about the priorities in his life.

Reflection
Questions ❓

REFLECTION QUESTIONS

- How had you intended to spend the time?
- Why did you choose the activities?
- How do these differ from your normal day?
- How do you compare with others in your group?

EXERCISE 3: PRIORITIES RANKING

By identifying and comparing your existing priorities with your ideal, you should become more aware of what your true interests and values are. You may want to think about whether you need to rethink how you use your time and adjust what you do so that it is more in accord with your true values and interests.

Process

1. The group should discuss the ten needs listed below and how important they are to people in general.
2. Using column 1, each group member should rank them from 1 to 10 (1 is most satisfied with; 10 least satisfied) in the order in which they are now being satisfied.
3. Next, each member should rank the needs again in column 2, this time in the order in which she would like to have them met (1 most satisfied and 10 least satisfied).
4. Group members should share how they ranked their needs in the two lists and explore as a group how the members could accomplish their ideal.

Column 1	Column 2
Rank needs (1 to 10) in the order in which they are now being satisfied.	Rank needs (1 to 10) in the order in which you would like to have them met.
_____ support group	_____ support group
_____ intimacy	_____ intimacy
_____ exercise	_____ exercise
_____ nutrition	_____ nutrition
_____ sleep	_____ sleep
_____ recreation	_____ recreation
_____ alone time	_____ alone time
_____ time for what I love to do	_____ time for what I love to do
_____ variety of work	_____ variety of work
_____ brave questions, brave answers	_____ brave questions, brave answers

Source: Simon, S., Howe, L., & Kirschenbaum, H. (1995).

chapter 4

Professional Obligations and Duty to Clients

In previous chapters we have worked with the CASW (2005a) and NASW (1999) codes of ethics, which identify core values and principles. We have also looked at the companion documents or sections of the codes, which include guidelines, commentaries, or standards that explicate the values and principles for professional practice. The codes and companion documents provide broad guidelines on how professional values are to be translated into ethical professional behaviour. In this chapter we focus on those documents in professional ethical codes that contribute to our understanding of what professional judgment means in the context of carrying out the "essential professional duties and obligations to clients"—that is, practising in a nonjudgmental, objective, and competent manner for the best interests of clients.

CASW *Guidelines for Ethical Practice* (2005b) gives priority to clients' interests; client self-determination is supported in the section on "respect for the inherent dignity and worth of persons" (sec. 1.0). In the area of professional "competency," the CASW *Guidelines* discuss ethical responsibility in research (6.0) and to the profession (7.0). In the standards document of the NASW (1999) *Code of Ethics,* the commentary on self-determination (1.02), competence (1.04), and cultural competence and social diversity (1.06) give direction for practising in a nonjudgmental, objective, and competent manner.

INQUIRY PROJECT

In addition to CASW and NASW codes of ethics, examine documents in at least one other professional code of ethics, and locate the discussion of acting in the "best interests" of clients or acting in a nonjudgmental, objective, and competent manner. You will probably need to go to discussions of associated values, such as respect for diversity, self-determination, and integrity in practice. Given what you have found in your review of the professional code of ethics, as well as in the CASW and NASW codes of ethics, respond to the following questions:

- What is your understanding of what it means to practise in the best interests of clients or in a nonjudgmental and objective manner?
- Does acting in the best interests of clients or in a nonjudgmental manner always mean doing what the client views is in her best interests or having no judgment at all? Please explain your response.
- What do you think is required to be competent as a professional?
- What questions are you left with after reading the documents in these codes?
- Develop a strategy to gather information and guidance for deepening your understanding about practising in the best interests of a client or in a non-judgmental and objective manner.

Practice Situation: **The Joneses**

Read the practice situation described below and think about what it means for the social worker to act in the best interests of a client or to be nonjudgmental, objective, and competent. Apply one or more of the ethical decision-making models in Chapter 2 to work through practice questions provided at the conclusion of the discussion. Note that there is a significant amount of background information on the mental illness Mr. Jones may be experiencing. As you read, reflect on whether you think it is too much or not enough in order for the social worker to carry out her role in the mental health team. Is information not provided that you think you would want if you were the professional?

POSSIBLE MISDIAGNOSIS

A social worker/counsellor works for an agency that serves mentally ill patients and their families. Currently, she is working on a multi-professional team that includes members from social work, psychiatry, nursing, and psychology. Her client is Mr. Jones and his family. Mr. Jones has been in and out of psychiatric institutions for years, and the family needs considerable support from mental health professionals. Mr. Jones has been diagnosed with several disorders including generalized anxiety disorder, panic disorder, and, most recently, a personality disorder. He has had problems with alcohol abuse in the past and has made several suicide attempts. The professional team is growing quite frustrated with Mr. Jones, and the worker feels that this frustration is due to his apparent lack of progress.

The professional has observed some characteristics in Mr. Jones that do not seem to fit with his previous and current diagnoses. For example, he has very erratic behaviour; at times he acts like he is functioning fine; at other times he is childlike. She has also observed that he can be very angry at one moment and very cooperative at another.

The professional thinks that Mr. Jones may have been misdiagnosed. She believes that his symptoms are consistent with a diagnosis of dissociative identity disorder (DID). When she approaches her supervisor with this possibility, the supervisor dismisses it, stating that DID is extremely rare and not even a proven valid diagnosis.

BACKGROUND INFORMATION

According to the *DSM-IV-TR* (APA 2000), dissociative identity disorder (DID) is defined as follows:

> The essential features of dissociative identity disorder is the presence of two or more distinct identities or personality traits (Criterion A) that recurrently take control of behaviour (Criterion B). There is an inability to recall important personal information, the extent of which is too great to be explained by ordinary forgetfulness (Criterion C). The disturbance is not due to the direct physiological effects of a substance or a general medical condition (Criterion D). (p. 526)

In her book *The Myth of Sanity: Divided Consciousness and the Promise of Awareness* (2001) Martha Stout explains why an individual may develop a dissociative disorder:

> The answer, paradoxically, lies in a perfectly normal function of the mind known as dissociation, which is the universal reaction to extreme fear and pain. In traumatic situations, dissociation mercifully allows us to disconnect emotional content—the feeling part of our "selves"—from our conscious awareness. Disconnected from feelings in this way, we stand a better chance of surviving the ordeal, of doing what we have to do, of getting through a critical moment in which our emotions would only be in the way. Dissociation causes a person to view an ongoing traumatic event almost as if she/[he] were a spectator. (p. 8)

Steinberg and Schnall support this description of DID in their book *Stranger in the Mirror* (2000). They state that "symptoms of DID are fascinating because they express the universal language of pain in an intensely imaginative and metaphorical way, yet at the same time they seem so bizarre and theatrical as to arouse incredulity" (p. 19). They further state:

> Another basis for skepticism many clinicians have towards dissociative disorders, especially DID, can be found in the philosophical underpinnings of their traditional training. The presence of a variety of personality states that take control of a person's thoughts and behaviour at different times contradicts a long-held assumption. For years the thinking was that we should have one unitary personality, and skeptics are reluctant to question such a fundamental concept. (p. 19)

Many people are intrigued by DID, yet many deny its existence. It is often thought of as a fictitious disorder because of the way it has been presented in and perceived by the general public. "No other field of medicine in modern times has been buried under such a mudslide of misconception, skepticism, and plain ignorance" (Steinberg & Schnall, 2000, p. 19). However, in recent years there has been a change in attitude toward this disorder, and many believe that DID is actually much more common than once thought. According to the Sidran Institute (2003), "Dissociative identity disorder (DID) (previously known as Multiple Personality Disorder MPD) and other dissociative disorders are now understood to be fairly common effects of severe trauma in early childhood, most typically extreme, repeated physical, emotional, and sexual abuse" (p. 1). In addition, according to Steinberg and Schnall (2000), "recent studies have shown that far from being rare, dissociative disorders are much more prevalent than previously realized. Individuals with DID number as much as one percent of the general population, or more than 2.5 million people. This is a conservative estimate considering how under diagnosed dissociative disorders are. The true figure for the dissociation disorder is probably closer to ten percent" (p. 21). If we apply these statistics to the Canadian population of 30 million, anywhere between 300,000 and 3 million people could be affected with this disorder. The American Psychological Association (2000) states that "the sharp rise in reported cases of dissociative identity disorder in the United States in recent years has been subject to very different interpretations" (p. 528), and Steinberg and Schnall (2000) report that a group of experts believe that greater awareness of the diagnosis among mental health professional has resulted in the identification of cases that were previously undiagnosed.

Several studies have focused on DID. As a result of this research, new tools have emerged that can be used to test and diagnose this disorder. "Many research reports support the view that DID is a real illness with a consistent pattern of symptoms, a characteristic course, and chronic impairment if untreated. The Steinberg Clinical Interview for *DSM-IV* dissociative disorders (2000) field trials provides evidence that DID is a real illness with clinically measurable symptoms" (Steinberg & Schnall, 2000, p. 26). This study further notes that "the idea that people can successfully fake or exaggerate multiple personalities was soundly disproved by Dr. George Fraser, M.D., and associates in a 1999 study. Using the SCID-D and other psychological tests, their research project detected individuals who were directed to fake multiple personalities in a group consisting of the pretenders, DID patients, schizophrenics, and normal people. On the SCID-D 100 percent of the true DID patients were diagnosed with DID, and none of the pretenders and normals were" (Steinberg & Schnall, 2000, pp. 26–27).

The Sidran Institute (2003) reports that many professionals in different contexts often see people who live with this disorder:

> They change from therapist to therapist and from medication to medication, getting treatment for symptoms but making little or no actual progress. Research has documented that on average, people with dissociative disorders have spent seven years in the mental health system prior to accurate diagnosis. . . . In fact, many people who are diagnosed with dissociative disorders also have secondary diagnoses of depression, anxiety, or panic disorders. (pp. 3–4)

Research shows that DID is a curable disorder. Steinberg and Schnall state that "DID patients have a good prognosis for recovery once they are accurately diagnosed and treated appropriately." The problem, according to Steinberg and Schnall (2000), is "the failure of many clinicians to make an accurate diagnosis" (p. 27). They further claim that "recovery is a challenging process that takes time—an average of three to five years of weekly sessions. The results can be enormously gratifying and transformative, especially when you consider that many people with DID spend long years of their lives in treatment for panic attacks, OCD, depression, anxiety disorder, bipolar disorder, ADHD, and even schizophrenia without this kind of progress" (p. 27).

Other research supports the view that a favourable outcome is possible if DID is treated appropriately. "Dissociative disorders are highly responsive to individual psychotherapy, or talk therapy. . . . In fact, among comparable severe psychiatric disorders, dissociative disorder may be the condition that carries the best prognosis if proper treatment is undertaken and completed . . . individuals with dissociative disorders have been successfully treated by therapists of all professional backgrounds working in a variety of settings" (Sidran, 2003, p. 4).

Despite the evidence that DID is a valid disorder, a great deal of controversy associated with the diagnosis of the disorder remains. Currently, DID is listed in the *DSM-IV* as a diagnostic category, but not everyone believes it should be. Lalonde's (2001) research on the controversy surrounding DID found that "both Canadian and American psychiatrists show little consensus regarding the diagnostic status of scientific validity of dissociative amnesia and dissociative identity disorder" (p. 1). The diagnosis of dissociative identity disorder is still under scrutiny by many professionals in the mental health field.

PROFESSIONAL'S USE OF BACKGROUND INFORMATION AND IDENTIFICATION OF OPTIONS

As the summary of background information indicates, DID is currently a prime area of research. The level of professional understanding about DID is much more advanced than it was even a few years ago. It has also been shown that aspects of DID are widely accepted as effects of severe trauma, and that continued trauma can affect some individuals to the point of hiding or altering parts of their personality.

To add to the complexities of this disorder, misdiagnosis is often a part of the process. The *DSM-IV-TR* (APA, 2000) discusses the difficulty in diagnosing this disorder:

> The differential diagnosis between dissociative identity disorder and a variety of other mental disorders (including Schizophrenia and other psychotic disorders, Bipolar Disorder, Anxiety Disorder, Somatization Disorders, and Personality Disorder) is complicated by the apparently overlapping symptom presentations. For example, the presence of more than one dissociated personality state may be mistaken for a delusion or the communication from one identity to another may be mistaken for an auditory hallucination, leading to confusion with the psychotic disorders, and shifts between identity states may be confused with cyclical mood fluctuations leading to confusion with bipolar disorder. (p. 529)

In Mr. Jones's case, the professional notes that Mr. Jones's experiences are quite similar to other disorders, resulting in misunderstanding and consequent misdiagnosis. He has been in and out of mental institutions for years with multiple diagnoses and without much success or progress. He has made several suicide attempts and has abused alcohol. The research shows that DID is a legitimate disorder that can be accurately diagnosed if tested and treated properly, and it can be cured.

The professional reflects on the background information she has examined, her place on the treatment team, and the views of her supervisor. She thinks she has three options in her work with Mr. Jones and the team:

1. Follow the instructions of her supervisor and accept the diagnosis of the team, particularly the psychiatrist on the team.
2. Attempt to find appropriate assistance outside of the team and arrange for reassessment of Mr. Jones.
3. Make a proposal to the team regarding why she thinks that Mr. Jones should be reassessed.

PROFESSIONAL'S REFERENCE TO CODE OF ETHICS

The professional examines the CASW *Code of Ethics* (2005a), with the companion document, *Guidelines for Ethical Practice* (2005b), as important information to consider in her decision making. The worker finds many applicable sections in both of these documents. For example, the section on "Ethical Responsibilities to the Workplace" in the *Guidelines* states: "Social workers work toward the best possible standards of service provision and are accountable for their practice" (4.1.2). It also states that "social workers appropriately challenge and work to improve policies, procedures, practices and service provisions that are not in the best interests of clients" (4.1.4). The worker feels that this statement supports her desire to have Mr. Jones assessed in order to protect his interests yet also supports the need for her to discuss the matter among the team members.

The professional also thinks the section of the CASW *Guidelines* on "Ethical Responsibilities to Colleagues" provides support for options two and three but also could be used to support option one. Statements in these sections provide guidance on collaboration and consultation with other professionals: "Social workers relate to both social work colleagues and colleagues from other disciplines with respect, integrity and courtesy, and seek to understand differences in viewpoints and practice" (3.1). In addition, "when collaborating with other professionals, social workers utilize the expertise of other disciplines for the benefit of their clients" (3.2).

INQUIRY QUESTIONS

- Do you think the background information given for this situation is appropriate? Do you think it is either too much or insufficient in relation to the diagnosis and alternatives for the diagnosis? Is information missing that you think is critical? If yes, identify this information and where you might obtain it.
- Given what you know at this point, what would you advise the professional to do? What is the ethical basis for your recommendation? What other sections in the CASW *Guidelines* or in other relevant professional codes of ethics can you use to support your recommendation?

THE OBLIGATION TO BE NONJUDGMENTAL AND OBJECTIVE: HOW IT RELATES TO PROFESSIONAL JUDGMENT

The importance of professional judgment in ethical decision making has been noted in the previous chapters and is cited frequently in professional codes of ethics. For example, the introduction to the CASW *Guidelines for Ethical Practice* (2005b) states that "the extent to which each responsibility is enforceable is a matter of professional judgment" (p. 1). The last paragraph of the NASW *Code of Ethics* (1999) also emphasizes the importance of professional judgment: "Principles and standards must be applied by individuals of good character who discern moral questions and, in good faith, seek to make reliable ethical judgments" (p. 3).

INQUIRY QUESTION

- What does it mean, within the context of professional judgment, to state that ethical practice requires the worker to be "nonjudgmental" and "objective"? Is this a contradiction, or do these requirements work together? Explain your answer.

THE ROLE OF BACKGROUND INFORMATION AND CRITICAL THINKING IN PROFESSIONAL JUDGMENT

For many of the previous practice situations we have attempted to provide background information that a professional may find helpful in thinking through what she or he should do in a particular situation. The background information brings in relevant research and at times examples of similar practice situations reported in the literature. The information is provided so that the professional can be as informed as possible in terms of current research and "state-of-the-art" practice knowledge.

INQUIRY QUESTION

Think about the "lens" we use to filter information, and then respond to this question:

- How do the requirements for being nonjudgmental and objective fit within the context of accessing and applying relevant information? Are there strategies you could use to monitor and evaluate the types and quality of information you gather for making decisions?

One approach to understanding the "negative" role of judgment in decision making is to think about what it means to be "biased" in how we view events and people in our life. To be biased means to have a set of beliefs or perceptions, shaped by values, through which we view a person or event. Biases predetermine our feelings and ideas. This "lens" or set of biases prevents us from seeing people or events for what they are. For example, a prejudice creates a negative "lens" for viewing people of colour or other minorities, whom we "prejudge" based on their membership in these groups. A "lens" can also cause us to "idealize" what we experience so that we emphasize the positive features and are unable to appreciate a more complex view of the experience. We are no longer able to assess the individual talents and contributions of individuals because of the barriers our positive or negative prejudices create. For example, suppose you are working with a youth from a neighbourhood in which you were previously a community worker and you had a very positive experience in that community and in particular with the youth's family. The youth has been referred because of misconduct in school. Given your past experience, you come to a quick judgment that the behaviour must be the result of school dynamics rather than personal issues of the youth. Although this may be the case, the judgment you have made can potentially hinder you from gathering the types of information that would help you understand the situation more deeply.

A helpful way to think about being nonjudgmental may be to think about a professional as one who continually examines himself in terms of the biases or prejudices he brings to practice that would prevent him from fairly and objectively assessing the contributions and needs of people he works with. So being nonjudgmental does not preclude using professional judgment but rather entails laying aside biases or prejudgments that would hinder the professional from being able to access and evaluate objectively background information and personal client information to inform decision making.

CRITICAL THINKING AND ETHICAL REASONING

One approach for becoming sensitive to the role of biases in our thinking and for gaining a degree of control over the negative role of biases in ethical reasoning is to use a critical-thinking approach to critique our own thinking. This brief section on critical thinking will leave you with the responsibility to continually assess and challenge your thought processes and encourage you to increase your ability to be nonjudgmental and objective.

Reflection Questions ? REFLECTION QUESTION

As you work on the ideas in this section and the practice situation that follows, reflect on whether you agree or disagree with this statement:

• Critically assessing the thought processes underlying your reactions to ideas and events as well as your ability to interpret, evaluate, and make informed judgments, will enable you to continually grow as an ethical practitioner.

Definitions of critical thinking all include the ability to "interpret, evaluate, and make informed judgments about the adequacy of arguments, data and conclusions" (Pascarella & Terenzini, 1991, p. 118). In addition to the "rational" abilities identified with critical thinking, many researchers also identify emotions and feelings as central components of critical thinking and of our values, ideas, behaviours, and sources of resistance to alternative perspectives (Brookfield, 1987). Richard Paul, director of research and professional development at the Center for Critical Thinking, argues that critical thinking skills are the foundation of ethical reasoning (Paul & Elder, 2002). Paul's critical-thinking framework involves applying elements and standards of thinking to our own thoughts as well as the thoughts others in order to attain a deeper reflection about our ideas, feelings, and beliefs.

INQUIRY PROJECT

REFLECTING ON YOUR CRITICAL-THINKING ABILITIES

1. Assess your own thinking by responding to following:
   - What biases or prejudices influence your thinking, even to a small degree? How do you deal with these influences?
   - How much of your thinking is vague, muddled, inconsistent, inaccurate, illogical, or superficial?
   - Do you have any conscious standards for determining when you are thinking well and when you are thinking poorly?
2. What is the relation of critical thinking skills to ethical practice? Explain your response.
3. Using one or two of the references on critical thinking provided at the end of this chapter or others you locate on your own,
   - identify at least one approach to critical thinking that you can apply to reflect on your own thinking;
   - describe how you would apply this approach and how it would help you to advance your ability to make sound professional ethical judgments.

Along with tools for critical thinking, the work you have completed, particularly in Chapter 3, on reflecting on your personal values contributes to your ability to be non-judgmental and in turn to be effective in reasoning through the ethical dimensions of practice.

INQUIRY QUESTIONS

Review the work you completed in Chapter 3 and reflect on what you discovered about your personal values and how this contributes to your ability to be nonjudgmental.

- What biases do you bring to practice that could interfere with your ability to be non-judgmental and objective?
- Given the importance of professional judgment and the critical-thinking work described previously, what do you view as important practices that would help you to continually monitor how your values impact your judgments?

Practice Situation: **Roxanne—Mental Illness, Medication, and Client Self-Determination**

The Acme Community Supports Organization is a publicly funded organization with the mandate to provide community living services to clients released from active-care psychiatric hospitals. The mission of the organization is to provide services and links to services to assist clients who suffer from mental illness. Social workers in this organization are expected to integrate and maintain these persons in the community. One of the goals of this organization is to reduce expensive active-care hospital use by decreasing the relapse rates of psychiatric patients and providing active supports for independent living.

Roxanne is a thirty-six-year-old client who suffers from schizophrenia, paranoid type. She is a single mother with two children: a girl age twelve and a boy age eight. Roxanne functions well when on her medications and maintains a three-bedroom townhouse in low-income cooperative housing. Roxanne has been taking her medications for one and a half years and attends parent support groups and appropriate counselling. She has been hospitalized eight times in the last ten years. Her children have been apprehended by social services once when Roxanne had an active episode and left them alone for two days, but for the most part she has been a loving and devoted mother.

Recently Roxanne told her social worker that she does not need to continue her medications. She complains of weight gain, blunted affect, agitation, and body shakes as some of the more intolerable side effects of her medications. She also says she is unhappy: she has no extended family support, which she feels is due to her past erratic behaviour during her active psychiatric episodes. Her ex-husband lives in another town and sees the children infrequently, partly because the children are settled in their home and school and partly due to animosity between him and Roxanne. Roxanne is lonely and feels her excess weight caused by the medications makes her unattractive and unable to find a romantic partner. She is also "fed up" with her neighbours in her housing unit and believes they get overly involved in her affairs and talk about her behind her back.

Inquiry
Questions

INQUIRY QUESTIONS

- What is your initial reaction to Roxanne's desire not to continue with medication? What is the basis of your reaction and what values underlie your reaction?
- What are the primary ethical issues in this situation? Why have you chosen these?
- What sections of your professional code of ethics apply to the issues you have identified?

BACKGROUND INFORMATION

According to Carson, Butcher, & Mineka (2000), schizophrenia is defined as "psychosis characterized by the break down of integrated personality functioning, withdrawal from reality, emotional blunting and distortion, and disturbances in thought and behaviour" (p. G-23). They go on to define schizophrenia, paranoid type, as a "type of schizophrenia in which a person is increasingly suspicious, has severe difficulties in interpersonal relationships, and experiences, absurd, illogical, and often changing delusions. Other types are: catatonic, disorganized, residual and undifferentiated" (p. G-23).

It is important to note that schizophrenia tends to be chronic, and "loss of hope is a common reaction to chronic, debilitating diseases" (Noordsy et al., 2002, p. 319). Further deleterious effects are that "individuals with severe mental illness frequently find themselves impoverished, stigmatized and excluded from opportunities to participate in community roles in addition to suffering the symptoms of their illness" (Noordsy et al., 2002, p. 318). Research indicates that schizophrenia is best managed by a biopsychosocial approach to managed care to reduce psychiatric crisis (Falloon, Held, Roncone, Coverdale, & Laidlaw, 1998). Studies of schizophrenics in the community have shown that "[c]ontinuation of medication after remission from acute episodes prevents major occurrences." It is also important to note that "even with optimal adherence to medication, not all cases will respond and not all psychotic episodes can be prevented" (Falloon et al., 1998, p. 45).

WHO IS THE CLIENT? FURTHER INFORMATION ABOUT THE ILLNESS AND ROXANNE'S CHILDREN

In this situation, an argument can be made that the worker has more than one client: the mother and the children. The client has expressed the intention of discontinuing her medication, which may have adverse consequences for her two children.

As noted previously, Roxanne suffers from schizophrenia, paranoid type, with delusions and hallucinations. According to Carson et al. (2000), delusions are defined as "false beliefs about reality but maintained in spite of strong evidence to the contrary" (p. G-23). Delusions take innumerable forms. An affected person may be absolutely convinced that she is a victim of witchcraft or a target of organized crime. Roxanne feels she is being spied on by her neighbours. It is possible that her neighbours get overly involved in her affairs and talk about her behind her back, but she may also be suffering from a delusion. Hallucinations, on the other hand, are "false perceptions such as things seen or heard that are not real or present" (Carson et al., 2000, p. G-23). It could be inferred that Roxanne may experience any or all of these phenomena while alone with the children. Roxanne was left home for two days during an active episode in the past, and neighbours who were concerned about the children called social services. The children were placed in temporary foster care until it was determined Roxanne was able to care for them.

INQUIRY QUESTIONS

- Does the further information about schizophrenia, paranoid type, and about Roxanne's children change your initial reactions about how to respond to Roxanne's desire to discontinue medication? Why are your views the same or different given this information?
- What ethical issues does this information raise for you, and what in your professional code of ethics relates to the issues that are present in this situation?
- What further background information, if any, would be important to inform your decision making?
- What, if anything, have you done to critically monitor your thinking during your responses to these questions?

CONCLUSION

This chapter has focused on the "essential" professional responsibilities and duties to practise in a nonjudgmental, objective, and competent manner for the best interests of clients. The chapter has also addressed what it means to be nonjudgmental, objective, and competent as a practitioner in terms of accessing and using relevant information, working with colleagues, being aware of our biases, and evaluating our underlying thought processes. We have also reviewed the difficulty of defining what the client's "best interests" entail and discussed the related issue of deciding who defines best interests.

In the next two chapters we will continue to focus on professional obligations to clients as we examine the areas of protecting confidentiality, ensuring informed consent, and being honest with clients.

NOTES

_____

_____

_____

_____

_____

_____

_____

_____

_____

_____

_____

_____

_____

_____

NOTES

NOTES

NOTES

NOTES

NOTES

REFERENCES

American Psychiatric Association (APA). (2000). *Diagnostic and statistical manual of mental disorders (DSM-IV)* (4th ed.). Washington, DC: Author.

Canadian Association of Social Workers. (2005a). *Code of ethics.* Ottawa, ON: Author.

Canadian Association of Social Workers. (2005b). *Guidelines for ethical practice.* Ottawa, ON: Author.

Carson, R., Butcher, J., & Mineka, S. (2000). *Abnormal psychology and modern life* (11th ed.). Needham Heights: Pearson Education.

Falloon, I., Held, T., Roncone, R., Coverdale, J., & Laidlaw, T. (1998). Optimal treatment strategies to enhance recovery from schizophrenia. *Australian & New Zealand Journal of Psychiatry, 32,* 32–43.

Heston, L.L. (1996). *Mending minds.* New York: W.H. Freeman.

Lalonde, J.K. (2001). Canadian and American psychiatrists' attitudes toward dissociative disorders diagnoses. *Canadian Journal of Psychiatry, 46*(5), 407–412.

National Association of Social Workers. (1999). *Code of ethics of the National Association of Social Workers.* Washington, DC: Author.

National Institute of Mental Health. (2001). *Research on child neglect.* PA-01-060. Washington, DC: Various: Authors.

Noordsy, D., Torrey, W., Mueser, K., Mean, S., O'Keefe, C., & Fox, L. (2002). Recovery from severe mental illness; and intrapersonal and functional outcome definition. *International Review of Psychiatry, 14,* 318–326.

Sellwood, W., Thomas, C.S., Tarrier, N., Jones, S., Clewes, J., James, A., Welford, M., Palmer, J., & McCarthy, E. (1999). A randomized controlled trial of home-based rehabilitation versus outpatient-based rehabilitation for patients suffering from chronic schizophrenia. *Social Psychiatry, 34,* 250–253. Manchester: Steinkopff Verlag.

Sidran Institute. (2003). About trauma: Dissociative disorders. Retrieved October 27, 2003, from http://sidran.org/catalog/vegb.html

Steinberg, M., & Schnall, M. (2000). *Stranger in the mirror.* New York: Cliff Street Books.

Stout, M. (2001). *The myth of sanity: Divided consciousness and the promise of awareness.* New York: Penguin Books.

Treatment Advocacy Center. (1998). Schizophrenia treatment side effects may cause patients to discontinue medication. Retrieved October 29, 2003, from http://www.psychlaws.org/briefingpapers/bp15.htm

CRITICAL THINKING REFERENCES

Brookfield, Stephen D. (1987). *Developing critical thinkers*. San Francisco: Jossey-Bass.

Ennis, R. (1985). *Goals for critical thinking/resources curriculum*. Champaign: University of Illinois Press.

King, Patricia M., Strohm Kitchener, K. (1994). *Developing reflective judgment*. San Francisco: Jossey-Bass.

Nosich, Gerald M. (2001). *Learning to think things through*. Upper Saddle River, NJ: Prentice-Hall.

Pascarella, E.T., & Terenzini, P.T. (1991). *How college affects students: Findings and insights from twenty years of research*. San Francisco: Jossey-Bass.

Paul, Richard. (1995). *Critical thinking: How to prepare students for a rapidly changing world*. Santa Rosa, CA: Foundation for Critical Thinking.

Paul, Richard W., & Elder, L. (2002). *Critical thinking: Tools for taking charge of your professional and personal life*. Upper Saddle River, NJ: Prentice Hall.

Paul, Richard W., & Elder, L. (2005). *Miniature guide to understanding the foundations of ethical reasoning*. Dillon Beach, CA: Foundation for Critical Thinking.

Porter, Burton F. (2002). *Fundamentals of critical thinking*. New York: Oxford University Press.

Confidentiality in the Professional Relationship: Protecting Client Privacy

In this chapter we will examine what it means to protect a service user's right to privacy within the context of a professional relationship, particularly in social work or counselling. Privacy is a core value in many societies, and the ethical importance of protecting privacy in professional relationships was identified in physicians' first code of ethics: "What I may see or hear in the course of treatment . . . I will keep to myself, holding such things shameful to be spoken about" (Van Hoose & Kottler, 1985, p. 7).

CONFIDENTIALITY IN PROFESSIONAL CODES OF ETHICS AND ITS RELATION TO PRIVILEGED COMMUNICATION

Maintaining confidentiality is the primary means of protecting service users' privacy. The complexity, however, of defining confidentiality is reflected in the amount of space devoted to the topic in professional codes of ethics such as the NASW *Code of Ethics* (1999). The section on "Privacy and Confidentiality" is the longest section of the NASW code (sec. 1.07) and begins with the statement, "Social workers should respect clients' right to privacy. Social workers should not solicit private information from clients unless it is essential to providing services or conducting social work evaluation or research. Once private information is shared, standards of confidentiality apply" (sec. 1.07a). This section is followed by seventeen paragraphs describing what those "standards of confidentiality" are and what they entail for professional practice. In the CASW *Code of Ethics* (2005a) confidentiality is described as a "cornerstone of professional social work relationships" (Value 5).

Five principles in the CASW *Code of Ethics* clarify what confidentiality means in practice. They include instances when confidentiality may be violated in order to adhere to relevant laws, a court order, or ethical obligations to others. These obligations include the rights of certain individuals to obtain client information when it affects the well-being of others. In practice this means social workers and counsellors are often not able to guarantee to service users "absolute confidentiality." The American Counseling Association (ACA) *Code of Ethics* (1995), section B, covers six topics ranging from right to privacy to consultation.

Privileged communication, which resembles "absolute confidentiality," is a legal term that designates the "quality of certain specific types of relationships that prevent information, acquired from such relationships, from being disclosed in court or other legal proceedings" (Keith-Spiegel & Koocher, 1985, p. 58). Most counselling and social work "communications" do not meet all the criteria, as defined by Wigmore (1961), for privileged communication:

1. The communication must originate in confidence that it will not be disclosed.
2. The confidentiality of information must be essential to the full and satisfactory maintenance of the relationship.
3. The relationship must be one that should be sedulously fostered in the opinion of the community.
4. Injury to the relationship by disclosure of the communication must be greater than the benefit gained by the correct disposal of litigation regarding the information (Schwitzgebel & Schwitzgebel, 1980).

Because privileged communication is a legal and not an ethical concept, questions about whether a communication is privileged need to be resolved through legal consultation.

SHARING SERVICE-USER INFORMATION WITH THIRD PARTIES AND THE DUTY TO WARN AND PROTECT

Since social workers and counsellors often cannot guarantee privileged communication or "absolute" confidentiality, they must be clear with service users about the limits of confidentiality they are able to offer. The "relative" confidentiality that they can provide means ensuring service users that information and communications shared with third parties, such as supervisors and colleagues, is done in the interest of providing services and with the service user's understanding and consent. When appropriate, they should also let service users know that information that is shared with third parties within other contexts, such as through court order, must be done so within the bounds of legal mandates (Strom-Gottfried & Corcoran, 1998; Dickson, 1998). Duty to warn and consequently disclose confidential information to third parties when there is a danger of harm to others is a legal requirement and a critical issue that professionals must address. In a previous chapter we discussed the *Tarasoff* case (Perlin, 1997) in which the court decided that a professional has not only a "duty to warn but also a duty to protect" third parties who he thinks are in danger due to information they have gained from his service users. Other important court cases that have addressed the issue of duty to warn are the *Bradley* (Laughran & Bakken, 1984), *Jablonski* (Laughran & Bakken, 1984), and *Hedlund* (Laughran & Bakken, 1984) cases. In the end, counsellors and social workers "inform clients, to the extent possible, about the disclosure of confidential information and its potential consequences before the disclosure is made. This applies in all circumstances of disclosure, except when, in the professional judgment of the social worker, sharing this information with the client may bring about, or exacerbate, serious harm to individuals or the public" (CASW, 2005b, sec. 1.5.3).

Refer to one of the professional codes of ethics, such as CASW, NASW, or the American Counseling Association, and respond to the following:

- Given what you have found about confidentiality in the code of ethics you have chosen to review and what we have briefly described in the beginning of this chapter, in a short paragraph describe how you would characterize the responsibility of helping professionals to protect service users' privacy. In your description, explain why confidentiality is characterized as "relative" rather than "absolute" for social work and counselling and similar professions. In your explanation use citations from the professional code you are referencing to give examples of how it deals with the relative nature of confidentiality.

- Describe what you think are the two or three major issues you anticipate you will face, or have faced, as a professional in respecting service users' right to privacy as well as addressing the requirements of your employer, the community, and other third parties.

Practice Situation: **Sarah**

Sarah, a sixteen-year-old who works as a prostitute, was removed from the street under the Alberta government's Protection of Children Involved in Prostitution Act (1995). She was confined to a safe house, where she has spent the last twenty-one days. Sarah ran away from home a year ago after her mother's boyfriend moved into the home and started sexually abusing Sarah. While on the street she met other young girls who offered her a place to stay and introduced her to the life of prostitution.

Throughout her stay she has made progress with the social worker in the safe house and feels she can trust her worker. She has confided to the social worker about her cocaine abuse and has also disclosed information about her pimp, his whereabouts, and the location of a trick pad she had once been forced to work in. Sarah will be released in five days and has planned to move in with a girlfriend she met while working on the streets. Sarah claims that this friend has never worked in the sex industry and has a job at a local bar.

The social worker is concerned about the lives of the girls who are working in the trick pad Sarah identified and is aware of how difficult it is for the RCMP to locate these establishments in order to rescue the children forced to work there. She is also concerned about Sarah's well-being if she notifies the authorities about the "trick pad" and the whereabouts of the pimp. The social worker has reservations about Sarah's proposed living arrangements when she leaves the safe house, because her roommate may have ties to Sarah's former life of prostitution and drug abuse, causing Sarah to relapse.

BACKGROUND INFORMATION ON TEENAGE PROSTITUTION

Teenage prostitution is a worldwide social problem. Those who become involved in this life have run to the streets to escape abuse, abandonment, poverty, and neglect at home. According to Hodgson (1997), "36% of young prostitutes suffered physical abuse, 20% sexual abuse, 21% psychological abuse, and 16% reported all three types of abuse" (32). The abuse these girls suffer can affect their self-esteem and self-confidence and cause them to be more vulnerable to sexual exploitation.

The adolescents often feel that the street is their best option, but once the reality of lack of money, shelter, food, or companionship hits, they find it hard to cope. This is where the pimp appears. Because the young girl has no place to go, hasn't eaten, and is feeling helpless, she is extremely vulnerable to the displays of affection and concern the pimp offers. The pimp gains the child's trust and often further isolates her, thus increasing her dependency on him. After a child becomes financially and emotionally dependent on a pimp, he introduces her to the world of commercial sex.

Protective safe houses (secured facilities with restricted access) have been set up in Alberta to house children who have been removed from the street under the Protection of Children Involved in Prostitution Act (1995). The act enables police officers and social workers to detain the young prostitutes for a minimum of five days. They may then apply to the courts for a maximum of two additional confinement periods of up to twenty-one days each. Allowing more time is viewed as crucial because it obviously takes more than five days for most of these young prostitutes to be integrated back into society.

Once the adolescents are in a safe house they are given medical care and a social-psychological assessment. Sections 4A and C of the Protection of Children Involved in Prostitution Act (1995) states that in order to apply for an additional twenty-one-day confinement, "Release of the child from a protective safe house presents a risk to the life or safety of the child because the child is unable or unwilling to stop engaging in or attempting to engage in prostitution" and "it is in the best interests of the child to order a period of further confinement for the purposes of making programs or other services available to the child in a safe and secure environment" (p. 5). If, in the opinion of the director of a safe house, the child has reached the age of sixteen and is able to provide for his or her own needs and safety, the child must be released.

BACKGROUND INFORMATION ON CONFIDENTIALITY

Confidentiality is frequently described as the foundation on which the client–worker relationship is built because it is viewed as a precursor to building trust. In addition, the promise of confidentiality is often a central factor in a client's willingness to even approach a professional and to continue the relationship.

One of the consequences of a breach of confidentiality, therefore, is that those in need of services are less likely to seek them (Strom-Gottfried & Corcoran, 1998). Because of this, the limits of confidentiality must be communicated to ensure that the service user's expectations match the reality of what the worker can provide within the context of "relative" confidentiality.

As Rothman (2005) indicates, there are "exceptions to the obligation of workers to preserve confidentiality," one exception relevant to the present situation being "if the client is in danger of harming self or others" (p. 203). The CASW *Code of Ethics* (2005a) includes this exception: "The general expectation that social workers will keep information confidential does not apply when disclosure is necessary to prevent serious, foreseeable, and imminent harm to a client or others" (Value 5). It further states that information that is disclosed should be the "least amount" required to "achieve the desired purpose" (Value 5).

The professional's obligation to prevent harm is balanced with a need to preserve client self-determination, but most would claim that preventing harm takes precedence when there is an impending need to protect the individual from self-destructive behaviour. In Sarah's situation a life of prostitution may pose serious harm to her in the form of abuse or homicide. The vast majority of female prostitutes are beaten by their pimps and abused by their customers. According to the Missing Kids website (2003), "Rape is often a common occurrence for girls involved in prostitution, with up to seventy percent of female-juvenile prostitutes admitting that they have been raped by customers an average of thirty-one times per prostitute." In addition to rape, there is the potential for health risks from either sexually transmitted diseases or drug abuse.

INQUIRY QUESTIONS

- Use one of the decision-making models or a combination of models described in Chapter 2 to think through and develop a recommendation for the social worker in this situation. Give your rationale and include citations from sections from a professional code of ethics.
- What possible positive and negative consequences may ensue if your recommendation is followed?
- What ethical principles support your recommendation? What principles would direct the professional to take a different course of action?

RECORD KEEPING

Professional record keeping refers to the recording and storage of information about service users and who has access to the information. It is extremely important in the maintenance of confidentiality and respect for the privacy of service users. Professional codes of ethics emphasize that recorded information about service users should include only pertinent and essential information and access to this information denied to those who do not have a right to the information. The CASW *Guidelines for Ethical Practice* (2005b) has a section on maintaining and handling client records (sec. 1.7) and also includes guidelines for record keeping.

> Social workers maintain one written record of professional interventions and opinions, with due care to the obligations and standards of their employer and relevant regulatory body. Social workers document information impartially and accurately and with an appreciation that the record may be revealed to clients or disclosed during court proceedings. Social workers are encouraged to take care to:
>
> - Report only essential and relevant details
> - Refrain from using emotive or derogatory language
> - Acknowledge the basis of professional opinions
> - Protect clients' privacy and that of others involved. (sec. 1.7)

The NASW *Code of Ethics* (1999) includes three subsections on record keeping in the section on "Privacy and Communication" (sec. 1.07) and has separate sections on client records (sec. 3.04) and access to records (sec. 1.08). The section on client records emphasizes that "only information that is directly relevant to the delivery of services" should be included (3.04d), and the section on access to records directs professionals to provide clients "reasonable access to records" while "protect[ing] the confidentiality of other individuals identified or discussed in such records" (sec. 1.08a,b). The ACA *Code of Ethics* (1995) includes a section on records (sec. B4) that outlines five topics ranging from the requirement to maintain records to the need to respect privacy and record information obtained in consulting relationships.

The theme that runs throughout professional codes of ethics is that during the process of recording information about service users, professionals must be cognizant of how service user information should be recorded, stored, and used to protect the client's privacy. Given that social workers, counsellors, and similar professionals usually do not have "privileged" communication, third parties, such as courts, when legally sanctioned, may require us to share service user records in whatever form they are kept—print or electronic. In terms of confidentiality and privacy rights, even in the context of "relative" confidentiality, service user information should be secure from parties who should not have access to the information.

INQUIRY PROJECT

- Consult at least two professional codes of ethics and their companion documents, such as CASW, NASW, ACA, or the British Columbia Association of Social Workers. Find as many sections as you can that deal directly or indirectly with keeping records. Record what you find about record-keeping requirements.
- Compare what you found in the codes and identify what you think are the two or three core ideas or best practices for record keeping. Apply these to

either how you practise now or how you think you will practise when you graduate. What issues have you discovered in applying these to current or future practice?

CONSULTATION

For social workers, counsellors, and related professions, supervision and/or peer consultation is often assumed to be an essential part of practice. Even when a worker is working in relative isolation in a one-worker office, the assumption is that the professional will be connected with a supervisor or peers through phone and/or Internet connection, as well as through video conferencing or on-site, face-to-face meetings. Given the centrality of consultation in practice, sharing of information about service users needs to be considered in terms of service users' right to privacy. The CASW *Guidelines for Ethical Practice* (2005b) emphasizes the benefits of consultation for service users: "Social workers seek the advice and counsel of colleagues whenever such consultation is in the best interests of clients" (sec. 3.2.2). The NASW *Code of Ethics* (1999) clearly states that information about a service user during consultation sessions should not be disclosed unless the service user has approved the use of this information: "Social workers should not disclose identifying information when discussing clients with consultants unless the client has consented to disclosure of confidential information" (sec. 1.07q). In its section on confidentiality the American Counseling Association *Code of Ethics* (1995) delineates when and how client information should be used in a consultative session:

> Information obtained in a consulting relationship is discussed for professional purposes only with persons clearly concerned with the case. Written and oral reports present data germane to the purposes of the consultation, and every effort is made to protect client identity and avoid undue invasion of privacy. (sec. B6,a)

> Before sharing information, counselors make efforts to ensure that there are defined policies in other agencies serving the counselor's clients that effectively protect the confidentiality of information. (sec. B6,b)

INQUIRY PROJECT

Think about possible professional contexts in which you will work after you complete your degree. Imagine how you might use formal or informal sources of consultation—for example, with peers in the same or other agencies, through on-site meetings, on the Internet, and/or through regular meetings with a supervisor. How would you approach the professional requirement to protect service user privacy?

Practice Situation: **Amy**

Amy is a recent graduate of the University of Calgary Leadership in Human Services MSW specialization. She is a community developer for the city of Calgary and has been given the assignment of working in a low-income area in the city to identify their perceptions of service gaps as well as their reasons for not being able to use current services. One of her findings is that some residents have mentioned negative experiences with the professional Amy has replaced. That particular professional, Harry, is now Amy's supervisor. They report that Harry came to their area but did not listen to their concerns. They thought he was just "putting in time" before moving on to a higher-level position in the city. They report that, "in good faith," they gave him thorough accounts of their experiences with a "fragmented" service delivery system that often was not accessible when they needed services the most. Their view is that Harry did nothing to enhance their experiences with services and they have lost faith with the fact-finding process Amy is currently involved with. Harry did not report back what happened with the information they shared with him and they have seen no results.

Amy is in the process of thinking about how to use the information she has obtained about service gaps and Harry's apparent lack of attention so that the residents get the attention they desire. At the same time, Amy does not want to alienate the residents by violating their confidential information. She also does not want to alienate Harry, her supervisor.

INQUIRY PROJECT

Community practice is often not considered in discussions about confidentiality as the notion of confidentiality derives from a professional–client model that assumes a one-to-one interaction (Shuman, 1985; Strein & Hershenson, 1991; Millstein, Dare-Winters, & Sullivan, 1994). The challenge is to create guidelines or directives that fit more complex practice settings that involve multiple service users and a range of professionals.

- If Amy contacted you for advice, what would you recommend so that she can engage in effective, ethical practice? Support your recommendation with citations from one or more codes of ethics.

CONCLUSION

In the overview of confidentiality that has been given in this chapter, you should be aware of the importance of informed professional judgment in deciding who should know what, when, and to what extent, as well as the consequences for the participants involved. A critical factor in deciding how to proceed in terms of record keeping, use of consultants, and involvement of third parties is the impact of a course of action on the professional's relationship with service users. The prime consideration, of course, is professional responsibility to protect privacy and maintain confidentiality of service users. When the needs, rights, and safety of others are involved, the complexity of the decision process increases. Thus, the use of the decision-making processes available in Chapter 2, reference to professional codes of ethics, along with consultation with peers and supervisors are essential components of the professional's "toolkit."

In the next chapter we will extend our discussion of service users' right to privacy and the maintenance of confidentiality through a focus on informed consent. Many texts on ethics combine a discussion of confidentiality and informed consent, but the issues of competence, voluntary involvement, and disclosure of information deserve their own chapter.

NOTES

NOTES

_____

_____

_____

_____

_____

_____

_____

_____

_____

_____

_____

_____

_____

_____

_____

_____

_____

NOTES

NOTES

NOTES

NOTES

_____

_____

_____

_____

_____

_____

_____

_____

_____

_____

_____

_____

_____

_____

REFERENCES

American Counseling Association. (1995). *Code of ethics and standards of practice.* Alexandria, VA: author.

Backlar, P. (1996). Ethics in community mental health care: Confidentiality and common sense. *Community Mental Health Journal, 32*(6), 513–518.

Canadian Association of Social Workers. (2005a). *Code of ethics.* Ottawa, ON: Author.

Canadian Association of Social Workers. (2005b). *Guidelines for ethical practice.* Ottawa, ON: Author.

Dickson, D. (1998). *Confidentiality and privacy in social work.* New York: Free Press.

Gelman, R., Pollack, D., & Weiner, A. (1999). Confidentiality of social work records in the computer age. *Social Work, 44*(3), 243–252.

Government of Alberta. (1995). Protection of Children Involved in Prostitution Act. Edmonton, AB: Author.

Hodgson, J.F. (1997). *Games pimps play.* Toronto: Canadian Scholars' Press.

Jagim, R.D., Whittman, W.D., & Noll, J.O. (1978, August). Mental health professionals' attitudes toward confidentiality, privilege, and third party disclosure. *Professional Psychology,* 458–466.

Keith-Spiegel, P., & Koocher, G. (1985). *Ethics in psychology.* New York: Random House.

Laughran, W., & Bakken, G.M. (1984). The psychotherapist's responsibilities toward third parties under current California law. *Western State University Law Review, 12*(1), 1–33.

McMahon, M., & Knowles, A. (1995). Confidentiality in psychotherapy. *Professional Psychology: Research and Practice, 16*(1), 15–19.

Millstein, K., Dare-Winters, K., & Sullivan, S. (1994). The power of silence: Ethical dilemmas of informed consent in practice evaluation. *Clinical Social Work Journal, 22*(3), 317–329.

Missing Kids Web Page. (2003). Retrieved November 1, 2003, from http://www.missingkids.com/missingkids/servlet/PageServlet?LanguageCountry=en_US&PageId=992

National Association of Social Workers. (1999). *Code of ethics and standards of practice.* Washington, DC: Author.

Nicolai, K., & Scott, N. (1994). Provision of confidentiality information and its relation to child abuse reporting. *Professional Psychology: Research and Practice, 25*(2), 154–160.

Perlin, M.L. (1997). The "duty to protect" others from violence. In *The Hatherleigh guide to ethics in therapy* (pp. 127–147). New York: Hatherleigh Press.

Reamer, F. (1998). *Ethical standards in social work: A critical review of the NASW Code of Ethics*. Washington, DC: NASW.

Rothman, J.C. (2005). *From the frontline student cases in social work ethics*. Boston: Pearson Education.

Schwitzgebel, R.L., & Schwitzgebel, R.K. (1980). *Law and psychological practice*. New York: Wiley.

Shuman, D. (1985). The origins of the physician-patient privilege and professional secret. *Southwestern Law Review, 39*, 661–687.

Steinberg, K.L., Levine, M., & Doueck, H. (1997). Effects of legally mandated child-abuse reports on the therapeutic relationship: A survey of psychotherapists. *American Journal of Orthopsychiatry, 67*, 112–122.

Strein, W., & Hershenson, D. (1991). Confidentiality in nondyadic counseling situations. *Journal of Counseling and Development, 69*, 312–316.

Strom-Gottfried, K., & Corcoran, K. (1998). Confronting ethical dilemmas in managed care: Guidelines for students and faculty. *Journal of Social Work Education, 34*(1), 109–119.

Van Hoose, W.H., & Kottler, J.A. (1985). *Ethical and legal issues in counseling and psychotherapy* (2nd ed.). San Francisco: Jossey-Bass.

Wigmore, J. (1961). *Evidence in trials at common law* (Rev. ed.). Boston: Little, Brown.

chapter

Informed Consent

Informed consent is related to the confidentiality issues discussed in Chapter 5. Service users should be informed about and consent to how the information they share with professionals will be kept confidential and what information cannot be absolutely protected (the limits of confidentiality). They should also understand and consent to professional interventions, for example, medical and psychological treatments, activities with groups and communities, and involvement of third parties.

There are three major interrelated requirements for informed consent to take place:

1. **Competency:** How competent are the service users to understand the nature of what they are being asked to consent to? For example, can a person with a limited mental capacity be able to give informed consent to being placed in a residential treatment facility? Competency should determine both how information is given and the quality and quantity of information that is appropriate for informed consent.
2. **Disclosure of Information:** How much information should be given to service users so that they can make informed decisions about whether to proceed? We can give too much information so that the core issues are clouded and difficult for the service users to identify. We can also give too little information—service users may not understand the range of possible negative as well as positive consequences of the choices they are offered.
3. **Voluntariness:** Service users may "voluntarily" go to a professional, but if they feel they have few alternatives for accessing resources, they might go along with the professional so that they can gain entry into the service delivery system. In situations where service users' participation is not voluntary, such as corrections, juvenile justice, child protection, or court-ordered mental health and substance abuse treatment, the ethical issue of a severe curtailment of "consent" is tied to the often negative impacts of being coerced to participate in professional intervention (Ivanoff, Blythe, & Tripodi, 1994; Rooney, 1992).

ADDICTIONS AND INFORMED CONSENT

The topic of addictions exemplifies some of the major difficulties faced in more "coercive" practice contexts that impact the service user's ability to give complete informed consent. For example, if an individual chooses to accept treatment while struggling with an addiction, to what degree is he competent to make this decision? As Duval (2001) states, "ethical issues arise in determining decision-making capacity and when to give treatment without consent to a person who is incapable of making treatment decisions" (p. 16). If addiction is defined as a mental illness, should this affect how we perceive the competency of addicts? If they are suffering from a mental illness, can they be considered competent to consent to treatment? If not, is it ethical to provide treatment without that consent? When a client must accept treatment because it is court-mandated or they are given a "choice" to either "accept" treatment or lose their job, can "informed consent" take place?

RELEVANT SECTIONS OF PROFESSIONAL CODES OF ETHICS

Section 1.03a of the NASW *Code of Ethics* (1999) states that "social workers should provide services to clients only in the context of a professional relationship based, when appropriate, on valid informed consent." This sentiment is echoed in the CASW *Guidelines for Ethical Practice* (2005b) section, "Promoting Client Self-Determination and Informed Consent," which states that "social workers promote the self-determination and autonomy of clients, actively encouraging them to make informed decisions on their own behalf" (sec. 1.3.1) and "social workers provide services to clients only on valid informed consent or when required to by legislation or court-ordered" (sec. 1.3.5). In providing information to service users the CASW (2005b) further states: "Social workers, at the earliest opportunity, discuss with clients their rights and responsibilities and provide them with honest and accurate available information" (sec. 1.3.4). The American Counseling Association *Code of Ethics* (1995) addresses the issue of informed consent for service users in "Section A: The Counseling Relationship": "Counselors offer clients the freedom to choose whether to enter into counseling relationship and to determine which professional(s) will provide counseling. Restrictions that limit choices of clients are fully explained" (sec. A.3.b). Given these and similar directives in other professional codes of ethics, the following questions and issues are particularly important to consider.

INQUIRY PROJECT

For each of the questions and issues described below, write a brief response that reflects your best advice. In addition to the codes of ethics cited in this section, consult at least one other code for additional passages that relate to these questions.

- **Competency-Related Questions:** According to Duval (2001), when the service user is not cognitively impaired, "the problem isn't that they have a cognitive impairment. They understand the information, but may make bad decisions without good justification in terms of their own values and what they really want" (p. 16). If this is the case, should workers consider requesting consent again after a set time period has passed within treatment? How long should they wait before requesting a renewed consent and how often should they request it?

- **Questions Related to Competency and Voluntariness:** If a client signs a contract for treatment to take place over a set period of time, but at a certain point feels that he does not need to continue, should he be held to the initial contract? Was he competent to sign the contract in the first place? What if he has come to a private clinic and his failure to fulfill his contract causes financial problems for the clinic? In early recovery, a service user may often feel relief because his symptoms are diminished and mistake this feeling of relief for "recovery." If he decides not to complete the full treatment process, this creates staffing and financial problems for the treatment agency and increases the likelihood that the client will return to his addictions within a short period of time.
- **Questions Related to Voluntariness and Mandated Treatment:** What should be the "ethical" response to service users who are mandated to work with a professional? For example, should we minimize the effect of the client's being "mandated" into treatment by giving "choices"? If yes, what could these choices be? When responding to this question think of service users who either are court-ordered or have a de facto choice that for them does not appear to be a choice because of the alternatives given them—for example, loss of contact with their children or loss of employment.

BASIC CONCEPTS AND PEER REFLECTION ON RESPONSES

In the field of addictions, questions about service users' competency and the voluntariness of their participation in treatment are core ethical issues professionals often struggle with. How workers define and perceive addiction, mental illness, self-determination, and informed consent will play a major role in how they involve service users in the decision-making/problem-solving process.

- Review your responses to the previous questions. What do they say about your understanding of service-user competency, voluntariness, and self-determination, especially in the field of addictions?
- Share your responses with your peers and identify where you agree and disagree.

Practice Situation: **Angelina**

Angelina is a twenty-six-year-old woman who was diagnosed with early-onset schizophrenia at the age of eighteen. She had her first major episode while attending her first semester of university and subsequently dropped out. She has been hospitalized several times. Though she responds well to medication, she often is not drug compliant and has been certified at risk for herself or others while off drugs, which has resulted in most of her hospitalizations. She currently resides at a group home for individuals with mental illnesses and receives residential support and counselling.

Angelina has expressed interest in going back to school, but the stress of exams and other obligations makes it difficult. She is currently attending a local college's vocational training program targeted for those with mental health issues. Angelina comes from a large family and has expressed a wish to have a family of her own when she gets "better." She often acts as a "mother" to the other residents of the home regardless of their age. Angelina's family live 500 km away and do not see her often, though they will often spend hours on the phone talking.

Angelina also has another significant social contact—Scott, her boyfriend, who was diagnosed as bipolar in his teens. When experiencing extreme mania, he would engage in high-risk behaviours that resulted in significant financial debt. He is currently taking lithium, which for the last four years has controlled his symptoms. Scott and Angelina have been dating for a year, and he has provided emotional support for her.

The agency that runs the group home where Angelina lives employs several social workers who handle case management and case supervision. In a recent case assessment during which three professionals from the house met with Angelina, she expressed a desire to move in with Scott and to start her own family. She says that she is better now and would like to get off the medications and become the homemaker she wants to be. Scott has put together a down-payment for a house in a remote area of town and has expressed interest in this plan. According to the frontline workers in the house, Angelina is not yet ready to live on her own, as she needs prompts to help her with the routine details of daily living. Angelina's family has raised concerns about Scott's ability to care for their daughter and have doubts about Angelina's competency to make a decision to live with Scott. Angelina's doctors have stated that if she goes off medication for her disorder, which is necessary to prevent harm to a fetus, she is at high risk of becoming psychotic.

At the next supervisory meeting, the social worker must present a recommendation to the board of directors at the halfway house about Angelina's desire to live with Scott.

INQUIRY PROJECT

If you were the social worker in this situation, what would your recommend to the board of directors? In your response describe the ethical foundation (ethical reasons) for your recommendation and include in your argument any other practice-related reasons you would give to persuade the board to accept your recommendation.

BACKGROUND INFORMATION ON SCHIZOPHRENIA AND BIPOLAR DISORDER

There is no test to determine if an individual has schizophrenia. The diagnosis is usually made by a psychiatrist and is based on symptoms the person displays. According to the *DSM-IV-TR,* schizophrenia is a psychotic brain disease characterized by, but not limited to, such symptoms as delusions, hallucinations, disorganized speech, severely disorganized or catatonic behaviour, and other manifestations such as flat affect and reduced speech (Psychiatry24x7, 2004).

A person with bipolar disorder, also know as manic depressive disorder, experiences rapid mood changes, from mania (feeling high and invincible) to depression (uncontrollable sadness). The criteria for determining mania or depression are outlined in the *DSM-IV* (Psychiatry24x7, 2004). People who are diagnosed bipolar will often have at least ten cycles of mania and depression in their lifetime. Bipolar disorder is difficult to treat as the medications are used in a "Russian roulette" fashion: once a consumer switches off of a medication onto a new one; the original medication's effectiveness dramatically decreases. Over time, medications can lose their effectiveness due to drug tolerance (Bipolar Home, 2004).

SELF-DETERMINATION, COMPETENCY, VOLUNTARINESS, AND DISCLOSURE OF INFORMATION

The following core ethical principles are emphasized in mental health practice across professions:

- protection of human rights,
- practice with least intrusion in a service user's life, and
- protection of the community.

People with mental illnesses, like all "patients" or service users, have rights that must be respected. The Canadian Patients' Bill of Rights (2002) covers the rights of people, including the mentally ill, who receive public health services in and out of the hospital. Patients "have the right to be fully informed as to their medical condition, the right to be advised of the treatment options that are available to them, the right to be involved in the decision as to which treatment to receive, the right to designate a person to exercise their rights on their behalf if they are not able to do so as a result of a physical or mental incapacity" (p. 2). Patients have the responsibility to "cooperate with health professionals who are rendering public health services to them and either to follow their reasonable instructions and advice respecting the public health services and behaviour that relates to health or to advise the professionals when they have not done so" (p. 2). The human rights of the mentally ill are also codified in the United Nations General Assembly Resolution 46/119 (1991), "Principles for the Protection of Persons with Mental Illness and the Improvement of Mental Health Care.

GUARDIANSHIP, LEAST-INTRUSIVE TREATMENT, AND HUMAN RIGHTS OF SERVICE USERS

Under the Canadian Patients' Bill of Rights people can designate a guardian to exercise their rights for them. Guardians are appointed by the courts and are expected to provide full opportunity for the dependent adult to contribute to his or her care or other life decisions. A guardianship order is made when the court is satisfied that the appointment is in the "best interests" of the dependent adult. Family members, friends, or any other individuals may make application for guardianship, but the courts prefer the nearest relative.

A person needs guardianship if she is over the age of eighteen and has been repeatedly or continuously unable to care for herself and cannot make reasonable judgment about matters relating to her person. The dependent adult must sign an agreement for a guardianship. In cases of mental illness a person may be involuntarily hospitalized by a psychiatrist. If the individual is in and out of the hospital frequently, a guardian may be appointed. If there are no suitable applications for guardianship, then the court may appoint a public guardian. Information on this process is available in each province. For example, information about Alberta's legal requirements for guardianship can be obtained from the Alberta Law Foundation (1996).

A person diagnosed with severe mental illness may be certified at risk to themselves and a guardian may be appointed to determine the "right course" of treatment. There are increasing concerns that guardians or decision makers may abuse their power when the mentally ill are unable to advocate for themselves. As a result, mental health policy has focused on supporting the "least-intrusive" method of treatment.

Each province has its own mental health policy. Alberta's Mental Health Act contains a section about how to determine treatment for those who cannot decide on their own and includes a provision for least-intrusive treatment. In order to consider the best interests of the patient in relation to treatment, professionals are to determine

(a) whether the mental condition of the patient will be or is likely to be improved by the treatment;
(b) whether the patient's condition will deteriorate or is likely to deteriorate without the treatment;
(c) whether the anticipated benefit from the treatment outweighs the risk of harm to the patient;
(d) whether the treatment is the least restrictive and least intrusive treatment that meets the requirements of clauses (1)(a) or (c)..

COMPLIANCE WITH TREATMENT AND WHY IT IS A CRITICAL ISSUE

Many mentally ill individuals may not comply with treatment medications. According to Petkova and Dimitrov (2000) the rate of noncompliance among those prescribed antipsychotic medications in Canada in 1998 was upwards of 69 percent. Curson et al. (2001), in a study of sixty-three patients for the Medical Research Council fluphenazine/placebo trial, found that 40 percent of patients practised noncompliance at some point over a period of seven years. In a related study they found that as many as 60 percent of service users who were diagnosed with schizophrenia and were outpatients of psychiatric facilities practised noncompliance with treatment medications.

Noncompliance with medications is important because resistance of mentally ill service users to treatment plans, combined with the difficulty of determining their competency, often makes it more difficult to support independent decision making by these service users. Their ability to make sound judgments or to perceive their situation clearly, while not making them incompetent, may make it difficult for them to assess consequences or to consistently follow up on treatment decisions. It is easier to say "the professional or guardian knows best" when you are working with people of limited capacity.

LEAST-INTRUSIVE TREATMENT, COMPLIANCE, AND HUMAN RIGHTS

The issue of least intrusion is germane to the issue of compliance, independence, and risk of harm. When practitioners follow the policy of least-intrusive intervention, the risk of "abuse" to a service user's "human rights" by the system or agency is diminished.

The policy of least-intrusive measures can be said to be a reaction to the eugenics movement in Canada in the late 1800s and early 1900s. At one time it was believed that the simplest method for treating mental illness was to sterilize those diagnosed as mentally ill so that they would not reproduce and pass the defects onto their children. It was also feared that an able-bodied, feeble-minded man might attack a "normal" woman, and any offspring would carry the defect of the father. The government supported the arguments for sterilization of the mentally ill, with the result that anyone who was considered undesirable was sterilized.

In 1965 Lelani Muir took the Alberta government to court over the policy of sterilization of "undesirables." She had been sterilized as a child after being mistakenly labelled as mentally incompetent after one badly administered IQ test. She won the case and the government has compensated both her and others for wrongful sterilization (Economica, 1996). Currently, if a woman who has a diagnosed mental illness requests sterilization, a special committee of doctors must determine whether it is the best treatment, the request is passed through an ethics board, and if approved can be challenged in court by a third party.

INQUIRY QUESTIONS: FOLLOW-UP TO ANGELINA'S SITUATION

Reflect on Angelina's situation and related information on ethical practice in the field of mental health.

- Given this information, would you as the social worker change your recommendation to the board regarding Angelina?
- If yes, explain why. If not, what information you have reviewed supports your initial recommendation?

INQUIRY PROJECT

Informed Consent and Confidentiality in a Correctional Setting

Issues about informed consent and confidentiality occur on a regular basis in correctional facilities, affecting not only the inmates themselves but their families. When an inmate is incarcerated, his basic human rights are compromised, and depending on how informed consent and confidentiality are addressed, those rights may be further eroded.

One question that a professional working in the field of corrections should consider is how to behave when an inmate confesses to previously unreported crimes.

- Is it the professional's duty to report these crimes?
- Does informed consent enter into this communication, and if so how?
- If an inmate discloses, for example, the smuggling of contraband items into the correctional facility, is the professional obligated to report and risk losing the inmate's trust?

In your response to these questions, cite references to at least one code of ethics to support your position and describe how you think informed consent and confidentiality are important dimensions of this situation.

Practice Situation: Ellen

Ellen Adams, age twenty, is the mother of two-year-old Shane. Ellen is currently serving a sentence in the women's federal correction facility in Prince Albert, Saskatchewan, on manslaughter charges. Ellen is only in the second month of her ten-year sentence. She was charged with manslaughter four months after an incident at a nightclub in Saskatoon that resulted in the death of a thirty-two-year-old woman. On the night of the incident Ellen had been drinking heavily with a group of men when she became involved in an altercation with the victim. The altercation became physical and ended when Ellen stabbed the victim with a broken beer bottle, resulting in the death of the victim that same evening in the Saskatoon University Hospital. The judge ruled manslaughter rather than murder because of Ellen's impaired state and proof of self-defence.

ELLEN'S DESIRE TO KEEP HER PARENTING ROLE: THE COUNSELLOR'S VIEW

Shane is currently living with Ellen's grandmother, who is unwilling to obtain guardianship of him. Ellen would like to resume her role as Shane's mother when she is released from her sentence and has discussed this with the counsellor at the correctional facility. She has also discussed her problems with alcohol addiction in confidence and is concerned that her addiction will become a barrier if the child welfare social worker is informed about her addiction problem.

The counsellor at the correctional facility feels that it may be in Shane's best interests to place him for adoption due to several factors. The first factor is an unsafe environment that Shane has been subjected to because of Ellen's previous alcohol dependency. It has been reported that prior to Ellen's incarceration her lifestyle often placed Shane in situations that compromised his health and safety. This includes possible neglect and mistreatment due to alcohol and illegal drug use in the child's presence. The counsellor is also concerned about Ellen's possible violent tendencies due to the nature of her crime. Because Shane is a healthy and happy child, the likelihood of successful adoption is high.

FURTHER BACKGROUND ON ELLEN

Ellen is currently involved in an Alcoholics Anonymous support group and other rehabilitative training. She is also part of anger management and parenting workshops and is working towards a high-school equivalency degree. Despite the lifestyle Ellen led previous to her incarceration, her son was always well fed and properly clothed. Although neglect was suspected, it was never confirmed, and there has never been any evidence of physical abuse.

INQUIRY PROJECT

There are several ethical issues that the counsellor needs to reflect on and process in working with Ellen. One of these is informed consent.

- Describe how informed consent enters into this scenario.
- If the counsellor came to you for peer consultation what questions would you ask him and what would be the primary areas for discussion? Include as many ethical issues as you think are relevant, being sure to include informed consent and confidentiality concerns.
- Refer back to the decision-making approaches discussed in Chapter 2 and choose one that you think would be helpful in thinking through informed consent issues. Describe how you would use the decision-making approach when you are consulting with this counsellor.

CONCLUSION

In this chapter we have worked on the concept of informed consent in relation to the requirements for competency, the sharing of relevant information, and voluntariness. The difficulty of ensuring informed consent for service users in more coercive practice settings, such as correctional institutions, has been highlighted to illustrate the effect of the absence of one or more of the requirements for informed consent.

The next chapter shifts our focus from individual and small-group practice scenarios to situations that challenge professionals to consider their social responsibilities and to be involved in social justice concerns. We will look at anti-oppressive practice as an important concept for ethical practice in a multicultural society such as Canada.

NOTES

NOTES

_____

_____

_____

_____

_____

_____

_____

_____

_____

_____

_____

_____

_____

NOTES

NOTES

NOTES

_____

_____

_____

_____

_____

_____

_____

_____

_____

_____

_____

_____

_____

_____

_____

NOTES

_____

_____

_____

_____

_____

_____

_____

_____

_____

_____

_____

_____

_____

REFERENCES

Alberta Law Foundation. (1996). Retrieved July 2004 from http://www.law-faqs.org/ab/guar.htm

Alberta Mental Health Act. (2004). Retrieved July 2004 from http://www.qp.gov.ab.ca/documents/Acts/M13.cfm?frm_isbn=0779721012

American Counseling Association. (1995). *Code of ethics and standards of practice.* Alexandria, VA: Author.

Bipolar Home (n.d.). Retrieved July 2004 from http://www.bipolarhome.org

Bissell, LeClair, & Royce, James E. (1978). *Ethics for addictions professionals.* Center City, MN: Hazelden Information and Educational Services.

Canadian Association of Social Workers. (2005a). *Code of ethics.* Ottawa, ON: Author.

Canadian Association of Social Workers. (2005b). *Guidelines for ethical practice.* Ottawa, ON: Author.

Canadian Patients' Bill of Rights. (2002). Bill C-238, 2nd Session, 37th Parliament. Retrieved July 2004 from http://www.parl.gc.ca/37/2/parlbus/chambus/house/bills/private/c-238/c-238_1/372021bE.html

Curson, P., et al. (2001). National Institute of Mental Health, U.S. Department of Health and Human Services. *Schizophrenia Bulletin, 27*(1), 149.

Duval, G. (2001). Q&A: Integrating ethics into the mental health and addiction fields. *Journal of Addiction and Mental Health, 6*(1), 16–17.

Economica Ltd. (1996). *Expert Witness Newsletter.* Retrieved July 2004 from http://www.economica.ca/ew.htm

Furman, R. (2003). Frame work for understanding value discrepancies. *International Social Work, 46,* 1.

Ivanoff, A., Blythe, B.J., & Tripodi, T. (1994). *Involuntary clients in social work practice: A research-based approach.* New York: Aldine de Gruyter.

National Association of Social Workers. (1999). *Code of ethics and standards of practice.* Washington, DC: Author.

Petkova, Nina, & Dimitrov, Simeon. (2000). Retrieved July 2004 from http://www.psychiatry24x7.com

Rooney, R.H. (1992). *Strategies for work with involuntary clients.* New York: Columbia University Press.

United Nations General Assembly. (1991). Resolution 46/119. *Principles for the protection of persons with mental illness and the improvement of mental health care.* Retrieved July 2004 from http://www.unhchr.ch/html/menu3/b/68.htm

Social Justice as a Professional Ethical Responsibility

In this chapter we will shift our focus from professional responsibilities to service users to address professional obligations to society. We will also apply the strategies for decision making that we employed in previous chapters to the issues we will discuss in this chapter. The decision-making strategy includes gathering background information, identifying and responding to inquiry questions throughout the decision process, and applying professional codes of ethics to identified issues. Thus, strategy occurs whenever possible within a deliberative structure and process of decision making—specifically, the application of one of the decision-making models described in Chapter 2.

SOCIAL JUSTICE, SOCIAL WELFARE, AND THE PROFESSION OF SOCIAL WORK

The social work profession is unique in incorporating social justice as a core professional responsibility. The American Counseling Association *Code of Ethics* (1995) section on public responsibility states that counsellors cannot discriminate "against clients, students, or supervisees in a manner that has a negative impact based on their age, color, culture, disability, ethnic group, gender, face, religion, sexual orientation, or socioeconomic status, or any other reason" (C5). It does not, however, mention responsibility for social justice or society in general. The Canadian Association of Social Workers *Code of Ethics* (2005a), however, identifies "pursuit of justice" and "service to humanity" as among the core values for social workers in Canada (Values 2 and 3). Section 8 of the CASW *Guidelines for Ethical Practice* (2005b) focuses on "ethical responsibility to society" with directives on social worker responsibilities to provide meaningful information on social problems to policymakers and the public, to participate in social action, and to encourage public participation in shaping policies and institutions (secs. 8.1–8.5). The National Association of Social Workers *Code of Ethics* (1999) provides similar views on social justice as a core value and provides supporting practice standards (sec. 6.04). Social justice is also a core value for social workers in other countries such as Australia (Australian Association of Social Workers, 2002) and Turkey (Association of Social Workers in Turkey, 2002).

Social justice has been a hallmark of social work since its inception as a profession in the early twentieth century. It has sought change in social and organizational policies and practices in order to assist groups of people. The early settlement house workers, who contributed to the development of social work as a profession, were leaders in social reform in North America during the Progressive Era (the late 1800s and early 1900s). The profession of social work also traces its origins to the charity organization workers of the same period, who took a "charity" or "social welfare" approach to working with immigrants and the newly displaced urban dwellers.

The "charity" or "social welfare" approach frequently consisted of helping individuals to adapt to society and to access existing resources. The leaders of the charity organization movement often joined with the settlement house leaders in advocating for social reform, drawing on what they had learned about the living conditions of immigrants. The "casework" method or individualistic approach to working with people was developed in a systematic way by Mary Richmond, a leader in the charity organization movement who sought to professionalize social work (Goldstein, 1990; Margolin, 1997).

The social justice and social welfare orientations have resulted in conflicting values for the social work profession. The social justice approach looks to societal, community, or organizational solutions to problems, while the social welfare philosophy focuses on assisting individuals to change (George & Wilding, 1994). The tension between these two orientations plays out in the practice of individual social workers when they are faced with limited time and resources and feel they cannot adequately implement both in their practice.

REFLECTION QUESTIONS

A social worker whose primary practice involves working with individual service users is faced with several complex questions. For example: Is there a time when the interests of individual service users can or should be minimized so that I can be engaged in institutional or organizational change that will ultimately benefit a group of service users, such as single parents? Can I justify taking time away from working with my service users to be involved with social action for change at even the organizational level? How can this "time away" be explained to my service users, who want me to be responsive to their needs and interests?

- How would you respond to these questions if a colleague came to you for peer consultation? Would you need further information from your colleague before giving her your opinion? If yes, what information would you need and from what source?
- What is "social justice for social worker practice"?

In addition to deciding how to allocate time and resources to address professional responsibilities to both individual service users and society at large, Michael Reisch (2002) points out that the ambiguity in defining social justice presents another difficulty in integrating larger-scale change into practice. The term social justice, he points out, can be used by those with very different views about individual and group entitlements and social obligations, with the result that "liberals and conservatives, religious fundamentalists, and radical secularists all regard their causes as 'socially just'" (p. 343). There is agreement that social justice involves questions about allocations of roles, rights, goods, and responsibilities in a society. Differences emerge, however, in discussions about what allocation means in terms of "just distribution" and "fairness."

Reflection
Questions
REFLECTION QUESTIONS

Jot down your responses to the following questions and reflect on what social justice means for you.

- Do you think all members of a society should have equal rights to "intangibles" such as liberty and freedom? Should they also have equal opportunity to obtain social goods such as property, health, and education?
- Should there be equal distribution of rewards and resources based on merit?
- Should there be equal distribution of rewards and resources based on equal productivity so that those who produce at the same level receive the same level of resources?
- Should there be unequal distribution of resources based on an individual's needs or requirements?
- Should there be unequal distribution of resources based on an individual's status or position?
- Should there be an unequal distribution of resources based on different "contractual" agreements that result in more benefits for certain individuals or groups of people?

John Rawls, in a classic text on justice, *A Theory of Justice* (1999), argues that the measure of justice of a society should be determined by "how fundamental rights and duties are assigned and on the economic opportunities and social conditions in various sectors of society" (p. 7). Part of his conception of a just society is the notion of distribution in which "all social values . . . are to be distributed equally unless an unequal distribution of any, or all, of these values is to everyone's advantage" (p. 62). Underlying this concept of distribution are two principles of justice:

> Each person has an equal right to the most extensive system of personal liberty, compatible with a system of total liberty for all.
>
> Social and economic inequality are to be arranged so that they are both (a) to the greatest benefit to the least advantaged in society and (b) attached to positions open to all under conditions of fair equality of opportunity. (p. 62)

For social workers, what is particularly salient in Rawls's conception of a just society is his "principle of redress," which provides a basis for policies directed to redress an unfair distribution of social goods because of "undeserved inequalities." Social goods include education, health care, employment, and housing:

> Undeserved inequalities call for redress; and since inequalities of birth and natural endowment are undeserved, these inequalities are to be somehow compensated for. Thus, the

principle of redress holds that in order to treat all persons equally, to provide genuine equality of opportunity, society must give more attention to those with fewer native assets and to those born into less favourable social positions. The idea is to redress the bias of contingencies in the direction of equality. (p. 100)

Reflection
Questions ?

REFLECTION QUESTIONS: YOUR VIEW OF SOCIAL JUSTICE

* Do you agree or disagree with Rawls's concept of a just society and principles for distribution and redress?
* What is the basis of your agreement or disagreement?
* What alternative to Rawls's idea of a just society would you propose to depict what a just society should be in terms of allocation of social goods?

A criticism of Rawls's approach to social justice is that it focuses predominantly on the expansion of individual rights and shares of societal resources; consequently, the need for policies and programs to address group concerns may be missed (Ryan, 1981). Authors who propose a less individual and more communitarian notion of social justice emphasize that race and racism are social constructs, rooted in the political-economic system and require societal and cultural change along with a change of power imbalances. Within a communitarian notion of justice, discussions about social justice and multiculturalism are essentially linked. Contemporary social work literature often links the attainment of social justice with the goals of social diversity or multiculturalism and with challenges to the normative power structure and the oppression it produces (Hyde, 1998).

MEANING OF SOCIAL JUSTICE FOR PRACTICE

Paranab Chatterjee and Amy D'Aprix (2002) claim that social work has for the most part been defined as supporting the redistribution of resources and thus often challenging the status quo. Freud and Krug (2002) argue that the opposite may be the case for social workers involved with direct or clinical practice: "few mental or physical health professionals, including social workers, have historically distinguished themselves as fighters for social justice. . . . Mental health professionals, far from being freedom fighters, have too often been obedient citizens cooperating with oppressions of their governments" (p. 475). Rossiter (2000) warns mental health professionals, including social workers, that the practice models they use may lead to a narrow definition of the source of problems and issues and result in disempowerment of service users.

The effects of organizational goals, budgets, and regulations have frequently been characterized as demoralizing for social workers who want to practise according to a social justice framework but feel compelled instead to practise within an exclusively social welfare or charity framework (Krug, 1994; Rhodes; 1992). The challenge for us is to continually reflect on what justice means in the context of our work so that we are continually redefining our notions of justice and evaluating our practice accordingly.

Social Justice in the Multicultural Canadian Context

Canada's multicultural society is growing in diversity and size, and many would argue that community services need to reflect and address this diversity. Currently, however, many services do not appear to be accessible to minority groups (Lecca, Quervalu, Nunes, & Gonzales, 1998). Examples of the barriers that block access to services include language differences between professionals and service users, agency regulations and processes that are not "user-friendly" to immigrant groups, oppressive financial requirements for services, and lack of transferability of immigrants' educational credentials from their countries of origin. In addition, a disproportionate percentage of immigrant, refugee, and Aboriginal families become involved with child welfare in Canada (Christensen, 2003).

One explanation for the higher percentage of Aboriginal and immigrant families involved with child welfare is related to the lack of cultural competency of human service professionals. This can result, for example, in inadequate understanding or appreciation of alternative child-rearing arrangements. Cultural competency involves a blend of values, attitudes, cultural knowledge, and cultural awareness, and is used to provide appropriate and effective service delivery in cross-cultural situations (Hurdle, 2002).

1. Do you support the view that inadequate cultural competency of service professionals explains the higher rate of children from certain groups involved in child welfare? State your reasons.
2. What other explanations can be given for the higher rate of involvement of Aboriginal and immigrant families in child welfare?
3. Given the increasingly complex cultural context of Canadian society, what are agencies' (including child welfare agencies) ethical responsibilities in ensuring culturally competent services? Examples of possible issues with agency responsibilities are
   - language barriers—access to trained, competent interpreters;
   - hiring policies that promote culturally diverse workers;
   - identification of cultural barriers in the agency's policies and procedures; and
   - professional development workshops/seminars that promote cultural competency.
4. Can you think of any other items to include in the above list? If so what are they and what priority would you give them related to the other items in the list? What ethical reasons would you give to justify advocating for agencies to take such measures?

5. What are social workers' ethical and practice-related responsibilities to ensure service users receive culturally competent services? Examples of possible responsibilities are

- referring service users to agencies that are culturally competent and able to provide effective services;
- ensuring that clients receive culturally competent service, while promoting informed referral to resources;
- addressing the barriers to services within an agency (including cultural, religious, socioeconomic, language, etc.); and
- taking advantage of (and insisting on) opportunities to develop cultural competency.

6. Can you think of any other responsibilities to include in this list? If so, what are they and what priority would you give them related to the other items in the list? What ethical reasons would you give to justify professionals incorporating such measures in their practice?

INQUIRY PROJECT

Application of Decision-Making Process

In this text we have followed a decision-making process that considers

- relevant background information that informs the decision-making process;
- alternative courses of action the professional could consider;
- areas in professional codes of ethics that should be considered in possible the deliberating about possible courses of action; and
- choosing one or a combination of the decision-making models described in Chapter 2.

Using the decision-making process we have used in the text, make recommendations to an agency using the background information given below concerning the needs of Aboriginals and immigrants who are moving to an urban area in Canada. In your response, take into account any issues of social justice and the limited agency resources available given the multiple and complex issues professionals face in meeting existing service-user needs.

Context and Questions

A Canadian city is increasingly finding itself ill prepared to address the socialization, housing, and general support needs of Aboriginals and immigrants who continue to flood its human service agencies. One of the agencies contracted by the Children's Ministry finds that the majority of the children it works with are from families who have recently immigrated to the city or from Aboriginal families who have moved off the reserve. You are a social worker who works in the agency and you have discovered a lack of cultural competency among your peers in the agency and in other agencies you work with. You have brought this up with your supervisor. She does not agree with you but has given you permission to make a presentation to the staff.

- What would be the goal of your presentation and how would you gather information? What sources would you use?
- How would you organize your presentation?
- How would issues of ethics and social justice enter into your presentation?
- Whom would you involve in the presentation?

In your responses, provide

1. Background information you would want to obtain on Aboriginals, immigrants, and child welfare. You do not necessarily need to obtain the information, but at least identify the types of information you would want to gather and consider.
2. Important sections of at least one professional code of ethics that you think are relevant to guide professionals in this situation.
3. Your thoughts on how you think social justice enters into this issue and contributes to the decision-making process. Identify what social justice means in this context.
4. Alternative courses of action (give at least two possibilities) that a professional could consider given the background information you would include and sections from the code you have cited. These alternatives may change once you have more background information.
5. A decision-making model from Chapter 2 that you would suggest to the agency, along with your reasons, to assist agency staff in thinking through prioritization of resources.

Finally, share your reflections on how helpful it was to adapt the approach to practice situations we have used in this text to the issue of social justice for aboriginal and immigrant families.

ANTI-OPPRESSIVE PRACTICE

One of the more recent frameworks to explain why service users seek professional help is the concept of oppression. Practice is said to be "anti-oppressive" when it seeks to help service users understand the factors that have led to their condition (Dominelli, 2002; Mullaly, 2002;). This framework attempts to address the time and resource concerns of practitioners so that they can focus on individual needs as well as social justice concerns. The proponents of anti-oppressive practice argue that it can promote social justice by "empowering" service users to be equal participants in the "helping" relationship with the professional. They argue that power imbalances between service users and professionals contribute to oppression whether the professional is aware of it or not. A professional can address this imbalance by transferring power back to the service users, by focusing on their strengths, and by placing them in decision-making roles. "Respecting clients' rights to make decisions requires social workers to treat them as capable, relatively autonomous individuals. And, rather than pathologizing clients for their plight, focusing on their strengths without undermining their responsibility for the choices they make . . . practitioners are expected to serve client-defined needs, not dictate to them what should be done" (Dominelli, 2002, p. 25).

It is clear, however, that in order for professionals to carry out an "anti-oppressive" approach to empowering service users a supportive organizational climate must be in place. Some would argue that the professional should be challenged and supported to engage in organizational, and possibly societal, change to create increased awareness about oppression or social injustice. "The working environment has to be an anti-oppressive one throughout. Employers have to treat their employees, the social workers, in anti-oppressive ways . . . the extent to which anti-oppressive practice can survive and flourish within organizations that are not committed to its precepts at the personal, institutional and cultural levels remains a crucial issue" (Dominelli, 2002, p. 33).

Finn and Jacobson (2003) have developed a practice framework with a focus on social justice in direct or clinical practice. Their framework, called "just practice," centres around five themes: meaning, context, power, history, and possibility. An example of implementation of the model is given in the context of working with individual service users. This involves a social worker in a family-service agency funded by the government. The social worker is required to determine a service user's eligibility for income and service benefits, to enforce sanctions in response to a service user's noncompliance to policy directives, and to address barriers that prevent a single mother from entering the workforce (p. 13). The authors ask us to think about how the "just practice" framework might guide the social worker's thinking and practice. In this example, the context includes how issues of class, race, and gender both inform the agency's policies and practices and consequently shape the interaction the social worker has with the mother. What seems to be clearly missing from the "just practice" framework is a discussion about what the social worker can or should do in the presence of organizational and societal policies that do not support practising according to the framework. Our challenge is to begin to fill in that gap.

CHANGE IN THE PERMANENCY POLICY FOR HIGH-RISK OR HIGH-NEEDS CHILDREN

A province is implementing major changes to its policy for permanency planning for high-needs children. Over 5000 children have permanent guardianship status (PGO) with the Ministry of Children and Family Services, which means that the ministry acts as the "guardian," or "parent," for these children. The majority of these children are high-needs children and are living in foster homes. A high percentage of them are Aboriginal. The change in policy will mean that children under permanent guardianship status will have to be adopted or placed under private guardianship. Foster parents who work with these high-needs children will be significantly affected by this change in policy.

On a weekly basis the Assistant Deputy Minister (ADM) of Service Quality sends out "View to Adoption (VTA) Placements, Websites Activity" to remind children service workers that they need to focus on targets that have been set for moving children out of foster care. The goal is to increase adoption placements by 15 percent over last year's figure of 302 placements. To reach this target, the workers need to place 347 children within a year. Foster parents are being pressured to take steps to either adopt their foster children or to apply for private guardianship. This has upset many foster parents for a number of reasons:

- If they do not adopt or apply for private guardianship, the children will be removed from their home.
- They cannot appeal this decision regardless of how long the children have been placed in their home when a child is targeted for "permanent" placement.
- When foster parents adopt or apply for private guardianship they will lose financial support to take care of the children.

Some foster parents have committed themselves to fostering and do not have another source of income. Many of these foster parents have taken numerous hours of training in order to raise high-needs children, and in turn they are financially compensated for their time. In addition to financial assistance, a number of other supports that sustain the placement of high-needs children (for example, respite, counselling, youth work placements, recreation and vacation allowances) will be eliminated or significantly reduced once the child is adopted or private guardianship is granted. Also, as a result of the policy, foster parents will lose their skill fees and receive only basic maintenance, but only if their gross annual income is under $60,000. This does not take into consideration the number of other children they may be supporting on this income, including their own children.

Professional Concerns

One of the professionals who has been working with foster parents is concerned that the new permanency policy seems adversarial and intrusive and not respectful of the professionals, the families, or the children. The worker also feels that the cultural needs of Aboriginal children are being forgotten. He would like to propose options for including foster parents in evaluating the new policy. The worker also thinks that policy about permanency planning for high-risk or high-needs children should be more flexible.

The government's push for permanency stems from a belief that every child needs a family and that long-term foster care does not provide them with that sense of permanence. For example, in Alberta the report from the Child Welfare Act Review: 2002 articulated the principle that every child in Alberta deserves a "safe, stable home where they are nurtured by healthy families within loving, stable, nurturing and sustainable relationships because children need permanence in their young lives as soon as possible" (AFPA, 2003, p. 2). It also stated: "The provision of permanent placements for children and youth who are unable to live in their birth families is of the utmost concern of child welfare professionals. The harm done to children through the instability in their life perpetrated by multiple placements and delayed decisions is well documented in the child welfare literature. The provision of successful, stable permanent homes substantially increases the life chances of the child-in-care" (p. 3).

The worker agrees that children need a permanent home but wonders if long-term foster care may not be the preferred option for children with high needs who have already lived in a foster home for a long period of time. The worker feels this is especially important when the foster family is part of the extended family of an Aboriginal child. The worker also questions whether anyone is asking children, especially those who are older (that is, twelve or older), how they feel about being adopted or possibly being removed from their long-term foster homes. If the children's current foster parents do not wish to pursue one of the two options—adoption or private guardianship—where will these long-term foster children, especially the older children, go?

INQUIRY QUESTIONS

- If you were working with these high-needs children and their foster parents, what ethical concerns would you have with this new policy?
- What social justice concerns would you have with this new policy?

REFLECTIONS OF A PROFESSIONAL WHO WORKS WITH ABORIGINAL YOUTH IN TROUBLE

A professional spent some time during her lunch hour gathering a few statistics on incarceration of Aboriginal youth. She found that "in Saskatchewan in 1992, 70% of the youth in custody were Aboriginal. In Manitoba in 1990, 64% of the population of the Manitoba Youth Centre and 74% of the population at the Agassiz Youth Centre were Aboriginal" (Statistics Canada, 1998, p. 12). She also found that the incarceration rate of Aboriginal youth has been increasing over time. The Cawsey report in 1991 estimated that "in Alberta, the Aboriginal population in youth jails in the province would increase to 40% by 2011" (p. 10).

The professional reflects that if jailing young Aboriginal people were the answer to youth criminality, one would expect to find a decrease in Aboriginal youth jail admissions. But this has not occurred, and she believes that placing Aboriginal youth in young offender facilities does not prevent occurrences of criminal behaviour when they become adults; it simply prepares them for life in adult correctional institutions.

Proposal to Address Underlying "Causes" of Youth in Trouble

The professional works on a reserve with youth and has been designated by her band to provide direction and training for staff in youth-related agencies under the new Youth Criminal Justice Act (YCJA). She supports a number of the YCJA's principles. These include limits to the use of custody or placement in a treatment facility in nonviolent matters; the use of alternatives to custody that concentrate on reintegration and rehabilitation; and the use of case-management services. However, she questions whether these positive steps will achieve what they set out to if policies and programs do not address the underlying conditions that push vulnerable children and youth into antisocial behaviour.

The worker would like to develop a proposal for the youth on her reserve that would provide them training so that they can take advantage of higher-education and employment opportunities. However, she is feeling overwhelmed with her current professional responsibilities to develop alternatives to incarceration for both current and future at-risk youth.

INQUIRY PROJECT

How to Be Involved with Reform while Being Responsive to Service Users

As we have seen, direct and clinical social work professionals are faced with the dilemma of how to respond to the needs of their service users while addressing their professional ethical and social responsibilities. In the practice situations described above, the professional working with foster parents of high-needs children and the worker involved with Aboriginal youth both have ideas about how to improve the "context" of their practice but are equally "busy" with the day-to-day caring for the individuals they work with.

- Choose either the children's services scenario (permanency planning for high-needs children) or the Aboriginal youth-in-trouble scenario (underlying social and economic causes of problem). List the possible daily responsibilities workers may face in fulfilling service users' needs and organizational requirements.
- Given what you have listed and the concerns identified by the professional in your scenario, identify the organizational/social justice responsibilities they might face. Using ethical justifications for your recommendation, what would you advise the professional to do to address the organizational/social justice dimensions of their concerns?
- How would you respond to the professional's concerns that becoming involved with organizational and/or social change would mean spending less time with the service users?

REFLECTION QUESTIONS

- Think about your own reasons for becoming involved in professional practice and write a brief paragraph on whether you would prefer to work with individuals (anti-oppressive practice) or with organizational and social practices (social justice for groups).

- Describe the basis of your orientation at this point in your life.
- Finally, do you think there should be a section on social responsibility in professional codes of ethics other than social work? Give reasons for your response.

CONCLUSION

In this chatper we have shifted our focus from working with individuals and families within organizational contexts to considering social justice as a primary focus of social work practice. After a brief review of selected literature on the meaning of social justice for social work practice, we looked at the often contradictory demands on direct-service practitioners who are challenged to address the needs of individual clients and at the same time become involved with social justice. We did not resolve this dilemma; however, we have identified the questions and issues that will require ongoing consideration and reflection.

In the next chapter we will consider our professional responsibilities to colleagues and employers.

NOTES

NOTES

NOTES

NOTES

_____

_____

_____

_____

_____

_____

_____

_____

_____

_____

_____

_____

_____

NOTES

NOTES

REFERENCES

Alberta Foster Parent Association (AFPA). (2003, September). Proposal to extend the mandate of the AFPA to include support to adoptive families. Retrieved April 1, 2004, from http://www.afpaonline.com/programs_adoption.htm

American Counseling Association. (1995). *Code of ethics and standards of practice.* Alexandria, VA: Author.

Association of Social Workers in Turkey. (2002). *Code of ethics.* Retrieved July 2004 from http://www.Ifsw.org/Publications/4.4.1.tc.pub.html

Australian Association of Social Workers. (2002). *Code of ethics.* Retrieved July 2004 from http://www.aasw.asn.au

Canadian Association of Social Workers. (2005a). *Code of ethics.* Ottawa, ON: Author.

Canadian Association of Social Workers. (2005b). *Guidelines for ethical practice.* Ottawa, ON: Author.

Cawsey, R.A. (Chairman). (1991). *Justice on trial: Report of the task force on the criminal justice system and its impact on the Indian and Métis people of Alberta.* Edmonton: Ministry of Solicitor General.

Chatterjee, Paranab, & D'Aprix, Amy. (2002). Two tails of justice. *Families in Society: The Journal of Contemporary Human Services, 83*(4), 374–386.

Christensen (2003). Canadian society: Social policy and ethno-racial diversity. In A. Al-Krenawi & J. Graham (Eds.), *Multicultural social work in Canada: Working with diverse ethno-racial communities* (pp. 251–282). Don Mills, ON: Oxford University Press.

Dominelli, Lena. (2002). *Anti-oppressive social work theory and practice.* New York: Palgrave MacMillan.

Finn, Janet L., & Jacobson, Maxine. (2003). Just practice: Steps toward a new social work paradigm. *Journal of Social Work Education, 39*(1), 1–19.

Freud, S., & Krug, S. (2002). Beyond the code of ethics, part 2: Complexities of ethical decision making in social work practice. *Families in Society: The Journal of Contemporary Human Services, 83,* 488–498.

George, Vic, & Wilding, Paul. (1994). *Globalization and human welfare.* Houndsmill, Hampshire: Palgrave MacMillan.

Goldstein, H. (1990). The knowledge base of social work practice: Theory, wisdom, analogue, or art? *Families in Society: The Journal of Contemporary Human Services, 71*(1), 32–43.

Hurdle, D.E. (2002). Native Hawaiian traditional healing: Culturally based interventions for social work practice. *Social Work 47*(2), 183–192.

Hyde, C. (1998). A model for diversity training in human service agencies. *Administration in Human Services 22*(4), 19–33.

Krug, S. (1994). *The moral ecology of protective service work.* Unpublished doctoral dissertation, Simmons College School of Social Work, Boston.

Lecca, P.J., Quervalu, I., Nunes, J.V., & Gonzales, H.F. (1998). *Cultural competency in health, social, and human services: Directions for the twenty-first century.* New York: Garland Publishing.

Linden, L. (2000). *Criminology: A Canadian perspective.* Toronto: Harcourt Brace.

Margolin, L. (1997). *Under the cover of kindness: The invention of social work.* Charolottesville: University Press of Virginia.

Mullaly, Bob. (2002). *Challenging oppression: A critical social work approach.* Toronto: Oxford University Press.

National Association of Social Workers. (1999). *Code of ethics and standards of practice.* Washington, DC: Author.

Rawls, John. (1999). *A theory of justice.* Boston, MA: Harvard University Press. (Original work published in 1971)

Reisch, Michael. (2002). Defining social justice in a socially unjust world. *Families in Society: The Journal of Contemporary Human Services, 83*(4), 343–354.

Rhodes, M.L. (1992). Social work challenges: The boundaries of ethics. *Families in Society: The Journal of Contemporary Human Services, 73*(1), 40–47.

Rossiter, A. (2000). The professional is political: An interpretation of the problem of the past in solution-focused therapy. *American Journal of Orthopsychiatry, 70*(2), 150–161.

Ryan, W. (1981). *Equality.* New York: Vintage Books.

Statistics Canada. (1998, January). 1996 census: Aboriginal data. *The Daily,* 10–19. Ottawa: Statistics Canada. Retrieved June 27, 2004, from http://www.statcan.ca/Daily/English/980113.htm

Responsibilities to the Profession: Accountability to Colleagues and Employers

In our discussion of ethical practice we have emphasized the importance of being grounded in a professional frame of reference that includes codes of ethics and a deliberative decision process. As noted in Chapter 7, professional practice can range from assisting service users to addressing social justice issues in policies that impact individuals and groups of people.

Another important dimension of professional practice is how we relate to colleagues and carry out our responsibilities to our profession and employers. In this chapter we will focus on the ethical dimensions of these relationships. In particular we ask you to think about professional codes of ethics and the directions they give on responsibilities professionals have to each other, their employing organization, and the community.

 INQUIRY QUESTIONS

- How should a professional respond if she or he thinks a colleague is engaging in unethical or unprofessional conduct?
- What should a professional do if organizational or government policies result in inadequate services within his or her employing organization?
- Are there limits to what professionals can do when their views conflict with their obligations to an employer?
- Do professionals have an ethical responsibility to address policies even if it puts them in conflict with their organization's priorities?

These questions are related to the focus of Chapter 7 on the professional's responsibility to engage in social justice activity and the sometimes conflicting obligations arising from multiple professional duties. As has been the case throughout our discussion of ethical decision making, there are no easy answers about how to resolve these conflicts, and good arguments can often result in disagreements about the appropriate resolution of such conflicts. The challenge you have in this chapter is to read the practice situations described below, discern what the important issues are, and apply professional codes of ethics in a deliberative decision strategy, as you have in previous chapters.

WHEN RESPONSIBILITIES TO SERVICE USERS AND COLLEAGUES COME IN CONFLICT

The BC Addictions Recovery and Wellness Centre (BCRWC) is a private, nonprofit organization that has been treating people with alcohol and addiction problems since 1989. The centre offers a wide range of treatment services, including detoxification and shelter; assessment and referral; individual, family, and group counselling; and day and residential treatment.

Employees of BCRWC are skilled professionals with degrees in social work, counselling, psychology, and sociology. Many of them have personal and/or family experience with substance and behavioural dependence, which is thought to increase their empathy for others who are facing similar struggles. However, this agency has reported difficulties with these employees when their personal experiences have hindered the effectiveness of their working relationship. For example, some staff members may have problems separating their experience from that of their clients or may be struggling with their own issues of substance use.

BCRWC staff members are required to abide by an in-house code of ethical conduct, specific to workers in the field of addictions, and the social workers in the agency are also expected to adhere to the Canadian Association of Social Workers *Code of Ethics* (2005a). Additionally, BCRWC maintains strict policies that forbid the use of alcohol or other recreational drugs to ensure the integrity of their staff. The rationale for this practice is to provide service users with positive role models and protect them from triggering effects, which often occur when a service user detects substance use by someone in their immediate surroundings.

As you read the following practice situation jot down your first thoughts about the important ethical dimensions and how you think professional codes of ethics apply to the issues you have identified.

Practice Situation: **Christine and Rachel**

Christine is a social worker who has worked for BCRWC in Vancouver for sixteen years. She considers herself a recovered alcoholic. She regularly attends Alcoholics Anonymous (AA) meetings; this recovery community comprises most of her social network. Their support group meetings provide a place to share common problems and encourage one another in alcohol recovery. The primary purpose of AA is to help alcoholics achieve sobriety.

Christine first met her colleague Rachel at AA. Rachel had just transferred to Vancouver from a northern BC community, where she lived the first six and a half years of her recovery and began working for BCRWC before transferring to Vancouver.

Christine and Rachel have been friends and colleagues for almost two years since they first met at AA. Christine and Rachel realize that their relationship has many dimensions, but they concede that these are beneficial to their service users, their agency, and each other.

Recently, at one of their AA meetings, Rachel disclosed that she had had a relapse. Since then Christine has been concerned because Rachel had also expressed feeling overwhelmed and concerned about her marriage. Christine has been a supportive friend, but today she noticed that Rachel became defensive when discussing a service-user problem at the morning staff meeting. Later, Rachel returned from her lunch break with alcohol on her breath. Christine asked Rachel about the smell, but Rachel was indignant and denied that she had consumed alcohol during her lunch break. Christine is beginning to wonder about Rachel's history of sobriety, particularly in regards to her first six and a half years in northern BC.

BACKGROUND INFORMATION

The use of alcohol is a serious concern to BCRWC. The agency recognizes that alcohol use by employees during working hours could potentially trigger their service users to drink. Depending on the amount consumed, it may also impair workers' judgment. If workers claim to be in recovery from alcoholism, their use of alcohol may lower their credentials in the eyes of the service users, potentially making them ineffective role models.

The agency's policy is clear: workers cannot use alcohol during office hours and workers in recovery from alcoholism must remain completely abstinent. The responsibility rests with all staff members to monitor each other's actions. However, agency policy does not state specifically what actions workers should take if they suspect another staff member is using alcohol.

The agency sets out rules regarding triggers that are known to be dangerous to service users' recovery process. For example, sounds such as the jingling of coins may mentally remind, or "trigger," gambling addicts and thereby reintroduce craving for the addiction; therefore, no vending machines are allowed on the premises. Cell phones are not allowed on the property because narcotics addicts may be triggered by the sound of the ringing. The sense of sight, heavily used in advertising, may trigger many addicts, so there are no pictures of alcohol, cigarettes, drugs, or drug paraphernalia allowed on the bulletin boards. Because smells are also a concern, workers are cautioned about certain candy and are not allowed to have tobacco or alcohol on their breath. All staff members are reminded to be sensitive to additional triggers that are known to service users but not identified in the policy.

Nine years ago the agency restructured, and a group consisting of workers, alumni, board members, and the director, formulated the mission statement, goals, and policies of BCRWC. Participants believed in the power of "addicts helping addicts," and the agency committed itself to employing a number of workers who are in addictions recovery. The agency believes that such workers are in a unique position to demonstrate wellness behaviours, to motivate, inspire, and offer hope to their clients. However, because the workers are at risk of relapsing, the agency requires staff members to abide by two codes of ethical conduct: one specific to addictions and another specific to their profession within the agency. There are three versions of the in-house code of ethical conduct: one for professionals, one for volunteers, and another for the clients. All clients receive a copy of these three codes when they enter treatment. This is to ensure they are aware of BCRWC's serious commitment to the wellness of clients and staff.

While many addiction treatment centres take a reactive position by implementing random drug testing of their staff, this agency takes a proactive stance by setting up weekly staff support sessions facilitated by an outside therapist. At these weekly meetings, workers have a safe place to discuss issues that could threaten or challenge their work environment. Additionally, the professionals who are in addictions recovery are expected to have regular contact with their sponsor for personal support and to attend twelve-step meetings. Further, the agency encourages these staff members to appropriately disclose their personal stories to the service users.

APPLYING PROFESSIONAL CODES OF ETHICS

As discussed in previous practice situations, all professionals adhere to ethical codes specific to their profession. In this case both Christine and Rachel are social workers and members of the BC Association of Social Workers. They are expected to follow the CASW *Code of Ethics* (2005a). The agency also requires all staff members to follow an approved in-house code of ethical conduct specific to work in the field of addictions that is based on work by Bissell and Royce (1987). Two clauses in the agency code apply to this situation:

- In my use of alcohol and other mood-altering drugs, I will serve as a responsible role model for clients, staff, and community. If I have been chemically dependent in the past, I will maintain total abstinence while employed at BCRWC.
- I will exhibit responsible concern for the well being of my peers and the BCRWC community by not ignoring manifestations of illness or unethical conduct in colleagues.

Rachel and Christine are bound by the BCRWC *Code of Ethical Conduct*, which states: "As a member of the BCRWC professional staff, I will place the welfare of our clients . . . above all other concerns" and "To this end, I will deliver kind and humane treatment to all in my care." Additionally, "I will not deliberately do harm to a client, either physically or psychologically. I will not . . . endanger a patient, nor will I allow other patients or staff to do so."

As far as Alcoholics Anonymous is concerned, it is the ethical responsibility of each AA member to protect the anonymity of other members by not revealing who attends meetings and what is said there. Signs are found at meetings with variations of the message, "Who you see here—What you hear here—When you leave here—Let it stay here." A person may only disclose his or her own membership (Alcoholics Anonymous, 2000). In this case, Christine knows that she would be violating AA's core ethic of maintaining members' anonymity by telling her supervisor, or anyone else, about Rachel's relapse.

INQUIRY QUESTIONS

- Is Christine's knowledge of Rachel's relapse, which she detected during the AA meeting in itself sufficient ethical justification for her to speak to an authority at the agency? If yes, what is the justification, and if not, what is the ethical rationale for not talking with agency authorities about Rachel's relapse?
- Does Christine have an obligation to report Rachel to agency authorities when she detected alcohol on her breath during office hours?
- Did you arrive at the same conclusion for both questions? If you reach the same conclusion about disclosure for both questions, what are the core similarities that cause you to reach the same conclusion? If your conclusions about the responsibility to disclose are different, what has caused that difference? In explaining your response, include a rationale grounded in ethics.

The following practice situation describes a rather complex situation impacting practice in a remote community. It involves provincial policies and related program activities as they affect workers and service users in a transition house. As you read this situation, jot down what you think are the important ethical dimensions a practitioner would need to address. In particular, keep in mind possible obligations and responsibilities to the employer (the local nonprofit agency), co-workers in the house, service users, the profession, and the community.

Practice Situation: **A Transition House for Women and Children in British Columbia**

A seven-bed transition house is located in a remote northern community of 11,000 in BC It is partially funded by the provincial government as well as by local community grants and donations. On average 270 women and children from diverse backgrounds and circumstances are sheltered each year, with an average bed stay of nine days. The house is run by a local nonprofit agency that has been in operation for thirty years. The agency also provides services in the areas of child/family counselling, victim services, youth services, supported child care, and community living services. The varied programming has enabled the agency to survive fiscal challenges such as the most recent cutbacks by the provincial government. Yet such diversity in services can result in a "watering down" of values inherent to particular programs. In this case, it has meant a move away from the "feminist practice" that has been an identifying focus of the house.

Services are primarily targeted toward providing safety for women and children in abusive relationships, but due to cuts in other community and government services more women are turning to the transition house for nonabuse issues. As a result of this increase in demand, transition house workers are faced with the challenge of balancing all women's rights to safety, support, and respect with the mandate of the house, which is to focus on women and children in abusive relationships. The workers must assess their capacity to adequately assist women who come with non-abuse-related issues. Service guidelines do not take into consideration the complexity of issues experienced by these other groups of women and consequently give insufficient direction to the workers.

IMPACT OF GOVERNMENT AND AGENCY SERVICE EXPECTATIONS ON PRACTICE

The impact of the move away from a feminist practice model and a focus on women and children in abusive relationships is evident in the treatment of women who do not fit the original mandate of the house. For example, adult women with mental health issues are often evicted from the house because they do not (or cannot) abide by house guidelines and are viewed as compromising the house rules. The province's Ministry of Human Resources usually steps in to provide one night's accommodation for such women at a local motel, but this response is viewed as inadequate by many of the workers in the house because these women are no longer safe or supported. In the face of what they view as an unmet need, workers often feel powerless.

When a woman is attempting to flee an abusive relationship, most of the house workers think she should have access to services that have been developed using a gender analysis and centred within women's experience. If she does not have access to these "women-centred" services, she may encounter mainstream attitudes that will perpetuate her victimization and oppression (for example, "if you don't obey the rules you will be punished"). For women who do not have abuse issues, the impact is similar to being blamed for her situation. Whatever her circumstances—mental health issues, addiction problems, homelessness, unemployment, poverty—if a woman is blamed for her situation, she may feel hopeless about making the needed changes.

From the workers' perspective, the provincial government seems to be more interested in a balanced budget and economic growth than in social justice or human rights. The provincial funding contract for the house states that service principles are based on women's safety; respect for women's rights to make choices based on their own understanding of their options, needs, and goals; and respect for the individual situation, perspective, and needs of the women. Yet the funding provided to fulfill the contract restricts the services the house can offer and is inadequate to fund support services in the community. As a result, the workers' view is that women's choices are in reality not respected and their individual situations are not considered since there are few resources for them to access. For example, the house is the only option for many women in the sex trade who are dealing with drug/alcohol issues and/or mental health issues or are trying to get off the street, yet the service structure is not capable of providing these women the support services they request.

One worker put the issue succinctly during a staff meeting when she stated that "respecting rights to make choices" is an empty statement when the larger society is structured so that options are not available to these women. During the same staff meeting another worker questioned whether the programs offered in the house can enhance women's autonomy when government policy may be eroding women's rights.

As an example, the worker cited a statement by the BC Group of the United Nations Committee on the Elimination of Discrimination Against Women (CEDAW) about the effects of the elimination of the Human Rights Commission in BC: "Discrimination in B.C. society is experienced predominantly by women, people with disabilities, Aboriginal peoples, and visible minorities . . . the elimination of the [Human Rights] Commission removes a central institution relied on by women and other vulnerable members of British Columbian society to articulate and defend their right to equality, and to prevent its perpetuation" (BC CEDAW, 2003, p. 7).

WORKERS' RESPONSES

As a result of their growing frustration, workers in the house have discussed the possibility of involving women in the development of policy and community resources so that they are able to make choices for themselves. One of the important aspects of their thinking is that women who are service users, along with professionals involved with transition houses, should be involved in the policymaking process and there should be a commitment to consistently apply a gender analysis to an examination of policy and resources. Their proposal would recommend ongoing participatory evaluation of services/programs for women in the province based on value criteria that consider "policy's impact on rights, statuses, and social justice, including the ability of service users to be self-determining" (Wharf & McKenzie, 2004, p. 57).

Although this proposal has many features that workers support, most view it as unrealistic. At the provincial level the movement toward women's equality has been sliding backwards, and for this reason attempts to allow service users to participate in policy formation and evaluation might not prove effective. A report submitted by the BC group of CEDAW notes the lack of support for the rights of women and children: "the Government of British Columbia is not fulfilling its specific obligations to women and girls, as set out in the Convention. Secondly, the drastic and discriminatory changes to provincial legislation and programs which have been made since May 2001 violate the obligation. . . . Central to the fulfillment of CEDAW obligations is the understanding that governments will progressively advance women's exercise and enjoyment of their human rights. However, the Government of British Columbia is moving backwards. It has dismantled the very programs and protections that it points to in the Fifth Report as demonstrating its compliance with CEDAW" (BC CEDAW, 2003, p. 2).

Another group of workers argues that change would be best initiated from the "grassroots" level, focusing on the local community. Policy change in their view would begin within a tangible sphere of influence by identifying and addressing policy issues at the local program/agency level. This strategy is in keeping with the historical development of community women's organizations in BC. Most women's groups in British Columbia today are a result of this grassroots approach. The workers are not sure what this "grassroots" approach would look like, and they are not sure if they have time to develop it given their responsibilities in working with women and children at the house.

INQUIRY QUESTIONS

- If you were a consultant called in to help the workers, what key ethical dimensions would you ask the workers to consider?
- How would you help them come to a resolution? What role would professional codes of ethics play in the process?

THE IMPACT OF SERVICE CENTRALIZATION IN A RURAL CONTEXT

The following practice situation focuses on the tension between funding policies and access to services. The professional in this situation is concerned about changes that in her view have created barriers to accessing critical services for adolescents. Think about how you would respond if you were the worker and what ethical issues you would need to consider in developing your response.

Professional Experience and Analysis of Experience

The social worker notes that the centralization of adolescent mental health services in Nova Scotia has significantly impacted young people living in rural areas. She practises in a small community on the eastern shore of the province, where, in her experience, adolescents have experienced diminished access to crucial mental health services. Adolescents seeking services are referred to a central intake worker at the Health Centre in Halifax, who determines if the potential service user meets the criteria for a referral for service (designated on a priority type scale). If a referral is warranted, the adolescent is placed on a waiting list, which often takes up to six months to process. An appointment is then scheduled with a mental health worker in an urban centre (anywhere between 85 km and 120 km away). High demand and shortages in health care professionals often give rise to brief interventions scheduled on a bi-weekly or tri-weekly basis.

According to the social worker, many adolescents are not receiving adequate and timely responses to their service needs. Transportation for appointments in the urban centres is a real concern for service users and has detracted from their success in resolving their mental health problems. Subsequently, service users are left with unmet needs, which may become intensified in times of crisis.

The social worker perceives that the disparity in services for rural adolescents also applies to other residents of rural communities, who often feel unimportant and undervalued in relation to access to mental health services. They are also left with a lack of knowledge regarding diagnosis, the benefits of early intervention, and treatment options. It is this lack of knowledge that many professionals in rural communities claim disempowers rural service users and strengthens the cycle of stigma surrounding mental health treatment that often prevails in isolated communities. In addition, the ramifications of a central access policy impact the rural service professionals. For example, the social worker describes a sense of obligation to support those service users who are unable to access specialized services. The worker also expresses feelings of isolation, workload stress, and burnout, which she claims often limit her effectiveness in working with service users.

Conflicts in Policy

Canadians have voiced their support for the core values on which our health care system is built: equity, fairness, and solidarity. Canada's citizens want and expect their governments to work collaboratively to ensure that the policies and programs that define their health care system remain true to these values. Testimonials from the Romanow report, *Building on Values: The Future of Health Care in Canada,* suggest that "Canadians consider equal and timely access to medically necessary health care services on the basis of need as a right of citizenship, not a privilege of status or wealth" (Romanow, 2002). The report also contains recommendations to ensure the sustainability of a universally accessible, publicly funded health system that will offer quality services to all Canadians.

On a provincial level, it would appear that these same core values prevail. Of particular interest for the professionals in this rural Nova Scotia community is the contradiction between the mission statements of provincial, organizational, and departmental health authorities that promote access and the policy of centralization that has been adopted by the health region for mental health services, which from a rural perspective creates barriers to access.

Professional Response

The social worker has determined that the best way to address the problem of accessibility is to explore new ways of delivering care rather than expanding hospital-based programs in urban areas. At the same time, her supervisor has told her that she needs to increase her caseload and help the social workers in the urban centre facilitate adolescent referrals to hospital services. The professional is thinking of possible responses to the conflict between her supervisor's wishes and the needs of rural adolescents. One of the core questions facing her is: "Whose views and interests should come first?"

The social worker takes this question apart and considers her loyalties:

- to the adolescents she is currently working with;
- to her supervisor and the organization that employs her; or
- to herself as a professional—someone who wants to place service to the adolescents as the highest priority and who also wants to retain her position and move up in the organization?

INQUIRY PROJECT

Map Out and Apply a Decision Strategy

Put yourself in the place of the social worker in this scenario and map out a decision strategy for thinking through alternatives and arriving at a decision that is supported by sound ethical reasons. From Chapter 2, recall the following core elements that are part of any decision framework:

- having "real" options that are in contention, one or more of which the professional must choose;

- identifying goals, values, and interests;
- developing key questions to direct information gathering;
- devising an information-gathering strategy (Where will you get the information? How? When? In what form?);
- gathering and assessing information;
- developing criteria to decide on a course of action;
- assessing each option and selecting an option(s);
- implementing the course of action;
- evaluating the implementation;
- using what has been learned about implementation to adjust actions and decision making.

Given these core elements, you then reviewed *decision frameworks* from both absolutist and relativist ethical perspectives:

Ethical Absolutist Frameworks	Ethical Relativist Frameworks
Ethical Principles Screen	ETHIC Model
Hierarchy of Duties and Rights	Tracking Harms Model
Bioethics Principle and Rules Model	Ethical Problem-Solving Model

In the decision strategy you map out, refer to one or more of these frameworks or use the core elements to design a course of action supported by sound ethical reasoning. As you go through the decision process, incorporate the topic of this chapter—responsibilities to colleagues, the profession, and the employer—and refer to relevant sections of professional codes of ethics that are relevant for your decision process.

CONCLUSION

This chapter has incorporated the theme of Chapter 7—about integrating social justice in practice—with a discussion of our obligations to our profession, employers, and colleagues. The potential for conflict among these multiple obligations has been highlighted in the practice situations you have worked on in this chapter. The chapter concluded with an application of the decision-making models outlined in Chapter 2. Decision models are important conceptual tools to have before you as you work through complex practice issues, especially those that have important ethical components.

The next chapter focuses on a core concern facing all workers in the helping professions: identifying and maintaining relationship boundaries to advance the welfare of service users.

NOTES

NOTES

NOTES

NOTES

NOTES

NOTES

REFERENCES

Alberta Human Rights and Citizenship Commission. (1996). Diversity and equality. Retrieved October 31, 2003, from http://www.albertahumanrights.ab.ca/diversity

Alcoholics Anonymous. (2000). *AA guidelines for AA members employed in the alcoholism field*. Retrieved November 2, 2003, from http://www.alcoholics-anonymous.org/default/em-pdfs/mg-10_foraamembers.pdf

BC CEDAW. (2003). Group of the United Nations Committee on the Elimination of Discrimination Against Women on the occasion of the Committee's review of Canada's 5th Report. *BC moves backwards on women's equality*. Retrieved July 8, 2004, from http://www.treatyjustice.org/poverty.html

BC Coalition of Women's Centres. (2002, March). *Impact of BC government cutbacks on women*. Retrieved July 8, 2004, from http://www3.telus.net/bcwomen/archives/impact_of_cuts_on_women_mar_02.html

BC Ministry of Community, Aboriginal, and Women's Services. (2004). *Transition house program transfer under agreement*. Contract no. C05STVS0000079, Schedule A. Victoria: Province of British Columbia.

BC Ministry of Women's Equality. (1998). *Transition house program agreement*. Contract no. 199011, Schedule A. Victoria: Province of British Columbia.

BC Women's Hospital and Health Centre. (2003, March). *Woman abuse response program training and resource guide*. Vancouver.

BC/Yukon Society of Transition Houses. (2002). *Occupational competencies within women-serving organizations: Specific to transition houses, safe homes, second stage homes*. Retrieved July 8, 2004, from http://www.bcysth.ca/resources/resources.htm

BC/Yukon Society of Transition Houses. (2004). *Building bridges: Weaving women's wisdom: A response to government cutbacks through the voice of community*. Retrieved July 8, 2004, from http://www.bcysth.ca/resources/documents/Weaving%20Women's%20Wisdom%20Kit2.doc

Bissell, LeClair, & Royce, James E. (1987). *Ethics for addictions professionals*. Center City, MN: Hazelden Information and Educational Services.

Canadian Association of Social Workers. (2005a). *Code of ethics*. Ottawa, ON: Author.

Canadian Association of Social Workers. (2005b). *Guidelines for ethical practice*. Ottawa, ON: Author.

Houston Family Resource Center. (1995). *Substance abuse professional procedure guidelines for transportation workplace drug and alcohol testing programs*. Retrieved October 3, 2003 from http://www.helptochange.com/sap.htm

MacLeod, L. (1990). *Counselling for change: Evolutionary trends in counselling services for women who are abused and for their children in Canada.* Retrieved August 3, 2004, from http://www.hc-sc.gc.ca/hppb/familyviolence/femabus_e.html

Osmond, Bradley. (2004, June). *Rural communities impacting policy.* Retrieved July 28, 2004, from http://www.ruralnovascotia.ca/ruralhealth.asp

Romanow, Roy. (2002, November). *Building on values: The future of health care in Canada.* Retrieved July 26, 2004, from http://www.hc-sc.gc.ca

South Peace Community Resources Society. (2004, March). *Annual program evaluations and year end statistics report.* Dawson Creek, BC.

Statistics Canada. (2004, March). *Health status and behaviours of Canada's youth: A rural–urban comparison.* Retrieved July 30, 2004, from http://www.statcan.ca/start.html

Wharf, B., & McKenzie, B. (2004). *Connecting policy to practice in the human services.* New York: Oxford University Press.

chapter

Professional Relationships, Use of Power, and Boundaries

An essential ethical dimension in all the practice situations we have examined is the importance of being sensitive to boundaries and to the role of power in the professional–service user relationship. In Chapter 7 we addressed power imbalances in professional relationships from the perspective of an anti-oppressive model of practice.

This chapter revisits power issues within the context of a discussion of boundaries in professional relationships. We identify typical boundary problems and power issues faced by professionals and ask you to work with practice situations that exemplify these issues. Using a deliberate decision process, you will develop responses to the issues and will be challenged to give sound ethical reasons for the positions you take.

BOUNDARY ISSUES IN PROFESSIONAL RELATIONSHIPS

In a professional relationship the concerns and needs of the service user have priority over the personal needs of the professional. The worker, therefore, must be able to separate his or her own needs from those of the service user. Setting and maintaining professional boundaries are essential in preventing personal involvement and maintaining a professional relationship.

Boundary problems occur when roles change. For example, when a professional–service user relationship becomes a business partnership or friendship, this could be viewed as a "crossing" of professional boundaries. Boundary "violations," on the other hand, are considered to be more serious than "crossings." Boundary violations are characterized by exploitation of the service user in a misuse of power on the part of the professional. Examples of exploitation can be as subtle as seating arrangements in a professional's office designed to bring the professional physically closer to an attractive service user. Sexual exploitation is an example of a more extreme form of boundary violation, as is the financial or emotional exploitation of the vulnerability of service users. In rural and remote areas, professionals typically have more difficulty with boundary crossing given the multiple roles they play in a small community, such as school board member, church member, scout leader, and so forth. The question becomes not whether they can avoid boundary crossing but how they can minimize any problems this may create for service users.

In response to issues arising from boundary crossings and violations, Redlich and Pope (1980) offer seven principles for psychologists and psychiatrists to help them coordinate ethical guidelines with other standards of professional practice: (1) above all, do no harm; (2) practise only with competence; (3) do not exploit; (4) treat people with respect for their dignity as human beings; (5) protect confidentiality; (6) act, except in the most extreme instances, only after obtaining informed consent; and (7) practise, insofar as possible, within the framework of social equity and justice. The first five are mentioned explicitly in the "Hippocratic oath" for physicians. The seventh, although not universally accepted by human service professionals, is a core element in the social work profession's code of ethics (see Chapter 7).

DUAL RELATIONSHIPS

A dual relationship is a type of boundary crossing in which professionals have two or more overlapping roles with service users, one of which is the professional role. In a survey of dual relationships among 4800 psychologists, psychiatrists, and social workers Borys and Pope (1989) found that the majority of respondents reported that most forms of dual relationships were not ethical. Although this may indicate the urban nature of the sample, in general there was agreement across professions with the exception of slight differences based on profession and gender.

In response to the potential for exploitation in dual relationships, Kagle and Giebelhausen (1994) state that a dual relationship of any sort should result in the revocation of the social worker's licence. Brownlee and Delaney (1997), however, in their study of social work in northern areas, respond that this point of view does not apply to the northern practice setting. They support the argument that it is inevitable for social workers in small-town settings to be consistently faced with the challenges of dual relationships. A more realistic stance is for the professional to develop strategies for protecting service users from the direct or indirect negative consequences of duality. Given that dual relationships are difficult to avoid in rural and remote areas and in fact if a professional removes him or herself too much from the community to avoid dual relationships it may lower their effectiveness in the community, it is important to examine some of the risks that need to be considered in dual relationships and develop strategies to avoid such risks.

Practice Situation: **Rural Practice and Dual Relationships**

Imagine that you live in a small rural community and have accepted an invitation to be a member of a board for a community group that is engaged in the type of activism you value. During the first board meeting you discover that one of the service users you work with is also on the board. The service user comes over at a break to tell you how pleased she is that you share similar values and that the two of you will be working closely together.

RELATED QUESTIONS

- How do you feel?
- What feelings do you think the service user might be experiencing?
- What do you think are important issues to consider?
- What would you say to the service user?
- Would you remain on the board or not? What reasoning leads you to this decision?
- What additional information would you need to determine how you would proceed?

RISKS IN DUAL RELATIONSHIPS

Some of the major risks associated with dual relationships are

- impairment of professional judgment;
- conflict of interests;
- potential for exploitation of service user since the professional is in a more powerful position; and
- blurring of the professional nature of the worker.

INQUIRY PROJECT

In addition to the example described above, think of any actual or imagined situations in which you found yourself in a dual relationship with a service user. How did you or would you handle the situation so that you avoid the risks associated with dual relationships and do not compromise your professional role?

GUIDELINES FOR REDUCING THE RISKS OF DUAL RELATIONSHIPS

Compare your strategies above with the following guidelines for reducing risks associated with dual relationships:

- Set healthy boundaries from the outset of the relationship.
- Fully inform service users about potential risks.

- Discuss with service users any potential problematic relationship and clarify areas of concern.
- Consult with other professionals periodically if you are engaged in a dual relationship to help you maintain perspective.
- Work under supervision in situations where the potential for harm is high.
- Document discussions about any dual relationships and relevant steps taken.
- If necessary, refer the service user to another professional.

Factors to Consider when Entering into Dual Relationships

The following are questions to consider when you are faced with the possibility of entering into a dual relationship with service users:

- Are there legal or ethical issues with the relationship?
- Is there a possibility of negative effects for the service user or another party as a result of the dual relationship?
- What differences in power are there between the professional and service user?
- What are the risks for the professional?
- What are the benefits for the service user?
- What is the impact on professional boundaries?
- What is the potential effect on the goal(s) of the professional relationship?
- Are alternative solutions (referrals) available?

Practice Situation: **Surprise Thanksgiving Date**

You live by yourself in a small town, and a family with whom you are close friends is aware that you will probably be spending Thanksgiving alone. They invite you to share the day with them: preparing the meal during the morning, feasting at lunch, going for a leisurely walk in the woods during the afternoon, then returning for a light dinner. You show up to discover that they have, without letting you know, invited another "unattached" person who is presumably your blind date for the day. That person is a former service user with whom you completed your work a little over a month ago.

INQUIRY QUESTIONS

- What are your options?
- Given those options, what would you do?
- How would the situation be different if the person were a current service user? Would it matter what type of services the person was using?
- What if the person were your supervisor?
- What if the person were a professional who was treating you for depression?
- What additional information would you need to think through this situation?

PROFESSIONAL OBJECTIVITY

One risk that can result from boundary crossing or violation or can itself lead to boundary issues is loss of professional objectivity. If the worker's objectivity becomes compromised, the essence of the professional relationship, with its focus on service users' needs and concerns, is at risk. Loss of objectivity can occur when some element of the service user's experience causes the professional to identify with that experience. For example, if the service user had a particularly difficult time as a young parent and the worker begins to view the client's situation as similar to his or her own experience as a single parent, the identification may diminish the worker's objectivity, ultimately affecting the quality of the professional's work.

INQUIRY PROJECT

Think about particular types of issues service users could bring to you that would cause you to lose objectivity.

- What strategies would you use to retain your objectivity?
- What additional professional strategies could help you monitor whether you are maintaining objectivity in your professional work?

Practice Situation: **Teresa**

Teresa has been assigned the role of parole officer for a small town in rural northern Ontario. The service users she works with include some of the town's residents, the majority of whom are Aboriginal. Teresa often finds herself interacting with her clients on a personal level, mainly because there is only one grocery store, hardware store, gas station, community centre, and post office in the town. Tom, one of Teresa's clients, has recently been released from jail for a violent offence while under the influence of alcohol. He was given accelerated parole so that he could have a better opportunity to build stronger relationships with his family members in the community. He has been ordered to abstain from alcohol while on parole, and he can be subjected to unscheduled drug and alcohol testing to ensure he is clean. It is part of Teresa's role to assist Tom with his successful reintegration into the community and his adherence to the correctional release plan.

One day while grocery shopping, Teresa ran into Tom in the store. Tom approached her and began idle chitchat. Teresa noticed the strong smell of alcohol on Tom's breath. Teresa politely continued the conversation but was plagued with an ethical dilemma surrounding what her course of action should be: to report or not to report. As his parole officer, she knows a great deal about Tom's history and that he should not be under the influence of any substance; it is in fact a direct violation of his correctional release plan. Teresa also realizes that if she reports this incident to the authorities, Tom's parole could be revoked, and she could shatter the trust that she has developed in their professional relationship. Teresa is struggling with her obligation to her profession and community, and also her work with Tom. Another possible consequence is that her other clients may feel that Teresa is observing them as they carry out their daily lives and passing judgment on them because of the confidential information she knows about them.

BACKGROUND

Social workers in remote northern communities are faced with unique challenges in their professional careers. "Social work educators are slowly coming to the realization that practice in remote, isolated communities requires a different level or type of awareness that is not usually a requirement in an urban environment" (Schmidt, 2000, p. 343). The following are examples of challenges faced by social workers in these communities.

The first challenge stems from conflicts arising when professionals from urban areas apply their education to remote contexts. There is a "poor fit between urban edu-cated social workers and northern communities and clients" (Schmidt, 2000, p. 342). Many social workers often do not realize that their urban experience may not be totally applicable to an area with extremely different demographics. For example, whereas many members of urban communities appreciate autonomy, members of rural com-munities may value a sense of community more (Zapf, 1993). Programs that are based on an "autonomy" model of assisting individuals to become independent may not be effective in some rural communities, which may respond more positively to a program oriented to community capacity-building. In order to be effective, the social worker must adapt his or her professional style to the needs of the community.

A second challenge that the professional may have to face in a rural setting is mis-trust of strangers. For example, the members of the community may have a precon-ceived notion about the professional's intentions due to his or her membership in a different culture. This can be problematic given the small size of the community and the consequent likelihood of the worker to have both professional and personal roles with the same group of people. Schmidt (2000) suggests that the "issue of power as well as the integration of the social worker into the community are critical considerations" (p. 344). To gain respect from the community, the social worker must learn about and appreciate the community's values in order to be able to work with them toward a common goal. Should a social worker be unable to surmount these cultural differences, there is a good chance that he or she may stay only temporarily. This may result in a high staff turnover rate, further diminishing an already precarious trust between com-munity members and professionals.

A third challenge is identifying the balance between private and professional rela-tionships. Encompassed in this challenge is the need to maintain professional bound-aries and at the same time achieve a sense of personal belonging in the community. "Social workers in remote isolated communities experience high visibility and often feel that they are living in a fish bowl where each and every aspect of their behaviour is observed, recorded and measured by a critical community" (Schmidt, 2000, p. 344). This fish bowl analogy applies not only to the social worker, but to all members of the community. It is common for the social worker to encounter a client in a nonprofessional capacity.

SUMMARY OF ETHICAL DILEMMA

Teresa detects that Tom has used alcohol, which violates his parole. She is unsure whether this information should be disregarded since she obtained this information in a public, nonprofessional setting.

Teresa realizes that as a professional she has a responsibility to draw upon her training and act according to the professional code of ethics and her knowledge as a social worker when she is in a professional role. The Canadian Association of Social Workers *Code of Ethics* (2005a) clearly states that she has a professional obligation to maintain professional integrity and commitment to her employing agency, but what this means is not clear to her given the lack of agency policy about boundary issues and dual relationships.

Besides considering the consequences of reporting Tom's use of alcohol for her work with Tom and for other clients, Teresa is well aware of the possible repercussions that she may face as a member of the community outside of her professional role. She knows that in reporting Tom she may be perceived as blurring the lines between her professional and personal roles. As a consequence, some community members may avoid talking to her on a personal level for fear that what they say may be interpreted in a professional context, ultimately affecting the trust that she has worked hard to build in the community. The relationships and support she has developed in the community could be in jeopardy if residents no longer trust her. Given the size of the community, it is likely that people will find out about her reporting very quickly.

 Inquiry Questions

INQUIRY QUESTIONS

- If you were consulting with Teresa on how to proceed, what are the two or three most important ethical issues that you would bring up?
- As you did in Chapter 8, map out a decision strategy you would use to help Teresa think through her situation. Explain why you chose this strategy.
- What further information would help you as you work with Teresa?

INQUIRY PROJECT

Place yourself in the following two situations and respond to the questions as if you were the professional in the situation. Think about the ethical rationale you would give for each of your responses.

Situation 1: Sale of a House to a Service User

For financial reasons you need to sell your house, but so far you have been unsuccessful. Your house has been on the market for over a year and you are worried about debts you have incurred since moving to take your present position in a family service agency. The only person who comes to your open house is one of the service users you are currently working with. The client states that she thinks the house is wonderful and that she would like to buy it for the asking price. She thinks it's great that you will be the one getting the money and wonders if you should not be asking more for it.

- What options would you consider in responding to your client's interest in buying your house?
- What kinds of feelings would you be experiencing?
- How would you respond?

Situation 2: Tickets to a Performance

During a self-help group session that you facilitate at a child welfare agency, a single mother mentions that because of her job she receives free tickets to concerts, plays, and other events. She likes to give them to her friends or to people who have helped her. You find out at the end of the support group session that she has mailed you tickets to a folk concert because you had mentioned at a previous meeting that you like the artist and this is the first time this artist will perform in this region. You had actually tried to purchase tickets but the concert was sold out.

- What are your options for responding to the service user's gift?
- What feelings and thoughts did you have when the service user told you about mailing the tickets?
- What further information would you need before making a decision about how to proceed?
- How do you think you should proceed, and under what conditions do you think you might accept the gift?

INQUIRY PROJECT

Given the practice situations and related inquiry work you have been asked to respond to in this chapter as well as the previous chapters, you should now be able to create a scenario of your own that challenges you and your peers to think through and apply a decision process to a set of boundary issues.

Task

Create a scenario in which a professional confronts at least one boundary issue for which there is more than one possible ethical response. There should be no obvious "right" response for the professional in your situation. Also, make sure that the scenario you develop has enough information for your peers to work through the issues involved. You may include inquiry questions as we have provided in our practice situations, but do not create so many questions that your scenario is overwhelming for your peers. Work through the scenario yourself and come up with your own responses.

- If possible, share your scenario with at least one of your peers or a group of peers for them to work through using a decision process of their choosing. Compare their responses with the ones you have developed to see where you agree and disagree.

CONCLUSION

In this chapter we have looked at the role boundaries play in maintaining the integrity of professional relationships. We have also explored the nature of dual relationships, in which the workers and service users have a relationship outside of the professional context. Professionals working in rural, northern, and Aboriginal Canadian contexts are often involved in dual relationships.

The integrity of our work as professionals depends on the extent to which we can regulate our own behaviour. Our ability to engage in effective and ethical regulation, in turn, is contingent on our willingness to study our own behaviour and beliefs within the context of a deliberative decision process. Throughout your work in this text you have been asked to reflect on practice situations that involve ethical problems and issues you may face as a practitioner.

In the next and final chapter we revisit the concept of virtue ethics as we examine the notion of a professional relationship as a "covenant" that involves commitment, responsibility, and judgment. Along with self-awareness, self-care is foundational for all aspects of professional practice, including practising within an ethical framework. The final chapter concludes with a discussion of how we can monitor and take care of ourselves within a covenant notion of professional relationships.

NOTES

NOTES

NOTES

NOTES

NOTES

NOTES

_____

_____

_____

_____

_____

_____

_____

_____

_____

_____

_____

_____

_____

REFERENCES

Bernsen, A., Tabachnick, B., & Pope, K. (1994). National survey of social workers' sexual attraction to their clients: Results, implications, and comparison to psychologists. *Ethics & Behavior, 4,* 369–388. Retrieved May 2004 from http://kspope.com/sexiss/research3.php

Borys, D.S., & Pope, K.S. (1989). Dual relationships between therapist and client: A national study of psychologists, psychiatrists, and social workers. *Professional Psychology: Research and Practice, 20,* 283–293. Retrieved May 2004 from http://kspope.com/dual/research2.php

Brownlee, Keith, & Delaney, Roger. (1997). Developing our own: Inside versus outside expertise in northern social work practice. In Keith Brownlee, Roger Delaney, & John R. Graham (Eds.), *Strategies for northern social work practice.* Thunder Bay, ON: Lakehead University Northern Studies.

Canadian Association of Social Workers. (2005a). *Code of ethics.* Ottawa, ON: Author.

Canadian Association of Social Workers. (2005b). *Guidelines for ethical practice.* Ottawa, ON: Author.

Kagle, J.D., & Giebelhausen, P.N. (1994). Dual relationships and professional boundaries. *Social Work, 39*(2), 213–220.

Pope, K.S. (1994). Sexual involvement between therapists and patients: Patient assessment, subsequent therapy, forensics. Washington, DC: American Psychological Association. Retrieved May 2004 from http://kspope.com/sexiss/involv.php

Pope, K.S. (2000). Therapists' sexual feelings and behaviors: Research, trends, and quandries. In L. Szuchman & F. Muscarella (Eds.), *Psychological perspectives on human sexuality* (pp. 603–658). New York: John Wiley and Sons. Retrieved June 2004 from http://kspope.com/sexiss/sxchpabs.php

Pope, K.S., & Vasquez, M.J.T. (1999). *Ethics in psychotherapy and counseling: A practical guide* (2nd ed.). San Francisco: Jossey-Bass. Retrieved June 2004 from http://kspope.com/ethics/ethics.php

Redlich, F. C., & Pope, K.S. (1980). Ethics of mental health training. *Journal of Nervous and Mental Disease, 168,* 709–714.

Schmidt, Glen G. (2000). Remote northern communities. *International Social Work 43*(3), 337–349.

Younggren, J.N. (2002). Ethical decision-making and dual relationships. Retrieved June 2004 from http://kspope.com/dual/younggren.php

Zapf, Kim. (1993). Remote practice and cultural shock. *Social Work 38*(6), 694–704.

chapter

Ethics of Self-Care, Preventing Burnout, and the Covenant Model of Professional Relationships

This text has used decision procedures as tools in the process of deliberating about a course of action in practice situations that present ethical conflicts or dilemmas. The source of these conflicts can be found in disagreements about which values, principles, and interests should guide action. In arriving at our decisions, we have referred to professional codes of ethics. While these codes are critical in providing direction, at best they provide only broad guidelines for decision making in specific contexts. Although the decision models and procedures you have worked with are helpful in structuring your thinking, they are only tools: it is not the tool itself that will determine whether it is used for good or ill but rather how it is applied; and that, of course, is dependent on the expertise and character of the tool user—the professional.

In this chapter we will focus specifically on the qualities of character that are important for ethical practice within a covenant model of professional relationships. But first we will examine personal and organizational factors that contribute to burnout in the helping professions. If we do not take care of ourselves, then qualities of character may not matter if we do not have the energy to perform at our best. To engage positively in a professional context and use decision procedures effectively, we must care for ourselves and develop positive work environments.

BURNOUT, SELF-CARE, AND ORGANIZATIONAL ENVIRONMENTS

Freudenberger first used the term "burnout" in 1974, although it has probably existed since people took on helping roles. It is now a common term that refers to disengagement with work. Maslach and Leiter (1997) define burnout as a

> dislocation between what people are and what they have to do. It represents an erosion of values, dignity, spirit, and will—an erosion of the human soul. It is a malady that spreads

gradually and continuously over time, putting people into a downward spiral from which it is hard to recover. . . . What might happen if you begin to burn out? Actually three things happen: you become chronically exhausted; you become cynical and detached from your work; and you feel increasingly ineffective on the job. (p. 17)

Although burnout takes an enormous toll on the professional, the agency and service users suffer as well. Those professionals suffering from burnout lose their enthusiasm for their work and are often overcome by a general level of frustration and apathy. If such professionals stay in the profession they are not able to give their best. In addition to preserving their own well being, professionals have a responsibility to take care of themselves for the sake of the service users and organizations within which they work. Richard Davies (1998) reports on a survey in which 524 social workers in the UK were asked to complete a self-assessment on burnout. Ninety-six percent found their jobs to be "stressful," 77 percent reported awareness of stress-related symptoms, and 58 percent felt they manifested physiological symptoms of stress (p. 159).

Burnout Self-Assessment

Below is a typical self-assessment for determining whether you are suffering from or are on the way to burnout. This is a very simple assessment, but it will nevertheless give you a sense of whether you have low or high burnout at this point in your life.

I feel tired and run down.
- ☐ Never
- ☐ Sometimes
- ☐ Often
- ☐ All of the time

I feel isolated.
- ☐ Never
- ☐ Sometimes
- ☐ Often
- ☐ All of the time

I get along well with my colleagues.
- ☐ Never
- ☐ Sometimes
- ☐ Often
- ☐ All of the time

I feel emotionally drained.
- ☐ Never
- ☐ Sometimes
- ☐ Often
- ☐ All of the time

I feel too much is expected of me.
- ☐ Never
- ☐ Sometimes
- ☐ Often
- ☐ All of the time

I am able to concentrate.
- ☐ Never
- ☐ Sometimes
- ☐ Often
- ☐ All of the time

If you scored "All of the time" or "Often" for the negative items, you may be experiencing some degree of burnout. Getting along well with colleagues and being able to concentrate should be marked "All of the time" or "Often." You can find similar, more detailed inventories on the Internet.

Strategies for Addressing and Preventing Burnout

Because burnout can have a negative impact on organizations and service users as well as on personal well-being, an argument could be made that professionals have an ethical duty to take care of themselves. Some strategies for preventing burnout are relevant to all of us in any demanding environment. These include eating well; exercising regularly; learning to relax; and finding time to be alone as well as time to connect with support groups (family, friends, and colleagues). Other common strategies are to pursue hobbies and take time off from work when you are feeling overly stressed or in need of a break from the routine.

Strategies to Address Burnout in Human Service Contexts

Although the common strategies for addressing burnout are helpful and necessary to include in a "toolbox" for self-care, it is critically important that employers provide organizational supports to sustain us in our professional work or, if they do not, that we develop strategies to provide them for ourselves and our colleagues.

Organizational Strategies to Reduce Burnout

At the organizational level, providing professionals assistance in setting realistic goals, objectives, and strategies for working with service workers has been identified as an important element that lessens burnout. Victor Savicki (2002) describes how young, entry-level workers in residential care expect "to make major improvements in the lives of their clients, but find themselves frustrated by their lack of skill and knowledge in fashioning a positive outcome" (p. 5). Provision of training and professional development to address the needs of entry-level practitioners should be part of an overall organizational and professional support strategy for both new and seasoned practitioners. A comprehensive strategy would include supervision and mentoring, which contribute to an atmosphere in which professionals are encouraged to grow. In such a climate the culture of the organization is often inviting and supportive.

Successful organizations also offer a setting where the demands and the hours are reasonable and the compensation is as good as possible. Finally, a team environment within an organization can help professionals feel engaged with each other, with the service users, and with the decisions being made in the organization. All of these organizational characteristics—training and professional development, mentoring and supervision, reasonable workload and compensation, and a team approach—decrease the possibility of burnout.

INQUIRY PROJECT

It is not uncommon to find ourselves working in organizations that lack one or more of the above strategies to reduce burnout. Think about your current situation or one in your past. What do you do, or what have you done, to create supports for yourself to address *deficiencies* in one or more of the following areas: supervision, mentoring, professional training and development opportunities, workload and compensation levels, team or peer collaboration?

- Identify strategies you think are effective to address organizational deficiencies in decreasing burnout.
- Give your rationale for why you think these strategies are effective.
- Find at least one article that discusses strategies for reducing burnout in an organization. What did you learn from this article, and does it support the strategies you have previously identified?

The Role of Boundary Maintenance in Reducing Burnout

In addition to self-care, one of the key personal characteristics that can lessen burnout is respect for professional boundaries. Savicki (2002) focuses on the need for professionals to pay attention to boundaries in their work with service users. He states that human service professionals are particularly vulnerable to burnout because "effective practice requires emotional contact between the professional and the client-patient-student." Those who have difficulty separating themselves from the "pain, anger, and anxiety of their clients are not likely to have a long career in the field" (p. 5).

What does it mean to set boundaries? We have discussed boundary issues within the context of boundary violations that were ethically problematic. In the context of burnout it involves setting realistic expectations with some emotional distance so that you continue to have positive energy in your work with service users.

Being passionate about your work does not necessarily require making a personal investment in each service user or allowing failure to take an emotional toll. In the human service environments we work in, the problems and issues we face are frequently larger than the resources we have to work with, which often means that professionals need to focus on the ways they are able to have an impact, even if it is a relatively small one. Part of setting boundaries is keeping a realistic focus on what is achievable given the constraints we work with such as regulations, limited time, and funding restrictions.

Lastly, humour has been identified by several authors as essential for maintaining a sense of perspective and appropriate boundaries. This is where the presence of teams, networking, good mentoring, and supervision can assist professionals in seeing the humour in themselves and others.

INQUIRY PROJECT

Take a moment and think about the human services work in which you have been involved, as either a professional, volunteer, or practicum student.

- Which of the characteristics to prevent or minimize burnout were present? Which were absent?
- What contributed to any positive experiences? What were the sources of any negative experiences?
- If your experiences were negative, what do you think you could have done to help create a more positive work environment for yourself and others? If they were positive, what did you do to contribute to the positive experiences?
- What job characteristics will you look for once you have completed your academic work?

JUDGMENT IN PROFESSIONAL RELATIONSHIPS

We now shift our attention to what lies at the heart of ethical decision making: professional judgment. In particular we examine what it means to be a professional and make judgments within a covenant model of professional relationships.

As you read the following section, think about the work you have completed in the previous chapters applying professional codes of ethics and ethical decision-making models to complex practice situations to arrive at a decision about a course of action.

Imagine that a nonprofessional is asking you the following questions. Give your best response to help the nonprofessional understand what it means to be a professional:

- How is a professional relationship different from a nonprofessional helping relationship?
- What is the responsibility and role of the professional in such a relationship?
- What role does judgment play in decisions that affect service users' lives?
- Why do you want to be a professional? What motivates you?

A CONTRACT APPROACH TO PROFESSIONAL RELATIONSHIPS

The use of contracts to reach agreements about roles, responsibilities, and rights can be traced back to the concept of treaty and was used in political contexts to denote an agreement, often between strangers, to join together for common interests and to create conditions for peace. In our contemporary context, contracts are frequently used to spell out what will be accomplished in a certain period of time, by whom, and under what conditions. In the litigious environment we live in, contracts are also frequently viewed as providing protection to both the service user and the professional to spell out what is agreed on in the contract. Service users are given assurance that the professional will fulfill certain responsibilities. Contracts provide clarity by delineating the roles, responsibilities, rights, and expectations for both service users and professional. In this sense, they have been a useful tool in human services.

William May (1977), one of the early proponents of a covenant approach to mapping professional relationships, argues that while a contract approach can be useful in providing clarity for professional boundary maintenance, it may also have negative effects. Contracts, May argues, can encourage the laicizing of authority and the legalization of professional relationships (p. 73). This means that such relationships come to resemble legally enforceable, formal agreements, with accountability to an external authority. One disadvantage of this "legalization" of professional relationships is the potential for workers to take a cautionary approach to their responsibilities and to perform only those services specified in the contract.

Robert Veatch (1981) describes professional relationships as potentially embedded in a "triple contract" (p. 110) that consists of three levels. The first and highest level is a society's agreement about basic principles for appropriate and ethical human interaction for members in that society. The next level is a contract between society and professional groups about role-specific duties of professionals in that society. The third and lowest-level contract is the agreement between a service user and a professional, which is shaped by the content of the contracts of the two higher levels.

Veatch illustrates how his concept of triple contract directs professional conduct. At the heart of the example is a physician who feels he is exempted from providing equitable treatment to clients and thus decides not to treat individuals from certain groups or minimizes his work with them. The physician is ethically justified in his discriminatory practice because society either has agreed that such inequity is not a moral concern or has decided that it is not part of physicians' professional duty to treat diverse groups equitably. The physician in this scenario is "unburdened" of the worry that someone may have an equity claim for his or her services because equity is not part of the profession's contract with society (p. 131). We could imagine that such a society could exempt certain professionals from other duties, such as continuing to see a service user beyond treatment for the primary symptoms.

INQUIRY PROJECT

The above descriptions certainly do not cover all the positive ways in which the notion of contract has been used in texts on professional practice. For example, a contract approach has been found to be helpful for delineating the roles, responsibilities, and expectations for professionals, service users, and others involved in a professional intervention.

Reflect on either May's view that the contract approach may result in the "legalizing" of professional relationships or Veatch's theory that a triple contract approach to professional relationships contributes to or supports ethical practice. You can refer to your own experience, or to a text or article on professional practice and professional contracts.

- Does the contract approach to professional relationships present a complete picture of what is required for a professional relationship?
- What would you argue is missing from a contract approach to professional relationships?

COVENANT APPROACH TO PROFESSIONAL RELATIONSHIPS

For May (2001) and others, what is missing from a contract account of professional relationships is an emphasis on the commitment of a worker to a professional community within which he or she functions and to which he or she responds and is accountable. The social work community, for example, has a value framework that requires professional social workers to go beyond a minimal, "legalistic" type of contract.

May (1983) has expressed concern that a triple contract approach may lead professionals to avoid going "the extra mile" when service users' needs become increasingly complex (p. 92). To counter what he views as a linear, limited notion of obligation and responsibility contained in some interpretations of contract relationships, May (2001) argues for the covenant concept of professional relationship that has been taken up by such professions as engineering (Kallenberg, 2002) and pharmacology (Ontario College of Pharmacists 1996). May (2001) claims that every profession is fundamentally governed by a "covenant" in which "the professional professes something (a body of knowledge); on behalf of someone (or some institution); in the setting of colleagues and promises to be faithful to the values and principles of the professional community" (p. 7). This "promise" to the professional community's value framework extends to faithfully carrying out these values in practice.

Unlike the potentially narrower contract approach, the covenant model emphasizes the inclusive and "gift" aspects of professional relationships. In such an approach the professional is not limited by a narrow definition of the service user's problem but is committed to staying with the service user throughout his or her troubles. The key element of the covenant is the professional's promise to be faithful to the gift that has been given to him or her in becoming a professional by giving it back to the service user and community. Noting that the Hebrew scriptures' meaning of covenant entails a notion of faithfulness or loyalty, Ramsay (1970) describes covenant as an ethic of keeping promises. He refers to the moral qualities in a covenant as *agape* or love and claims that it is "a quality of attitude and action owed to all by an individual who steps into a covenant relation with another" (p. xiii).

May (1983) completes his description of the covenant model by identifying the three virtues of practical wisdom, fidelity, and public spiritedness that a professional should embody (p. 7). It is these virtues that characterize a professional.

INQUIRY PROJECT

Think of the times when you have been especially influenced by a professional (teacher, doctor, nurse, social worker).

- What qualities of the relationship resulted in a positive or negative experience?
- What did you learn from this experience that you will take with you in your professional practice?

COVENANT WITHIN COMMUNITIES OF PRACTICE

Unlike a contract that has its roots in agreements formed between strangers for mutual interests, the concept of covenant was developed within the framework of communities of practice and highlighted the responsibilities and obligations that ensued from membership in that community. To be a member of the community of practice involved sharing a way of life and making a "pledge" or covenant to contribute to the "good" of the community. As noted earlier, it signified a commitment to go beyond the minimalism of contract agreements, with their "defensive" strictures to protect parties from litigation.

For the field of social work, as for other human service professions, the ethical core of "practice" is spelled out at the beginning of the profession's code of ethics. The remainder of the code provides proscriptions rather than prescriptions for decision making—that is, it offers open-ended directives and requires skillful judgments by practitioners about how these broad directives will be carried out in practice. To view a professional code of ethics as a set of proscriptions rather than as a list of commands suggests that much more is required for proper conduct than following a set of rules and procedures. As a proscriptive document the statements in a code have "authority," but what it means to behave according to the statements cannot be specified in advance.

We have emphasized the importance of applying decision models in a deliberative manner in this text because the proscriptive nature of professional codes requires practitioners to make judgments about how to proceed in the face of conflicting or ambiguous ethical directives. We have even noted that in certain practice situations the statements in the codes themselves provide conflicting directives. Aristotle's (1976) concept of *phronesis* (practical wisdom), or skilled judgment, provides a way to help us resolve these ambiguities. Aristotle related practical wisdom to moral virtue, and it is worth spending a short time summarizing his views about this relationship as they are foundational to the notion of practical wisdom, ethics, and the covenant model of professional relationships.

SKILLED JUDGMENT AS PRACTICAL WISDOM AND MORAL VIRTUE

For Aristotle, ethics was tied to practical wisdom and was concerned about the character of the actor rather than the nature of the acts. Moral virtue was related to practical wisdom because only the morally virtuous person can "perceive" what really matters in a situation and be "motivated" to carry out "appropriate action" derived from skilled judgment or practical wisdom. Since humans have to choose some actions over others, Aristotle argued they they need to deliberate about what actions are needed to bring about what is rightly desired; someone who has both moral virtue and practical wisdom will be able to perceive the good in a situation as well as deliberate about how to achieve it, and hence choose well.

Aristotle stated that a person acquires practical wisdom and moral virtue over a long period of training and instruction in a moral community. People acquire these qualities by being shown what things matter in a situation, how to feel about these things, and how to act appropriately. The relation of moral virtue to practical wisdom is so essential that without moral virtue a person cannot have practical wisdom. You can reason well without moral virtue but you will neither be able to perceive the situation you are in correctly nor desire the right end. Aristotle calls the person who can reason well to get to an end that is not rightly desired "clever" but not wise.

In the context of what we have been working with in this text, imagine that you can apply the decision models from Chapter 2 to a practice situation to reason through the situation and thus show that you can reason well. This ability to apply decision models and reason well shows that you are "clever," but, according to Aristotle's linking of practical wisdom with moral virtue, unless you are motivated by a perception of the "good"—choosing what needs to be accomplished for the sake of the "good"—you have not practised ethically.

The reverse is that practical wisdom is a necessary condition of moral virtue. Part of being morally virtuous is listening to what reason tells us about what a practical situation is like so that we are able to carry out good intentions through effective reasoning about means and ends. As May (1977; 1983) claimed in his early writing on the covenant model of professional relationships, being a professional is a "way of life" or, as Hauerwas (1982) characterized it, a "habit of the mind," that embodies the good of a "practice." Both of these concepts capture at least some of the dimensions of practical wisdom and moral virtue Aristotle viewed as necessary for living "well" within a community.

 INQUIRY QUESTIONS

As you proceed through the remainder of this chapter reflect on the following questions and jot down possible responses to each.

- What is "skilled judgment"?
- How do we recognize when skilled judgment is present? Can the judgment of one professional override the less skilled or unskilled judgment of another? Who sets the standards?
- What is "virtue" in professional practice, and what do you think its role should be in practice?

SKILLED JUDGMENT IN PROFESSIONAL PRACTICE

We have looked at arguments for approaching professional relationships as covenants. In that context we discussed Aristotle's notion of an ethical person as one who practises skilled judgment, which requires development of both virtue and reasoning. In this section we continue to examine the role of skilled judgment as a marker of what it means to be a professional and the importance of developing judgment within a community of practice.

Alasdair MacIntyre (1984) provides a definition of "practice" that stresses "standards of excellence." Good practice is defined within the community of practice. For example, the social work community, specifically expert social workers, define "good" social work practice. MacIntyre goes further and claims that discerning the "good" of practice requires a moral as well as technical ability and is always being developed (p. 187).

INQUIRY PROJECT

Reflect on your reactions to MacIntrye's claims that "standards of practice" originate in a community of practice. Also think about his view that ability to recognize "good" practice requires moral as well as technical abilities.

- Do you agree or disagree with MacIntrye's claims about standards of practice residing within a community of practice? Why do you agree or disagree?

- What are your reactions to MacIntrye's belief that discerning the "good" of a practice requires moral as well as technical abilities?
- Share both positive and negative reactions you have to MacIntye's views about discernment and give your reasons for your reactions.
- If you disagree with MacIntrye, what do you think should replace his notion of discernment? If you agree, how do you think we should develop discernment in social work education?

VIRTUE ETHICS

In Chapter 2 we considered the possibility that Aristotle's concept of virtue ethics, as developed by contemporary ethicists, particularly feminist philosophers, may have particular resonance when describing what it means to be an ethical practitioner. Professional development for ethical practice, within a virtue ethics perspective, should focus on the cultivation of virtuous traits of character so that the inner character and motivation of the agent align with the values and principles of the profession. This does not mean dismissing an ethical reasoning process during which principles, rights, and obligations as well as consequences are considered. From a virtue perspective, however, ethical reasoning alone cannot fully account for what it means to be an ethical practitioner. Cultivation of good character attributes and habits are essential. If virtuous character is practised over the course of a life, the virtuous person (agent) would "know" and do the "right" thing intuitively as a reflection of "who they are" rather than coming to a decision about what is right by applying some method of decision making.

Perhaps we need to consider that to live a "good" life personally and professionally requires that we have a certain character and that we practise ethical reasoning for ethical decision making in the face of ambiguous practice situations. For example, in the practice situations you have worked with, you have faced the challenge of balancing conflicting principles, rules, rights, and consequences of various course of actions. The practice situations required you to perform careful reflection and analysis to consider the moral "weight" of principles or rules and decide if one or more outweighed the others. What perhaps became clear to you is that many of the complex situations we face in practice come in shades of grey rather than in clear dichotomies of "right and wrong," "ethical or unethical," or "good or bad." In your practice you will be confronted more often with moral ambiguity than with clarity as you set out to determine the preferred or "good" course of action. Does this mean that we are stalemated and that there are no important distinctions to be made between the shades of grey or that we might as well flip a coin to make decisions? How do we determine what is "good" when it appears that any course of action we take will cause at least some harm to one or more of the participants?

When you reflect on the work you have completed in the inquiry projects and challenges in this text you have probably noticed that there is a range of choices between what is ethically acceptable and what is completely unacceptable. There were times when all of the options had elements that were harmful for those involved. In such situations, you needed to be able to discern which option caused the least harm. The harms reduction model of ethical decision making you have worked with stresses "least harm" as a core criterion. You may have been drawn to that model because of what you saw as a match between harms reduction and the ethical dilemma posed in the practice situations. It is also true that you may have found that the harms reduction model does not work equally well with all practice situations.

As a result of the moral ambiguities you have dealt with in the practice situations in this text you have probably started to broaden your language to describe this ethical complexity and are able to discern that one decision model does not fit all situations. The language you use to describe your experience with ethical issues reflects the moral ambiguity and complexity we are faced with in practice.

In Chapter 2 we noted that Osmo and Landau (2003), after surveying social workers to obtain their ranking of principles in social work, concluded that the best guidance for choice is probably, "What kind of person do I want to be?" Their work on principles in ethical decision making in social work led them to focus on the worker's character (virtue) along with his or her reasoning ability. In important ways, their focus on character and reasoning parallels Aristotle's discussion of "skilled judgment" as containing both virtue and reasoning qualities as well as the covenant model's emphasis on commitment, character, and membership in a professional community. Osmo and Landau subsequently recommended the development of self-knowledge to build character, which, they argued, can lead to sound ethical judgments. The following are their specific recommendations for self-development:

- Develop awareness of your own belief system.
- Be explicit about the principles that guide your ethical decisions.
- Develop a personal sense of accountability and personal responsibility.
- Provide explicit justification of your judgments and subject reasoning to careful scrutiny and evaluation. (p. 48)

The importance for ethical practice of ongoing development of self-knowledge and character, along with applying principle-based and consequentialist approaches to ethical decision, is perhaps becoming clearer to you. To summarize, decision-making approaches discussed in this text are tools to be used in a deliberative, thoughtful process. They require the self-knowledge and personal qualities described in this chapter.

LIFELONG INQUIRY PROJECT

Reflect on whether a focus on self-knowledge and character as described by Osmo and Landau matches your experience of what self-knowledge and personal qualities mean for lifelong development as an ethical practitioner.

- What two or three character traits do you think are especially important for a human service professional to develop to engage in ethical practice?

- Why have you chosen these traits and how do you see yourself pursuing them as you move through your professional career?
- What is the role of reasoning in ethical practice?
- How do you measure yourself in terms of reasoning ability and what are your plans for continual development of effective reasoning as a professional?

CONCLUSION

We conclude this text with an invitation for you to engage in a lifelong, ongoing process of self-development within the context of your commitment to engage in ethical practice. We are hopeful that your work in this text has at least started you on the journey of applying a deliberative process to ethical reasoning and taking responsibility for your development as an ethical human service professional.

NOTES

NOTES

_____

_____

_____

_____

_____

_____

_____

_____

_____

_____

_____

_____

_____

_____

NOTES

NOTES

NOTES

NOTES

REFERENCES

Aristotle. (1976). *The ethics of Aristotle: The Nicomachean ethics.* (J.A.K. Thomson, Trans.; revised by Hugh Tredennick). Toronto: Penguin Classics.

Canadian Association of Social Workers. (2005a). *Code of ethics.* Ottawa, ON: Author.

Canadian Association of Social Workers. (2005b) *Guidelines for ethical practice.* Ottawa, ON: Author.

Davies, R. (1998). *Stress in social work.* London: Jessica Kingsley.

Freudenberger, Herbert J. (1974). The staff burnout syndrome in alternative institutions. *Psychotherapy: Theory, Research and Practice, 12,* 73–82.

Hauerwas. S. (1982). *Responsibility in health care.* Dordrecht: D. Reidel.

Horowitz, Mark. (1998). Social work trauma: Building resilience in child protective workers. *Smith College Studies in Social Work, 68*(3), 1–25.

Kallenberg, Brad J. (2003). Professional or practitioner? What's missing from the codes? *Teaching Ethics 3*(1), 1–18.

MacIntyre, Alasdair. (1984). *After virtue.* Notre Dame, IN: University of Notre Dame Press.

Maslach, Christina, & Leiter, Michael. (1997). *The truth about burnout: How organizations cause personal stress and what to do about it.* San Francisco: Jossey-Bass.

May, William. (1977). Code and covenant or philanthropy and contract? In S.J. Reiser (Ed.), *Ethics in medicine: Historical perspectives and contemporary concerns* (pp. 67–76). Cambridge: MIT Press.

May, William. (1983). *The physician's covenant: Images of the healer in medical ethics.* Philadelphia: Westminster Press.

May, William. (2001). *Beleagured rulers: The public obligation of the professional.* Louisville, KY: Westminster/John Knox Press.

Ontario College of Pharmacists. (1996). *Code of ethics.* Retrieved July 2004 from http://www.ocpinfo.com/client/ocp/ocphome.nsf

Osmo R., & Landau, R. (2003). Professional and personal hierarchies of ethical principles. *International Social Welfare, 12,* 42–49.

Ramsay, P. (1970). *The patient as person.* New Haven, CT: Yale University Press.

Savicki, Victor (2002). *Burnout across thirteen cultures: Stress and coping in child and youth care workers.* Westport, CT: Praeger.

Veatch. R.M. (1981). *A theory of ethics.* New York: Basic Books.

Appendix A:
Canadian Association of Social Workers (CASW) Code of Ethics © 2005

PURPOSE OF THE CASW CODE OF ETHICS

Ethical behaviour lies at the core of every profession. The Canadian Association of Social Workers (CASW) *Code of Ethics* sets forth values and principles to guide social workers' professional conduct. A code of ethics cannot guarantee ethical behaviour. Ethical behaviour comes from a social worker's individual commitment to engage in ethical practice. Both the spirit and the letter of this *Code of Ethics* will guide social workers as they act in good faith and with a genuine desire to make sound judgments.

This *Code of Ethics* is consistent with the International Federation of Social Workers (IFSW) *International Declaration of Ethical Principles of Social Work* (1994, 2004), which requires members of the CASW to uphold the values and principles established by both the CASW and the IFSW. Other individuals, organizations, and bodies (such as regulatory boards, professional liability insurance providers, courts of law, boards of directors of organizations employing social workers, and government agencies) may also choose to adopt this *Code of Ethics* or use it as a basis for evaluating professional conduct. In Canada, each province and territory is responsible for regulating the professional conduct of social workers to ensure the protection of the public. Social workers are advised to contact the regulatory body in their province or territory to determine whether it has adopted this *Code of Ethics*. To find the IFSW declarations or information about your relevant regulatory body, visit the CASW website: http://www.casw-acts.ca.

Recognition of Individual and Professional Diversity

The CASW *Code of Ethics* does not provide a set of rules that prescribe how social workers should act in all situations. Further, the *Code of Ethics* does not specify which values and principles are most important and which outweigh others in instances of conflict. Reasonable differences of opinion exist among social workers with respect to which values and principles should be given priority in a particular situation. Further, a social worker's personal values,

---

This Social Work Code of Ethics, adopted by the Board of Directors of the Canadian Association of Social Workers (CASW), is effective March 2005 and replaces the CASW Code of Ethics (1994). The code is reprinted here with the permission of CASW. The copyright in the document has been registered with Canadian Intellectual Property Office, registration no. 1030330.

culture, religious beliefs, practices, and/or other important distinctions, such as age, ability, gender, or sexual orientation can affect his/her ethical choices. Thus, social workers need to be aware of any conflicts between personal and professional values and deal with them responsibly.

Ethical Behaviour Requires Due Consideration of Issues and Judgment

Social work is a multifaceted profession. As professionals, social workers are educated to exercise judgment in the face of complex and competing interests and claims. Ethical decision making in a given situation will involve the informed judgment of the individual social worker. Instances may arise when social workers' ethical obligations conflict with agency policies, or relevant laws or regulations. When such conflicts occur, social workers shall make a responsible effort to resolve the conflicts in a manner that is consistent with the values and principles expressed in this *Code of Ethics*. If a reasonable resolution of the conflict does not appear possible, social workers shall seek appropriate consultation before making a decision. This may involve consultation with an ethics committee, a regulatory body, a knowledgeable colleague, supervisor, or legal counsel.

PREAMBLE

The social work profession is dedicated to the welfare and self-realization of all people; the development and disciplined use of scientific and professional knowledge; the development of resources and skills to meet individual, group, national, and international changing needs and aspirations; and the achievement of social justice for all. The profession has a particular interest in the needs and empowerment of people who are vulnerable, oppressed, and/or living in poverty. Social workers are committed to human rights as enshrined in Canadian law, as well as in international conventions on human rights created or supported by the United Nations.

As professionals in a country that upholds respect for diversity, and in keeping with democratic rights and freedoms, social workers respect the distinct systems of beliefs and lifestyles of individuals, families, groups, communities, and nations without prejudice (United Nations Centre for Human Rights, 1992). Specifically, social workers do not tolerate discrimination (throughout this document, the term "discrimination" refers to treating people unfavourably or holding negative or prejudicial attitudes based on discernible differences or stereotypes; it does not refer to the positive intent behind programs, such as affirmative action, where one group may be given preferential treatment to address inequities created by discrimination). based on age, abilities, ethnic background, gender, language, marital status, national ancestry, political affiliation, race, religion, sexual orientation, or socioeconomic status.

CORE SOCIAL WORK VALUES AND PRINCIPLES

Social workers uphold the following core social work values:

Value 1: Respect for the Inherent Dignity and Worth of Persons

Value 2: Pursuit of Social Justice

Value 3: Service to Humanity

Value 4: Integrity in Professional Practice

Value 5: Confidentiality in Professional Practice

Value 6: Competence in Professional Practice

The following section describes each of these values and discusses their underlying principles.

Value 1: Respect for the Inherent Dignity and Worth of Persons

Social work is founded on a long-standing commitment to respect the inherent dignity and individual worth of all persons. When required by law to override a client's wishes, social workers take care to use the minimum coercion required. Social workers recognize and respect the diversity of Canadian society, taking into account the breadth of differences that exist among individuals, families, groups, and communities. Social workers uphold the human rights of individuals and groups as expressed in The *Canadian Charter of Rights and Freedoms* (1982) and the United Nations *Universal Declaration of Human Rights* (1948).

Principles

- Social workers respect the unique worth and inherent dignity of all people and uphold human rights.
- Social workers uphold each person's right to self-determination, consistent with that person's capacity and with the rights of others.
- Social workers respect the diversity among individuals in Canadian society and the right of individuals to their unique beliefs consistent with the rights of others.
- Social workers respect the client's right to make choices based on voluntary, informed consent.
- Social workers who have children as clients determine the child's ability to consent and, where appropriate, explain to the child and to the child's parents/guardians the nature of the social worker's relationship to the child.
- Social workers uphold the right of society to impose limitations on the self-determination of individuals, when such limitations protect individuals from self-harm and from harming others.
- Social workers uphold the right of every person to be free from violence and threat of violence.

Value 2: Pursuit of Social Justice

Social workers believe in the obligation of people, individually and collectively, to provide resources, services, and opportunities for the overall benefit of humanity and to afford them protection from harm. Social workers promote social fairness and the equitable distribution of resources, and act to reduce barriers and expand choice for all persons, with special regard for those who are marginalized, disadvantaged, vulnerable, and/or have exceptional needs. Social workers oppose prejudice and discrimination against any person or group of persons, on any grounds, and specifically challenge views and actions that stereotype particular persons or groups.

Principles

- Social workers uphold the right of people to have access to resources to meet basic human needs.
- Social workers advocate for fair and equitable access to public services and benefits.
- Social workers advocate for equal treatment and protection under the law and challenge injustices, especially injustices that affect the vulnerable and disadvantaged.
- Social workers promote social development and environmental management in the interests of all people.

Value 3: Service to Humanity

The social work profession upholds service in the interests of others, consistent with social justice, as a core professional objective. In professional practice, social workers balance individual needs, and rights and freedoms with collective interests in the service of humanity. When acting in a professional capacity, social workers place professional service before personal goals or advantage, and use their power and authority in disciplined and responsible ways that serve society. The social work profession contributes to knowledge and skills that assist in the management of conflicts and the wide-ranging consequences of conflict.

Principles

- Social workers place the needs of others above self-interest when acting in a professional capacity.
- Social workers strive to use the power and authority vested in them as professionals in responsible ways that serve the needs of clients and the promotion of social justice.
- Social workers promote individual development and pursuit of individual goals, as well as the development of a just society.
- Social workers use their knowledge and skills in bringing about fair resolutions to conflict and in assisting those affected by conflict.

Value 4: Integrity in Professional Practice

Social workers demonstrate respect for the profession's purpose, values, and ethical principles relevant to their field of practice. Social workers maintain a high level of professional conduct by acting honestly and responsibly, and promoting the values of the profession. Social workers strive for impartiality in their professional practice, and refrain from imposing their personal values, views, and preferences on clients. It is the responsibility of social workers to establish the tenor of their professional relationship with clients, and others to whom they have a professional duty, and to maintain professional boundaries. As individuals, social workers take care in their actions to not bring the reputation of the profession into disrepute. An essential element of integrity in professional practice is ethical accountability based on this *Code of Ethics,* the IFSW *International Declaration of Ethical Principles of Social Work,* and other relevant provincial/territorial standards and guidelines. Where conflicts exist with respect to these sources of ethical guidance, social workers are encouraged to seek advice, including consultation with their regulatory body.

Principles

- Social workers demonstrate and promote the qualities of honesty, reliability, impartiality, and diligence in their professional practice.
- Social workers demonstrate adherence to the values and ethical principles of the profession and promote respect for the profession's values and principles in organizations where they work or with which they have a professional affiliation.
- Social workers establish appropriate boundaries in relationships with clients and ensure that the relationship serves the needs of clients.
- Social workers value openness and transparency in professional practice and avoid relationships where their integrity or impartiality may be compromised, ensuring that should a conflict of interest be unavoidable, the nature of the conflict is fully disclosed.

Value 5: Confidentiality in Professional Practice

A cornerstone of professional social work relationships is confidentiality with respect to all matters associated with professional services to clients. Social workers demonstrate respect for the trust and confidence placed in them by clients, communities, and other professionals by protecting the privacy of client information and respecting the client's right to control when or whether this information will be shared with third parties. Social workers only disclose confidential information to other parties (including family members) with the informed consent of clients, clients' legally authorized representatives or when required by law or court order. The general expectation that social workers will keep information confidential does not apply when disclosure is necessary to prevent serious, foreseeable, and imminent harm to a client or others. In all instances, social workers disclose the least amount of confidential information necessary to achieve the desired purpose.

Principles

- Social workers respect the importance of the trust and confidence placed in the professional relationship by clients and members of the public.
- Social workers respect the client's right to confidentiality of information shared in a professional context.
- Social workers only disclose confidential information with the informed consent of the client or permission of client's legal representative.
- Social workers may break confidentiality and communicate client information without permission when required or permitted by relevant laws, court order, or this *Code.*

- Social workers demonstrate transparency with respect to limits to confidentiality that apply to their professional practice by clearly communicating these limitations to clients early in their relationship.

Value 6: Competence in Professional Practice

Social workers respect a client's right to competent social worker services. Social workers analyze the nature of social needs and problems, and encourage innovative, effective strategies and techniques to meet both new and existing needs and, where possible, contribute to the knowledge base of the profession. Social workers have a responsibility to maintain professional proficiency, to continually strive to increase their professional knowledge and skills, and to apply new knowledge in practice commensurate with their level of professional education, skill, and competency, seeking consultation and supervision as appropriate.

Principles

- Social workers uphold the right of clients to be offered the highest-quality service possible.
- Social workers strive to maintain and increase their professional knowledge and skill.
- Social workers demonstrate due care for client's interests and safety by limiting professional practice to areas of demonstrated competence.
- Social workers contribute to the ongoing development of the profession and its ability to serve humanity, where possible, by participating in the development of current and future social workers and the development of new professional knowledge.
- Social workers who engage in research minimize risks to participants, ensure informed consent, maintain confidentiality, and accurately report the results of their studies.

GLOSSARY

Capacity

The ability to understand information relevant to a decision and to appreciate the reasonably foreseeable consequences of choosing to act or not to act. Capacity is specific to each decision, and thus a person may be capable of deciding about a place of residence, for example, but not capable with respect to deciding about a treatment. Capacity can change over time (Etchells, Sharpe, Elliot, & Singer, 1996).

Recent references in law point to the concept of "a mature minor," which Rozovsky and Rozovsky (1990) define as "one with capacity to understand the nature and consequences of medical treatment. Such a person has the power to consent to medical treatment and parental consent is not necessary" (p. 55). They quote the comments by The Honorable Justice Lambert in *Van Mol v. Ashmore,* which help clarify common law with respect to a minor's capacity to consent. He states:

> At common law, without reference to statute law, a young person, still a minor, may give, on his or her own behalf, a fully informed consent to medical treatment if he or she has sufficient maturity, intelligence and capacity of understanding what is involved in making

informed choices about the proposed medical treatment . . . once the capacity to consent has been achieved by the young person reaching sufficient maturity, intelligence and capability of understanding, the discussions about the nature of the treatment, its gravity, the material risks and any special and unusual risks, and the decisions about undergoing treatment, and about the form of the treatment, must all take place with and be made by the young person whose bodily integrity is to be invaded and whose life and health will be affected by the outcome.

Child

The *Convention on the Rights of the Child* passed by the United Nations in 1959 and ratified by Canada in 1990, defines a child as a person under the age of eighteen years unless national law recognizes an earlier age of majority (Alberta Law Reform Institute, 1991). The age of majority differs in provinces and territories in Canada. Under the *Criminal Code of Canada* (1985), the age of consent is held to be over the age of fourteen years; age in the context of the criminal code frequently refers to capacity to consent to sexual relations. All jurisdictions in Canada have legislation regarding child protection, which defines the age of a child for the purposes of protection. In Canada, in the absence of provincial or territorial legislation, courts are governed by common law. Social workers are encouraged to maintain current knowledge with respect to legislation on the age of a child, as well as capacity and consent in their jurisdiction.

Client

A person, family, group of persons, incorporated body, association, or community on whose behalf a social worker provides or agrees to provide a service or to whom the social worker is legally obligated to provide a service. Examples of legal obligation to provide service include a legislated responsibility (such as in child welfare) or a valid court order. In the case of a valid court order, the judge/court is the client and the person(s) who is ordered by the court to participate in assessment is recognized as an involuntary client.

Conduct Unbecoming

Behaviour or conduct that does not meet social work standard of care requirements and is, therefore, subject to discipline. In reaching a decision in *Matthews vs. Board of Directors of Physiotherapy* (1986) 54 O.R. (2d) 375, Saunders J. makes three important statements regarding standards of practice, and by implication, professional codes of ethics:

1. Standards of practice are inherent characteristics of any profession.
2. Standards of practice may be written or unwritten.
3. Some conduct is clearly regarded as misconduct and need not be written down, whereas other conduct may be the subject of dispute within a profession.

(See "Standard of Practice.")

Confidentiality

A professional value that demands that professionally acquired information be kept private and not shared with third parties unless the client provides informed consent or a professional or legal obligation exists to share such information without client informed consent.

Discrimination

Treating people unfavourably or holding negative or prejudicial attitudes based on discernible differences or stereotypes (AASW, 1999).

Human Rights

The rights of an individual that are considered the basis for freedom and justice, and serve to protect people from discrimination and harassment. Social workers may refer to the *Canadian Charter of Rights and Freedoms* enacted as Schedule B to the *Canada Act* 1982 (U.K.) 1982, c. 11, which came into force on April 17, 1982, as well as the *Universal Declaration of Human Rights* (1948) proclaimed by the United Nations General Assembly December 10, 1948.

Informed Consent

Voluntary agreement reached by a capable client based on information about foreseeable risks and benefits associated with the agreement (e.g., participation in counselling or agreement to disclose social work report to a third party).

Malpractice and Negligence

Behaviour that is included in "conduct unbecoming" and relates to social work practice behaviour within the parameters of the professional relationship that falls below the standard of practice and results in, or aggravation of, injury to a client. It includes behaviour that results in assault, deceit, fraudulent misrepresentations, defamation of character, breach of contract, violation of human rights, malicious prosecution, false imprisonment, or criminal conviction.

Self-Determination

A core social work value that refers to the right to self-direction and freedom of choice without interference from others. Self-determination is codified in practice through mechanisms of informed consent. Social workers may be obligated to limit self-determination when a client lacks capacity or in order to prevent harm (Regehr & Antle, 1997).

Social Worker

A person who is duly registered to practise social work in a province or territory; or where mandatory registration does not exist, a person with social work education from an institution recognized by the Canadian Association of Schools of Social Work (CASSW) or an institution from outside of Canada that has been approved by the CASW, who is practising social work and who voluntarily agrees to be subject to this *Code of Ethics*. Note: Social workers living in Quebec and British Columbia, whose social work education was obtained outside of Canada, follow a separate approval process within their respective provinces.

Standard of Practice

The standard of care ordinarily expected of a competent social worker. It means that the public is assured that a social worker has the training, the skill, and the diligence to provide them with social work services. Social workers are urged to refer to standards of practice that have been set by their provincial or territorial regulatory body or relevant professional association (see "Conduct Unbecoming").

Voluntary

"In the context of consent, 'voluntariness' refers to a patient's right to make treatment decisions free of any undue influence, such as ability of others to exert control over a patient by force, coercion or manipulation. . . . The requirement for voluntariness does not imply that clinicians should refrain from persuading patients to accept advice. Persuasion involves appealing to the patient's reason in an attempt to convince him or her of the merits of a recommendation. In attempting to persuade the patient to follow a particular course of action, the clinician still leaves the patient free to accept or reject this advice" (Etchells, Sharpe, Dykeman, Meslin, & Singer, 1996, p. 1083).

REFERENCES

AASW. (1999). *AASW code of ethics*. Kingston: Australian Association of Social Workers (AASW).

Alberta Law Reform Institute. (1991). *Status of the child: Revised report* (Report No. 60). Edmonton, Alberta: Law Reform Institute.

BASW. (2002). *BASW: A code of ethics for social workers*. British Association of Social Workers (BASW).

Canadian Charter of Rights and Freedoms. Enacted as Schedule B to the *Canada Act* 1982, c.11 (1982). [http://laws.justice.gc.ca/en/charter.]

CASW. (1994). *Social work code of ethics*. Ottawa: Canadian Association of Social Workers (CASW).

Criminal Code, R.S., c. C-34, s.1. (1985). [http://laws.justice.gc.ca/en/C-46/40670.html]

Etchells, E., Sharpe, G., Dykeman, M.J., Meslin, E.M., & Singer, P. (1996). Bioethics for clinicians: 4: Voluntariness. *Canadian Medical Association Journal, 155*, 1083–1086.

Etchells, E., Sharpe, G., Elliott, C., & Singer, P. (1996). Bioethics for clinicians: 3: Capacity. *Canadian Medical Association Journal, 155*, 657–661.

IFSW. (1994). *The ethics of social work: Principles and standards*. Geneva, Switzerland: International Federation of Social Workers (IFSW).

IFSW. (2004). *Ethics in social work: Statement of principles*. Geneva, Switzerland: International Federation of Social Workers (IFSW).

Lens, V. (2000). Protecting the confidentiality of the therapeutic relationship: *Jaffe v. Redmond*. *Social Work, 45*(3), 273–276.

Matthews and Board of Directors of Physiotherapy (1986) 54 O.R. (2d) 375.

NASW. (1999). *Code of ethics*. Washington: National Association of Social Workers (NASW).

Regehr, C., & Antle, B.J. (1997). Coercive influences: Informed consent and court-mandated social work practice. *Social Work, 42*(3), 300–306.

Rozovsky, L.E., & Rozovsky, F.A. (1990). *The Canadian law of consent to treatment*. Toronto: Butterworths.

United Nations. (1948). *Universal Declaration of Human Rights*. New York: United Nations. [http://www.unhchr.ch/udhr]

United Nations Centre for Human Rights. (1992). Teaching and learning about human rights: A manual for schools of social work and the social work profession (Developed in co-operation with International Federation of Social Workers and International Association of Schools of Social Workers). New York: United Nations.

Appendix B: National Association of Social Workers (NASW) Code of Ethics

PREAMBLE

The primary mission of the social work profession is to enhance human well-being and help meet the basic needs of all people, with particular attention to the needs and empowerment of people who are vulnerable, oppressed, and living in poverty. A historic and defining feature of social work is the profession's focus on individual well-being in a social context and the well-being of society. Fundamental to social work is attention to the environmental forces that create, contribute to, and address problems in living.

Social workers promote social justice and social change with and on behalf of clients. "Clients" is used inclusively to refer to individuals, families, groups, organizations, and communities. Social workers are sensitive to cultural and ethnic diversity and strive to end discrimination, oppression, and other forms of social injustice. These activities may be in the form of direct practice, community organizing, supervision, consultation, administration, advocacy, social and political action, policy development and implementation, education, and research and evaluation. Social workers seek to enhance the capacity of people to address their own needs. Social workers also seek to promote the responsiveness of organizations, communities, and other social institutions to individuals' needs and social problems.

The mission of the social work professions is rooted in a set of core values. These core values, embraced by social workers throughout their profession's history, are the foundation of social work's unique purpose and perspective:

- Service
- Social justice
- Dignity and worth of the person
- Importance of human relationships
- Integrity
- Competence

This constellation of core values reflects what is unique to the social work profession. Core values, and the principles that flow form them, must be balanced within the context and complexity of the human experience.

Copyright © 1999, National Association of Social Workers, Inc., NASW Code of Ethics.

PURPOSE OF THE NASW CODE OF ETHICS

Professional ethics are at the core of social work. The profession has an obligation to articulate its basic values, ethical principles, and ethical standards. The NASW *Code of Ethics* sets forth these values, principles, and standards to guide social workers' conduct. The *Code* is relevant to all social workers and social work students, regardless of their professional functions, the setting in which they work, or the populations they serve.

The NASW *Code of Ethics* serves six purposes:

1. The *Code* identifies core values on which social work's mission is based.
2. The *Code* summarizes broad ethical principles that reflect the profession's core values and establishes a set of specific ethical standards that should be used to guide social work practice.
3. The *Code* is designed to help social workers identify relevant considerations when professional obligations conflict or ethical uncertainties arise.
4. The *Code* provides ethical standards to which the general public can hold the social work profession accountable.
5. The *Code* socializes practitioners new to the field to social work's mission, values, ethical principles, and ethical standards.
6. The *Code* articulates standards that the social work profession itself can use to assess whether social workers have engaged in unethical conduct. NASW has formal procedures to adjudicate ethics complaints filed against its members.* In subscribing to this *Code*, social workers are to participate in adjudication proceedings, and abide by any NASW disciplinary rulings or sanctions based on it.

The *Code* offers a set of values, principles, and standards to guide decision making and conduct when ethical issues arise. It does not provide a set of rules that prescribe how social workers should act in all situations. Specific applications of the *Code* must take into account the context in which it is being considered and the possibility of conflicts among the *Code's* values, principles, and standards. Ethical responsibilities flow from all human relationships, from the personal and familial to the social and professional.

Further, the NASW *Code of Ethics* does not specify which values, principles, and standards are most important and ought to outweigh others in instances when they conflict. Reasonable differences of opinion can and do exist among social workers with respect to the ways in which values, ethical principles, and ethical standards should be rank ordered when they conflict. Ethical decision making in a given situation must apply the informed judgment of the individual social worker and should also consider how the issues would be judged in a peer review process where the ethical standards of the profession would be applied.

Ethical decision making is a process. There are many instances in social work where simple answers are not available to resolve complex ethical issues. Social workers should take into consideration all the values, principles, and standards in this *Code* that are relevant to any

---

*For information on NASW adjudication procedures, see *NASW Procedures for the Adjudication of Grievances.*

situation in which ethical judgment is warranted. Social workers' decisions and actions should be consistent with the spirit as well as the letter of this *Code*.

In addition to this *Code,* there are many other sources of information about ethical thinking that may be useful. Social workers should consider ethical theory and principles generally, social work theory and research, laws, regulations, agency policies, and other relevant codes of ethics, recognizing that among codes of ethics social workers should consider the NASW *Code of Ethics* as their primary source. Social workers also should be aware of the impact on ethical decision making of their clients' and their own personal values and cultural and religious beliefs and practices. They should be aware of any conflicts between personal and professional values and deal with them responsibly. For additional guidance social workers should consult the relevant literature on professional ethics and ethical decision making and seek appropriate consultation when faced with ethical dilemmas. This may involve consultation with an agency-based or social work organization's ethics committee, a regulatory body, knowledgeable colleagues, supervisors, or legal counsel.

Instances may arise when social workers' ethical obligations conflict with agency policies or relevant laws or regulations. When such conflicts occur, social workers must make a responsible effort to resolve the conflict in a manner that is consistent with the values, principles, and standards expressed in this *Code*. If a reasonable resolution of the conflict does not appear possible, social workers should seek proper consultation before making a decision.

The NASW *Code of Ethics* is used by NASW and by individuals, agencies, organizations, and bodies (such as licensing and regulatory boards, professional liability insurance providers, courts of laws, agency boards of directors, government agencies, and other professional groups) that choose to adopt it or use it as a frame of reference. Violation of standards in this *Code* does not automatically imply legal liability or violation of the law. Such determination can only be made in the context of legal and judicial proceedings. Alleged violations of the *Code* would be subject to a peer review process. Such processes are generally separate from legal or administrative procedures and insulated from legal review of proceedings to allow the profession to counsel and discipline its own members.

A code of ethics cannot guarantee ethical behaviour. Moreover, a code of ethics cannot resolve all ethical issues or disputes or capture the richness and complexity involved in striving to make responsible choices within a moral community. Rather, a code of ethics sets forth values, ethical principles, and ethical standards to which professionals aspire and by which their actions can be judged. Social workers' ethical behaviour should result from their personal commitment to engage in ethical practice. The NASW *Code of Ethics* reflects the commitment of all social workers to uphold the profession's values and to act ethically. Principles and standards must be applied by individuals of good character who discern moral questions and, in good faith, seek to make reliable ethical judgments.

ETHICAL PRINCIPLES

The following broad ethical principles are based on social work's core values of service, social justice, dignity and worth of the person, importance of human relationships, integrity, and competence. These principles set forth ideals to which all social workers should aspire.

Value: *Service*
Ethical Principle: *Social workers' primary goal is to help people in need and to address social problems.*
Social workers elevate service to others above self-interest. Social workers draw on their knowledge, values, and skills to help people in need and to address social problems. Social workers are encouraged to volunteer some portion of their professional skills with no expectation of significant financial return (pro bono service).

Value: *Social Justice*
Ethical Principle: *Social workers challenge social injustice.*
Social workers pursue social change, particularly with and on behalf of vulnerable and oppressed individuals and groups of people. Social workers' social change efforts are focused primarily on issues of poverty, unemployment, discrimination, and other forms of social injustice. These activities seek to promote sensitivity to and knowledge about oppression and cultural and ethnic diversity. Social workers strive to ensure access to needed information, services, and resources; equality of opportunity; and meaningful participation in decision making for all people.

Value: *Dignity and Worth of the Person*
Ethical Principle: *Social workers respect the inherent dignity and worth of the person.*
Social workers treat each person in a caring and respectful fashion, mindful of individual differences and cultural and ethnic diversity. Social workers promote clients' socially responsible self-determination. Social workers seek to enhance clients' capacity and opportunity to change and to address their own needs. Social workers are cognizant of their dual responsibility to clients and to the broader society. They seek to resolve conflicts between clients' interests and the broader society's interests in a socially responsible manner consistent with the values, ethical principles, and ethical standards of the profession.

Value: *Importance of Human Relationships*
Ethical Principle: *Social workers recognize the central importance of human relationships.*
Social workers understand that relationships between and among people are an important vehicle for change. Social workers engage people as partners in the helping process. Social workers seek to strengthen relationships among people in a purposeful effort to promote, restore, maintain, and enhance the well-being of individuals, families, social groups, organizations, and communities.

Value: *Integrity*
Ethical Principle: *Social workers behave in a trustworthy manner.*
Social workers are continually aware of the profession's mission, values, ethical principles, and ethical standards and practise in a manner consistent with them. Social workers act honestly and responsibly and promote ethical practices on the part of the organizations with which they are affiliated.

Value: *Competence*
Ethical Principle: *Social workers practise within their areas of competence and develop and enhance their professional expertise.*

Social workers continually strive to increase their professional knowledge and skills and to apply them in practice. Social workers should aspire to contribute to the knowledge base of the profession.

ETHICAL STANDARDS

The following ethical standards are relevant to the professional activities of all social workers. These standards concern (1) social workers' ethical responsibilities to clients, (2) social workers' ethical responsibilities to colleagues, (3) social workers' ethical responsibilities in practice settings, (4) social workers' ethical responsibilities as professionals, (5) social workers' ethical responsibilities to the social work profession, and (6) social workers' ethical responsibilities to the broader society.

Some of the standards that follow are enforceable guidelines for professional conduct, and some are aspirational. The extent to which each standard is enforceable is a matter of professional judgment to be exercised by those responsible for reviewing alleged violations of ethical standards.

1. SOCIAL WORKERS' ETHICAL RESPONSIBILITIES TO CLIENTS

1.01 Commitment to Clients

Social workers' primary responsibility is to promote the well-being of clients. In general, clients' interests are primary. However, social workers' responsibility to the larger society or specific legal obligations may, on limited occasions, supersede the loyalty owed clients, and clients should be so advised. (Examples include when a social worker is required by law to report that a client has abused a child or has threatened to harm self or others.)

1.02 Self-Determination

Social workers respect and promote the right of clients to self-determination and assist clients in their efforts to identify and clarify their goals. Social workers may limit clients' right to self-determination when, in the social workers' professional judgment, clients' actions or potential actions pose a serious, foreseeable, and imminent risk to themselves or others.

1.03 Informed Consent

(a) Social workers should provide services to clients only in the context of a professional relationship based, when appropriate, on valid informed consent. Social workers should use clear and understandable language to inform clients of the purpose of the services, risks related to the services, limits to services because of the requirements of a third-party payer, relevant costs, reasonable alternatives, clients' right to refuse or withdraw consent, and the time frame covered by the consent. Social workers should provide clients with an opportunity to ask questions.

(b) In instances when clients are not literate or have difficulty understanding the primary language used in the practice setting, social workers should take steps to ensure clients' comprehension. This may include providing clients with a detailed verbal explanation or arranging for a qualified interpreter or translator whenever possible.

(c) In instances when clients lack the capacity to provide informed consent, social workers should protect clients' interests by seeking permission from an appropriate third party, informing clients consistent with the clients' level of understanding. In such instances social workers should seek to ensure that the third party acts in a manner consistent with clients' wishes and interests. Social workers should take reasonable steps to enhance such clients' ability to give informed consent.

(d) In instances when clients are receiving services involuntarily, social workers should provide information about the nature and extent of services and about the extent of clients' right to refuse service.

(e) Social workers who provide services via electronic media (such as computer, telephone, radio, and television) should inform recipients of the limitations and risks associated with such services.

(f) Social workers should obtain clients' informed consent before audiotaping or videotaping clients or permitting observation of services to clients by a third party.

1.04 Competence

(a) Social workers should provide services and represent themselves as competent only within the boundaries of their education, training, licence, certification, consultation received, supervised experience, or other relevant professional experience.

(b) Social workers should provide services in substantive areas or use intervention techniques or approaches that are new to them only after engaging in appropriate study, training, consultation, and supervision from people who are competent in those interventions or techniques.

(c) When generally recognized standards do not exist with respect to an emerging area of practice, social workers should exercise careful judgment and take responsible steps (including appropriate education, research, training, consultation, and supervision) to ensure the competence of their work and to protect clients from harm.

1.05 Cultural Competence and Social Diversity

(a) Social workers should understand culture and its function in human behaviour and society, recognizing the strengths that exist in all cultures.

(b) Social workers should have a knowledge base of their clients' cultures and be able to demonstrate competence in the provision of services that are sensitive to clients' cultures and to differences among people and cultural groups.

(c) Social workers should obtain education about and seek to understand the nature of social diversity and oppression with respect to race, ethnicity, national origin, color, sex, sexual orientation, age, marital status, political belief, religion, and mental or physical disability.

1.06 Conflicts of Interest

(a) Social workers should be alert to and avoid conflicts of interest that interfere with the exercise of professional discretion and impartial judgment. Social workers should inform clients when a real or potential conflict of interest arises and take reasonable steps to resolve the issue in a manner that makes the clients' interests primary and protects clients' interests to the greatest extent possible. In some cases, protecting clients' interests may require termination of the professional relationship with proper referral of the client.

(b) Social workers should not take unfair advantage of any professional relationship or exploit others to further their personal, religious, political, or business interests.

(c) Social workers should not engage in dual or multiple relationships with clients or former clients in which there is a risk of exploitation or potential harm to the client. In instances when dual or multiple relationships are unavoidable, social workers should take steps to protect clients and are responsible for setting clear, appropriate, and culturally sensitive boundaries. (Dual or multiple relationships occur when social workers relate to clients in more than one relationship, whether professional, social, or business. Dual or multiple relationships can occur simultaneously or consecutively.)

(d) When social workers provide services to two or more people who have a relationship with each other (for example, couples, family members), social workers should clarify with all parties which individuals will be considered clients and the nature of social workers' professional obligations to the various individuals who are receiving services. Social workers who anticipate a conflict of interest among the individuals receiving services or who anticipate having to perform in potentially conflicting roles (for example, when a social worker is asked to testify in a child custody dispute or divorce proceedings involving clients) should clarify their role with the parties involved and take appropriate action to minimize any conflict of interest.

1.07 Privacy and Confidentiality

(a) Social workers should respect clients' right to privacy. Social workers should not solicit private information from clients unless it is essential to providing services or conducting social work evaluation or research. Once private information is shared, standards of confidentiality apply.

(b) Social workers may disclose confidential information when appropriate with valid consent from a client or a person legally authorized to consent on behalf of a client.

(c) Social workers should protect the confidentiality of all information obtained in the course of professional service, except for compelling professional reasons. The general expectation that social workers will keep information confidential does not apply when disclosure is necessary to prevent serious, foreseeable, and imminent harm to a client or other identifiable person. In all instances, social workers should disclose the least amount of confidential information necessary to achieve the desired purpose; only information that is directly relevant to the purpose for which the disclosure is made should be revealed.

(d) Social workers should inform clients, to the extent possible, about the disclosure of confidential information and the potential consequences, when feasible before the disclosure is made. This applies whether social workers disclose confidential information on the basis of a legal requirement or client consent.

(e) Social workers should discuss with clients and other interested parties the nature of confidentiality and limitations of clients' right to confidentiality. Social workers should review with clients circumstances where confidential information may be requested and where disclosure of confidential information may be legally required. This discussion should occur as soon as possible in the social worker–client relationship and as needed throughout the course of the relationship.

(f) When social workers provide counselling services to families, couples, or groups, social workers should seek agreement among the parties involved concerning each individual's right to confidentiality and obligation to preserve the confidentiality of information shared by others. Social workers should inform participants in family, couples, or group counselling that social workers cannot guarantee that all participants will honour such agreements.

(g) Social workers should inform clients involved in family, couples, marital, or group counselling of the social worker's, employer's, and agency's policy concerning the social worker's disclosure of confidential information among the parties involved in the counselling.

(h) Social workers should not disclose confidential information to third-party payers unless clients have authorized such disclosure.

(i) Social workers should not discuss confidential information in any setting unless privacy can be ensured. Social workers should not discuss confidential information in public or semipublic areas such as hallways, waiting rooms, elevators, and restaurants.

(j) Social workers should protect the confidentiality of clients during legal proceedings to the extent permitted by law. When a court of law or other legally authorized body orders social workers to disclose confidential or privileged information without a client's consent and such disclosure could cause harm to the client, social workers should request that the court withdraw the order or limit the order as narrowly as possible or maintain the records under seal, unavailable for public inspection.

(k) Social workers should protect the confidentiality of clients when responding to requests from members of the media.

(l) Social workers should protect the confidentiality of clients' written and electronic records and other sensitive information. Social workers should take reasonable steps to ensure that clients' records are stored in a secure location and that clients' records are not available to others who are not authorized to have access.

(m) Social workers should take precautions to ensure and maintain the confidentiality of information transmitted to other parties through the use of computers, electronic mail, facsimile machines, telephones and telephone answering machines, and other electronic or computer technology. Disclosure of identifying information should be avoided whenever possible.

(n) Social workers should transfer or dispose of clients' records in a manner that protects clients' confidentiality and is consistent with state statutes governing records and social work licensure.

(o) Social workers should take reasonable precautions to protect client confidentiality in the event of the social worker's termination of practice, incapacitation, or death.

(p) Social workers should not disclose identifying information when discussing clients for teaching or training purposes unless the client has consented to disclosure of confidential information.

(q) Social workers should not disclose identifying information when discussing clients with consultants unless the client has consented to disclosure of confidential information or there is a compelling need for such disclosure.

(r) Social workers should protect the confidentiality of deceased clients consistent with the preceding standards.

1.08 Access to Records

(a) Social workers should provide clients with reasonable access to records concerning the clients. Social workers who are concerned that clients' access to their records could cause serious misunderstanding or harm to the client should provide assistance in interpreting the records and consultation with the client regarding the records. Social workers should limit clients' access to their records, or portions of their records, only in exceptional circumstances when there is compelling evidence that such access would cause serious harm to the client. Both clients' requests and the rationale for withholding some or all of the record should be documented in clients' files.

(b) When providing clients with access to their records, social workers should take steps to protect the confidentiality of other individuals identified or discussed in such records.

1.09 Sexual Relationships

(a) Social workers should under no circumstances engage in sexual activities or sexual contact with current clients, whether such contact is consensual or forced.

(b) Social workers should not engage in sexual activities or sexual contact with clients' relatives or other individuals with whom clients maintain a close personal relationship when there is a risk of exploitation or potential harm to the client. Sexual activity or sexual contact with clients' relatives or other individuals with whom clients maintain a personal relationship has the potential to be harmful to the client and may make it difficult for the social worker and client to maintain appropriate professional boundaries. Social workers—not their clients, their clients' relatives, or other individuals with whom the client maintains a personal relationship—assume the full burden for setting clear, appropriate, and culturally sensitive boundaries.

(c) Social workers should not engage in sexual activities or sexual contact with former clients because of the potential for harm to the client. If social workers engage in conduct contrary to this prohibition or claim that an exception to this prohibition is warranted because of extraordinary circumstances, it is social workers—not their clients—who assume the full burden of demonstrating that the former client has not been exploited, coerced, or manipulated, intentionally or unintentionally.

(d) Social workers should not provide clinical services to individuals with whom they have had a prior sexual relationship. Providing clinical services to a former sexual partner has the potential to be harmful to the individual and is likely to make it difficult for the social worker and individual to maintain appropriate professional boundaries.

1.10 Physical Contact

Social workers should not engage in physical contact with clients when there is a possibility of psychological harm to the client as a result of the contact (such as cradling or caressing clients). Social workers who engage in appropriate physical contact with clients are responsible for setting clear, appropriate, and culturally sensitive boundaries that govern such physical contact.

1.11 Sexual Harassment

Social workers should not sexually harass clients. Sexual harassment includes sexual advances, sexual solicitation, requests for sexual favours, and other verbal or physical conduct of a sexual nature.

1.12 Derogatory Language

Social workers should not use derogatory language in their written or verbal communications to or about clients. Social workers should use accurate and respectful language in all communications to and about clients.

1.13 Payment for Services

(a) When setting fees, social workers should ensure that the fees are fair, reasonable, and commensurate with the services performed. Consideration should be given to clients' ability to pay.

(b) Social workers should avoid accepting goods or services from clients as payment for professional services. Bartering arrangements, particularly involving services, create the potential for conflicts of interest, exploitation, and inappropriate boundaries in social workers' relationships with clients. Social workers should explore and may participate in bartering only in very limited circumstances when it can be demonstrated that such arrangements are an accepted practice among professionals in the local community, considered to be essential for the provision of services, negotiated without coercion, and entered into at the client's initiative and with the client's informed consent. Social workers who accept goods or services from clients as payment for professional services assume the full burden of demonstrating that this arrangement will not be detrimental to the client or the professional relationship.

(c) Social workers should not solicit a private fee or other remuneration for providing services to clients who are entitled to such available services through the social workers' employer or agency.

1.14 Clients Who Lack Decision-Making Capacity

When social workers act on behalf of clients who lack the capacity to make informed decisions, social workers should take reasonable steps to safeguard the interests and rights of those clients.

1.15 Interruption of Services

Social workers should make reasonable efforts to ensure continuity of services in the event that services are interrupted by factors such as unavailability, relocation, illness, disability, or death.

1.16 Termination of Services

(a) Social workers should terminate services to clients and professional relationships with them when such services and relationships are no longer required or no longer serve the clients' needs or interests.

(b) Social workers should take reasonable steps to avoid abandoning clients who are still in need of services. Social workers should withdraw services precipitously only under unusual circumstances, giving careful consideration to all factors in the situation and taking care to minimize possible adverse effects. Social workers should assist in making appropriate arrangements for continuation of services when necessary.

(c) Social workers in fee-for-service settings may terminate services to clients who are not paying an overdue balance if the financial contractual arrangements have been made clear to the client, if the client does not pose an imminent danger to self or others, and if the clinical and other consequences of the current nonpayment have been addressed and discussed with the client.

(d) Social workers should not terminate services to pursue a social, financial, or sexual relationship with a client.

(e) Social workers who anticipate the termination or interruption of services to clients should notify clients promptly and seek the transfer, referral, or continuation of services in relation to the clients' needs and preferences.

(f) Social workers who are leaving an employment setting should inform clients of appropriate options for the continuation of services and of the benefits and risks of the options.

2. SOCIAL WORKERS' ETHICAL RESPONSIBILITIES TO COLLEAGUES

2.01 Respect

(a) Social workers should treat colleagues with respect and should represent accurately and fairly the qualifications, views, and obligations of colleagues.

(b) Social workers should avoid unwarranted negative criticism of colleagues in communications with clients or with other professionals. Unwarranted negative criticism may include demeaning comments that refer to colleagues' level of competence or to individuals' attributes such as race, ethnicity, national origin, colour, sex, sexual orientation, age, marital status, political belief, religion, and mental or physical disability.

(c) Social workers should cooperate with social work colleagues and with colleagues of other professions when such cooperation serves the well-being of clients.

2.02 Confidentiality

Social workers should respect confidential information shared by colleagues in the course of their professional relationships and transactions. Social workers should ensure that such colleagues understand social workers' obligation to respect confidentiality and any exceptions related to it.

2.03 Interdisciplinary Collaboration

(a) Social workers who are members of an interdisciplinary team should participate in and contribute to decisions that affect the well-being of clients by drawing on the perspectives, values, and experiences of the social work profession. Professional and ethical obligations of the interdisciplinary team as a whole and of its individual members should be clearly established.

(b) Social workers for whom a team decision raises ethical concerns should attempt to resolve the disagreement through appropriate channels. If the disagreement cannot be resolved, social workers should pursue other avenues to address their concerns consistent with client well-being.

2.04 Disputes Involving Colleagues

(a) Social workers should not take advantage of a dispute between a colleague and an employer to obtain a position or otherwise advance the social workers' own interests.

(b) Social workers should not exploit clients in disputes with colleagues or engage clients in any inappropriate discussion of conflicts between social workers and their colleagues.

2.05 Consultation

(a) Social workers should seek the advice and counsel of colleagues whenever such consultation is in the best interests of clients.

(b) Social workers should keep themselves informed about colleagues' areas of expertise and competencies. Social workers should seek consultation only from colleagues who have demonstrated knowledge, expertise, and competence related to the subject of the consultation.

(c) When consulting with colleagues about clients, social workers should disclose the least amount of information necessary to achieve the purposes of the consultation.

2.06 Referral for Services

(a) Social workers should refer clients to other professionals when the other professionals' specialized knowledge or expertise is needed to serve clients fully or when social workers believe that they are not being effective or making reasonable progress with clients and that additional service is required.

(b) Social workers who refer clients to other professionals should take appropriate steps to facilitate an orderly transfer of responsibility. Social workers who refer clients to other professionals should disclose, with clients' consent, all pertinent information to the new service providers.

(c) Social workers are prohibited from giving or receiving payment for a referral when no professional service is provided by the referring social worker.

2.07 Sexual Relationships

(a) Social workers who function as supervisors or educators should not engage in sexual activities or contact with supervisees, students, trainees, or other colleagues over whom they exercise professional authority.

(b) Social workers should avoid engaging in sexual relationships with colleagues when there is potential for a conflict of interest. Social workers who become involved in, or anticipate becoming involved in, a sexual relationship with a colleague have a duty to transfer professional responsibilities, when necessary, to avoid a conflict of interest.

2.08 Sexual Harassment

Social workers should not sexually harass supervisees, students, trainees, or colleagues. Sexual harassment includes sexual advances, sexual solicitation, requests for sexual favours, and other verbal or physical conduct of a sexual nature.

2.09 Impairment of Colleagues

(a) Social workers who have direct knowledge of a social work colleague's impairment that is due to personal problems, psychosocial distress, substance abuse, or mental health difficulties and that interferes with practice effectiveness should consult with that colleague when feasible and assist the colleague in taking remedial action.

(b) Social workers who believe that a social work colleague's impairment interferes with practice effectiveness and that the colleague has not taken adequate steps to address the impairment should take action through appropriate channels established by employers, agencies, NASW, licensing and regulatory bodies, and other professional organizations.

2.10 Incompetence of Colleagues

(a) Social workers who have direct knowledge of a social work colleague's incompetence should consult with that colleague when feasible and assist the colleague in taking remedial action.

(b) Social workers who believe that a social work colleague is incompetent and has not taken adequate steps to address the incompetence should take action through appropriate channels established by employers, agencies, NASW, licensing and regulatory bodies, and other professional organizations.

2.11 Unethical Conduct of Colleagues

(a) Social workers should take adequate measures to discourage, prevent, expose, and correct the unethical conduct of colleagues.

(b) Social workers should be knowledgeable about established policies and procedures for handling concerns about colleagues' unethical behaviour. Social workers should be familiar with national, state, and local procedures for handling ethics complaints. These include policies and procedures created by NASW, licensing and regulatory bodies, employers, agencies, and other professional organizations.

(c) Social workers who believe that a colleague has acted unethically should seek resolution by discussing their concerns with the colleague when feasible and when such discussion is likely to be productive.

(d) When necessary, social workers who believe that a colleague has acted unethically should take action through appropriate formal channels (such as contacting a state licensing board or regulatory body, an NASW committee on inquiry, or other professional ethics committees).

(e) Social workers should defend and assist colleagues who are unjustly charged with unethical conduct.

3. SOCIAL WORKERS' ETHICAL RESPONSIBILITIES IN PRACTICE SETTINGS

3.01 Supervision and Consultation

(a) Social workers who provide supervision or consultation should have the necessary knowledge and skill to supervise or consult appropriately and should do so only within their areas of knowledge and competence.

(b) Social workers who provide supervision or consultation are responsible for setting clear, appropriate, and culturally sensitive boundaries.

(c) Social workers should not engage in any dual or multiple relationships with supervisees in which there is a risk of exploitation of or potential harm to the supervisee.

(d) Social workers who provide supervision should evaluate supervisees' performance in a manner that is fair and respectful.

3.02 Education and Training

(a) Social workers who function as educators, field instructors for students, or trainers should provide instruction only within their areas of knowledge and competence and should provide instruction based on the most current information and knowledge available in the profession.

(b) Social workers who function as educators or field instructors for students should evaluate students' performance in a manner that is fair and respectful.

(c) Social workers who function as educators or field instructors for students should take reasonable steps to ensure that clients are routinely informed when services are being provided by students.

(d) Social workers who function as educators or field instructors for students should not engage in any dual or multiple relationships with students in which there is a risk of exploitation or potential harm to the student. Social work educators and field instructors are responsible for setting clear, appropriate, and culturally sensitive boundaries.

3.03 Performance Evaluation

Social workers who have responsibility for evaluating the performance of others should fulfill such responsibility in a fair and considerate manner and on the basis of clearly stated criteria.

3.04 Client Records

(a) Social workers should take reasonable steps to ensure that documentation in records is accurate and reflects the services provided.

(b) Social workers should include sufficient and timely documentation in records to facilitate the delivery of services and to ensure continuity of services provided to clients in the future.

(c) Social workers' documentation should protect clients' privacy to the extent that is possible and appropriate and should include only information that is directly relevant to the delivery of services.

(d) Social workers should store records following the termination of services to ensure reasonable future access. Records should be maintained for the number of years required by state statutes or relevant contracts.

3.05 Billing

Social workers should establish and maintain billing practices that accurately reflect the nature and extent of services provided and that identify who provided the service in the practice setting.

3.06 Client Transfer

(a) When an individual who is receiving services from another agency or colleague contacts a social worker for services, the social worker should carefully consider the client's needs before agreeing to provide services. To minimize possible confusion and conflict, social workers should discuss with potential clients the nature of the clients' current relationship with other service providers and the implications, including possible benefits or risks, of entering into a relationship with a new service provider.

(b) If a new client has been served by another agency or colleague, social workers should discuss with the client whether consultation with the previous service provider is in the client's best interest.

3.07 Administration

(a) Social work administrators should advocate within and outside their agencies for adequate resources to meet clients' needs.

(b) Social workers should advocate for resource allocation procedures that are open and fair. When not all clients' needs can be met, an allocation procedure should be developed that is nondiscriminatory and based on appropriate and consistently applied principles.

(c) Social workers who are administrators should take reasonable steps to ensure that adequate agency or organizational resources are available to provide appropriate staff supervision.

(d) Social work administrators should take reasonable steps to ensure that the working environment for which they are responsible is consistent with and encourages compliance with the NASW *Code of Ethics*. Social work administrators should take reasonable steps to eliminate any conditions in their organizations that violate, interfere with, or discourage compliance with the *Code*.

3.08 Continuing Education and Staff Development

Social work administrators and supervisors should take reasonable steps to provide or arrange for continuing education and staff development for all staff for whom they are responsible. Continuing education and staff development should address current knowledge and emerging developments related to social work practice and ethics.

3.09 Commitments to Employers

(a) Social workers generally should adhere to commitments made to employers and employing organizations.

(b) Social workers should work to improve employing agencies' policies and procedures and the efficiency and effectiveness of their services.

(c) Social workers should take reasonable steps to ensure that employers are aware of social workers' ethical obligations as set forth in the NASW *Code of Ethics* and of the implications of those obligations for social work practice.

(d) Social workers should not allow an employing organization's policies, procedures, regulations, or administrative orders to interfere with their ethical practice of social work. Social workers should take reasonable steps to ensure that their employing organizations' practices are consistent with the NASW *Code of Ethics*.

(e) Social workers should act to prevent and eliminate discrimination in the employing organization's work assignments and in its employment policies and practices.

(f) Social workers should accept employment or arrange student field placements only in organizations that exercise fair personnel practices.

(g) Social workers should be diligent stewards of the resources of their employing organizations, wisely conserving funds where appropriate and never misappropriating funds or using them for unintended purposes.

3.10 Labour–Management Disputes

(a) Social workers may engage in organized action, including the formation of and participation in labour unions, to improve services to clients and working conditions.

(b) The actions of social workers who are involved in labour–management disputes, job actions, or labour strikes should be guided by the profession's values, ethical principles, and ethical standards. Reasonable differences of opinion exist among social workers concerning their primary obligation as professionals during an actual or threatened labour strike or job action. Social workers should carefully examine relevant issues and their possible impact on clients before deciding on a course of action.

4. SOCIAL WORKERS' ETHICAL RESPONSIBILITIES AS PROFESSIONALS

4.01 Competence

(a) Social workers should accept responsibility or employment only on the basis of existing competence or the intention to acquire the necessary competence.

(b) Social workers should strive to become and remain proficient in professional practice and the performance of professional functions. Social workers should critically examine and keep current with emerging knowledge relevant to social work. Social workers should routinely review the professional literature and participate in continuing education relevant to social work practice and social work ethics.

(c) Social workers should base practice on recognized knowledge, including empirically based knowledge, relevant to social work and social work ethics.

4.02 Discrimination

Social workers should not practise, condone, facilitate, or collaborate with any form of discrimination on the basis of race, ethnicity, national origin, colour, sex, sexual orientation, age, marital status, political belief, religion, or mental or physical disability.

4.03 Private Conduct

Social workers should not permit their private conduct to interfere with their ability to fulfill their professional responsibilities.

4.04 Dishonesty, Fraud, and Deception

Social workers should not participate in, condone, or be associated with dishonesty, fraud, or deception.

4.05 Impairment

(a) Social workers should not allow their own personal problems, psychosocial distress, legal problems, substance abuse, or mental health difficulties to interfere with their professional judgment and performance or to jeopardize the best interests of people for whom they have a professional responsibility.

(b) Social workers whose personal problems, psychosocial distress, legal problems, substance abuse, or mental health difficulties interfere with their professional judgment and performance should immediately seek consultation and take appropriate remedial action by seeking professional help, making adjustments in workload, terminating practice, or taking any other steps necessary to protect clients and others.

4.06 Misrepresentation

(a) Social workers should make clear distinctions between statements made and actions engaged in as a private individual and as a representative of the social work profession, a professional social work organization, or the social worker's employing agency.

(b) Social workers who speak on behalf of professional social work organizations should accurately represent the official and authorized positions of the organizations.

(c) Social workers should ensure that their representations to clients, agencies, and the public of professional qualifications, credentials, education, competence, affiliations, services provided, or results to be achieved are accurate. Social workers should claim only those relevant professional credentials they actually possess and take steps to correct any inaccuracies or misrepresentations of their credentials by others.

4.07 Solicitations

(a) Social workers should not engage in uninvited solicitation of potential clients who, because of their circumstances, are vulnerable to undue influence, manipulation, or coercion.

(b) Social workers should not engage in solicitation of testimonial endorsements (including solicitation of consent to use a client's prior statement as a testimonial endorsement) from current clients or from other people who, because of their particular circumstances, are vulnerable to undue influence.

4.08 Acknowledging Credit

(a) Social workers should take responsibility and credit, including authorship credit, only for work they have actually performed and to which they have contributed.

(b) Social workers should honestly acknowledge the work of and the contributions made by others.

5. SOCIAL WORKERS' ETHICAL RESPONSIBILITIES TO THE SOCIAL WORK PROFESSION

5.01 Integrity of the Profession

(a) Social workers should work toward the maintenance and promotion of high standards of practice.

(b) Social workers should uphold and advance the values, ethics, knowledge, and mission of the profession. Social workers should protect, enhance, and improve the integrity of the profession through appropriate study and research, active discussion, and responsible criticism of the profession.

(c) Social workers should contribute time and professional expertise to activities that promote respect for the value, integrity, and competence of the social work profession. These activities may include teaching, research, consultation, service, legislative testimony, presentations in the community, and participation in their professional organizations.

(d) Social workers should contribute to the knowledge base of social work and share with colleagues their knowledge related to practice, research, and ethics. Social workers should seek to contribute to the profession's literature and to share their knowledge at professional meetings and conferences.

(e) Social workers should act to prevent the unauthorized and unqualified practice of social work.

5.02 Evaluation and Research

(a) Social workers should monitor and evaluate policies, the implementation of programs, and practice interventions.

(b) Social workers should promote and facilitate evaluation and research to contribute to the development of knowledge.

(c) Social workers should critically examine and keep current with emerging knowledge relevant to social work and fully use evaluation and research evidence in their professional practice.

(d) Social workers engaged in evaluation or research should carefully consider possible consequences and should follow guidelines developed for the protection of evaluation and research participants. Appropriate institutional review boards should be consulted.

(e) Social workers engaged in evaluation or research should obtain voluntary and written informed consent from participants, when appropriate, without any implied or actual deprivation or penalty for refusal to participate; without undue inducement to participate; and with due regard for participants' well-being, privacy, and dignity. Informed consent should include information about the nature, extent, and duration of the participation requested and disclosure of the risks and benefits of participation in the research.

(f) When evaluation or research participants are incapable of giving informed consent, social workers should provide an appropriate explanation to the participants, obtain the participants' assent to the extent they are able, and obtain written consent from an appropriate proxy.

(g) Social workers should never design or conduct evaluation or research that does not use consent procedures, such as certain forms of naturalistic observation and archival research, unless rigorous and responsible review of the research has found it to be justified because of its prospective scientific, educational, or applied value and unless equally effective alternative procedures that do not involve waiver of consent are not feasible.

(h) Social workers should inform participants of their right to withdraw from evaluation and research at any time without penalty.

(i) Social workers should take appropriate steps to ensure that participants in evaluation and research have access to appropriate supportive services.

(j) Social workers engaged in evaluation or research should protect participants from unwarranted physical or mental distress, harm, danger, or deprivation.

(k) Social workers engaged in the evaluation of services should discuss collected information only for professional purposes and only with people professionally concerned with this information.

(l) Social workers engaged in evaluation or research should ensure the anonymity or confidentiality of participants and of the data obtained from them. Social workers should inform participants of any limits of confidentiality, the measures that will be taken to ensure confidentiality, and when any records containing research data will be destroyed.

(m) Social workers who report evaluation and research results should protect participants' confidentiality by omitting identifying information unless proper consent has been obtained authorizing disclosure.

(n) Social workers should report evaluation and research findings accurately. They should not fabricate or falsify results and should take steps to correct any errors later found in published data using standard publication methods.

(o) Social workers engaged in evaluation or research should be alert to and avoid conflicts of interest and dual relationships with participants, should inform participants when a real or potential conflict of interest arises, and should take steps to resolve the issue in a manner that makes participants' interests primary.

(p) Social workers should educate themselves, their students, and their colleagues about responsible research practices.

6. SOCIAL WORKERS' ETHICAL RESPONSIBILITIES TO THE BROADER SOCIETY

6.01 Social Welfare

Social workers should promote the general welfare of society, from local to global levels, and the development of people, their communities, and their environments. Social workers should advocate for living conditions conducive to the fulfillment of basic human needs and should promote social, economic, political, and cultural values and institutions that are compatible with the realization of social justice.

6.02 Public Participation

Social workers should facilitate informed participation by the public in shaping social policies and institutions.

6.03 Public Emergencies

Social workers should provide appropriate professional services in public emergencies to the greatest extent possible.

6.04 Social and Political Action

(a) Social workers should engage in social and political action that seeks to ensure that all people have equal access to the resources, employment, services, and opportunities they require to meet their basic human needs and to develop fully. Social workers should be aware of the impact of the political arena on practice and should advocate for changes in policy and legislation to improve social conditions in order to meet basic human needs and promote social justice.

(b) Social workers should act to expand choice and opportunity for all people, with special regard for vulnerable, disadvantaged, oppressed, and exploited people and groups.

(c) Social workers should promote conditions that encourage respect for cultural and social diversity within the United States and globally. Social workers should promote policies and practices that demonstrate respect for difference, support the expansion of cultural knowledge and resources, advocate for programs and institutions that demonstrate cultural competence, and promote policies that safeguard the rights of and confirm equity and social justice for all people.

(d) Social workers should act to prevent and eliminate domination of, exploitation of, and discrimination against any person, group, or class on the basis of race, ethnicity, national origin, colour, sex, sexual orientation, age, marital status, political belief, religion, or mental or physical disability

Appendix C: The American Psychological Association's Code of Conduct 2002

INTRODUCTION AND APPLICABILITY

The American Psychological Association's (APA's) *Ethical Principles of Psychologists and Code of Conduct* (hereinafter referred to as the *Ethics Code*) consists of an Introduction, a Preamble, five General Principles (A–E), and specific Ethical Standards. The Introduction discusses the intent, organization, procedural considerations, and scope of application of the *Ethics Code*. The Preamble and General Principles are aspirational goals to guide psychologists toward the highest ideals of psychology. Although the Preamble and General Principles are not themselves enforceable rules, they should be considered by psychologists in arriving at an ethical course of action. The Ethical Standards set forth enforceable rules for conduct as psychologists. Most of the Ethical Standards are written broadly, in order to apply to psychologists in varied roles, although the application of an Ethical Standard may vary depending on the context. The Ethical Standards are not exhaustive. The fact that a given conduct is not specifically addressed by an Ethical Standard does not mean that it is necessarily either ethical or unethical. This *Ethics Code* applies only to psychologists' activities that are part of their scientific, educational, or professional roles as psychologists. Areas covered include but are not limited to the clinical, counselling, and school practice of psychology; research; teaching; supervision of trainees; public service; policy development; social intervention; development of assessment instruments; conducting assessments; educational counselling; organizational consulting; forensic activities; program design and evaluation; and administration. This *Ethics Code* applies to these activities across a variety of contexts, such as in person, postal, telephone, Internet, and other electronic transmissions. These activities shall be distinguished from the purely private conduct of psychologists, which is not within the purview of the *Ethics Code*. Membership in the APA commits members and student affiliates to comply with the standards of the APA *Ethics Code* and to the rules and procedures used to enforce them. Lack of awareness or misunderstanding of an Ethical Standard is not itself a defence to a charge of unethical conduct. The procedures for filing, investigating, and resolving complaints of unethical conduct are described in the current *Rules and Procedures of the APA Ethics*

Committee. APA may impose sanctions on its members for violations of the standards of the *Ethics Code,* including termination of APA membership, and may notify other bodies and individuals of its actions. Actions that violate the standards of the *Ethics Code* may also lead to the imposition of sanctions on psychologists or students, whether or not they are APA members, by bodies other than APA, including state psychological associations, other professional groups, psychology boards, other state or federal agencies, and payors for health services. In addition, APA may take action against a member after his or her conviction of a felony, expulsion or suspension from an affiliated state psychological association, or suspension or loss of licensure. When the sanction to be imposed by APA is less than expulsion, the 2001 *Rules and Procedures* do not guarantee an opportunity for an in-person hearing, but generally provide that complaints will be resolved only on the basis of a submitted record. The *Ethics Code* is intended to provide guidance for psychologists and standards of professional conduct that can be applied by the APA and by other bodies that choose to adopt them. The *Ethics Code* is not intended to be a basis of civil liability. Whether a psychologist has violated the *Ethics Code* standards does not by itself determine whether the psychologist is legally liable in a court action, whether a contract is enforceable, or whether other legal consequences occur. The modifiers used in some of the standards of this *Ethics Code* (e.g., *reasonably, appropriate, potentially*) are included in the standards when they would (1) allow professional judgment on the part of psychologists, (2) eliminate injustice or inequality that would occur without the modifier, (3) ensure applicability across the broad range of activities conducted by psychologists, or (4) guard against a set of rigid rules that might be quickly outdated. As used in this *Ethics Code,* the term *reasonable* means the prevailing professional judgment of psychologists engaged in similar activities in similar circumstances, given the knowledge the psychologist had or should have had at the time. In the process of making decisions regarding their professional behaviour, psychologists must consider this *Ethics Code* in addition to applicable laws and psychology board regulations. In applying the *Ethics Code* to their professional work, psychologists may consider other materials and guidelines that have been adopted or endorsed by scientific and professional psychological organizations and the dictates of their own conscience, as well as consult with others within the field. If this *Ethics Code* establishes a higher standard of conduct than is required by law, psychologists must meet the higher ethical standard. If psychologists' ethical responsibilities conflict with law, regulations, or other governing legal authority, psychologists make known their commitment to this *Ethics Code* and take steps to resolve the conflict in a responsible manner. If the conflict is unresolvable via such means, psychologists may adhere to the requirements of the law, regulations, or other governing authority in keeping with basic principles of human rights.

PREAMBLE

Psychologists are committed to increasing scientific and professional knowledge of behaviour and people's understanding of themselves and others and to the use of such knowledge to improve the condition of individuals, organizations, and society. Psychologists respect and protect civil and human rights and the central importance of freedom of inquiry and expression in research, teaching, and publication. They strive to help the public in developing informed judgments and choices concerning human behaviour. In doing so, they perform many roles, such as researcher, educator, diagnostician, therapist, supervisor, consultant, administrator, social interventionist, and expert witness. This *Ethics Code* provides a common set of principles and standards upon which psychologists build their professional and scientific work. This *Ethics Code* is intended to provide specific standards to cover most situations encountered by psychologists. It has as its goals the welfare and protection of the individuals and groups with whom psychologists work and the education of members, students, and the public regarding ethical standards of the discipline. The development of a dynamic set of ethical standards for psychologists' work-related conduct requires a personal commitment and lifelong effort to act ethically; to encourage ethical behaviour by students, supervisees, employees, and colleagues; and to consult with others concerning ethical problems.

GENERAL PRINCIPLES

This section consists of General Principles. General Principles, as opposed to Ethical Standards, are aspirational in nature. Their intent is to guide and inspire psychologists toward the very highest ethical ideals of the profession. General Principles, in contrast to Ethical Standards, do not represent obligations and should not form the basis for imposing sanctions. Relying upon General Principles for either of these reasons distorts both their meaning and purpose.

Principle A: Beneficence and Nonmaleficence

Psychologists strive to benefit those with whom they work and take care to do no harm. In their professional actions, psychologists seek to safeguard the welfare and rights of those with whom they interact professionally and other affected persons, and the welfare of animal subjects of research. When conflicts occur among psychologists' obligations or concerns, they attempt to resolve these conflicts in a responsible fashion that avoids or minimizes harm. Because psychologists' scientific and professional judgments and actions may affect the lives of others, they are alert to and guard against personal, financial, social, organizational, or political factors that might lead to misuse of their influence. Psychologists strive to be aware of the possible effect of their own physical and mental health on their ability to help those with whom they work.

Principle B: Fidelity and Responsibility

Psychologists establish relationships of trust with those with whom they work. They are aware of their professional and scientific responsibilities to society and to the specific communities in which they work. Psychologists uphold professional standards of conduct, clarify their professional roles and obligations, accept appropriate responsibility for their behaviour, and seek to manage conflicts of interest that could lead to exploitation or harm. Psychologists consult with, refer to, or cooperate with other professionals and institutions to the extent needed to serve the best interests of those with whom they work. They are concerned about the ethical compliance of their colleagues' scientific and professional conduct. Psychologists strive to contribute a portion of their professional time for little or no compensation or personal advantage.

Principle C: Integrity

Psychologists seek to promote accuracy, honesty, and truthfulness in the science, teaching, and practice of psychology. In these activities psychologists do not steal, cheat, or engage in fraud, subterfuge, or intentional misrepresentation of fact. Psychologists strive to keep their promises and to avoid unwise or unclear commitments. In situations in which deception may be ethically justifiable to maximize benefits and minimize harm, psychologists have a serious obligation to consider the need for, the possible consequences of, and their responsibility to correct any resulting mistrust or other harmful effects that arise from the use of such techniques.

Principle D: Justice

Psychologists recognize that fairness and justice entitle all persons to access to and benefit from the contributions of psychology and to equal quality in the processes, procedures, and services being conducted by psychologists. Psychologists exercise reasonable judgment and take precautions to ensure that their potential biases, the boundaries of their competence, and the limitations of their expertise do not lead to or condone unjust practices.

Principle E: Respect for People's Rights and Dignity

Psychologists respect the dignity and worth of all people, and the rights of individuals to privacy, confidentiality, and self-determination. Psychologists are aware that special safeguards may be necessary to protect the rights and welfare of persons or communities whose vulnerabilities impair autonomous decision making. Psychologists are aware of and respect cultural, individual, and role differences, including those based on age, gender, gender identity, race, ethnicity, culture, national origin, religion, sexual orientation, disability, language, and socioeconomic status and consider these factors when working with members of such groups. Psychologists try to eliminate the effect on their work of biases based on those factors, and they do not knowingly participate in or condone activities of others based upon such prejudices.

ETHICAL STANDARDS

1. Resolving Ethical Issues

1.01 Misuse of Psychologists' Work

If psychologists learn of misuse or misrepresentation of their work, they take reasonable steps to correct or minimize the misuse or misrepresentation.

1.02 Conflicts between Ethics and Law, Regulations, or Other Governing Legal Authority

If psychologists' ethical responsibilities conflict with law, regulations, or other governing legal authority, psychologists make known their commitment to the *Ethics Code* and take steps to resolve the conflict. If the conflict is unresolvable via such means, psychologists may adhere to the requirements of the law, regulations, or other governing legal authority.

1.03 Conflicts between Ethics and Organizational Demands

If the demands of an organization with which psychologists are affiliated or for whom they are working conflict with this *Ethics Code,* psychologists clarify the nature of the conflict, make known their commitment to the *Ethics Code,* and to the extent feasible, resolve the conflict in a way that permits adherence to the *Ethics Code.*

1.04 Informal Resolution of Ethical Violations

When psychologists believe that there may have been an ethical violation by another psychologist, they attempt to resolve the issue by bringing it to the attention of that individual, if an informal resolution appears appropriate and the intervention does not violate any confidentiality rights that may be involved. (See also Standards 1.02, Conflicts between Ethics and Law, Regulations, or Other Governing Legal Authority, and 1.03, Conflicts between Ethics and Organizational Demands.)

1.05 Reporting Ethical Violations

If an apparent ethical violation has substantially harmed or is likely to substantially harm a person or organization and is not appropriate for informal resolution under Standard 1.04, Informal Resolution of Ethical Violations, or is not resolved properly in that fashion, psychologists take further action appropriate to the situation. Such action might include referral to state or national committees on professional ethics, to state licensing boards, or to the appropriate institutional authorities. This standard does not apply when an intervention would violate confidentiality rights or when psychologists have been retained to review the work of another psychologist whose professional conduct is in question. (See also Standard 1.02, Conflicts between Ethics and Law, Regulations, or Other Governing Legal Authority.)

1.06 Cooperating with Ethics Committees

Psychologists cooperate in ethics investigations, proceedings, and resulting requirements of the APA or any affiliated state psychological association to which they belong. In doing so, they address any confidentiality issues. Failure to cooperate is itself an ethics violation. However, making a request for deferment of adjudication of an ethics complaint pending the outcome of litigation does not alone constitute noncooperation.

1.07 Improper Complaints

Psychologists do not file or encourage the filing of ethics complaints that are made with reckless disregard for or willful ignorance of facts that would disprove the allegation.

1.08 Unfair Discrimination against Complainants and Respondents

Psychologists do not deny persons employment, advancement, admissions to academic or other programs, tenure, or promotion, based solely upon their having made or their being the subject of an ethics complaint. This does not preclude taking action based upon the outcome of such proceedings or considering other appropriate information.

2. Competence

2.01 Boundaries of Competence

(a) Psychologists provide services, teach, and conduct research with populations and in areas only within the boundaries of their competence, based on their education, training, supervised experience, consultation, study, or professional experience. (b) Where scientific or professional knowledge in the discipline of psychology establishes that an understanding of factors associated with age, gender, gender identity, race, ethnicity, culture, national origin, religion, sexual orientation, disability, language, or socioeconomic status is essential for effective implementation of their services or research, psychologists have or obtain the training, experience, consultation, or supervision necessary to ensure the competence of their services, or they make appropriate referrals, except as provided in Standard 2.02, Providing Services in Emergencies. (c) Psychologists planning to provide services, teach, or conduct research involving populations, areas, techniques, or technologies new to them undertake relevant education, training, supervised experience, consultation, or study. (d) When psychologists are asked to provide services to individuals for whom appropriate mental health services are not available and for which psychologists have not obtained the competence necessary, psychologists with closely related prior training or experience may provide such services in order to ensure that services are not denied if they make a reasonable effort to obtain the competence required by using relevant research, training, consultation, or study. (e) In those emerging areas in which generally recognized standards for preparatory training do not yet exist, psychologists nevertheless take reasonable steps to ensure the competence of their work and to protect clients/patients, students, supervisees, research participants, organizational clients, and others from harm. (f) When assuming forensic roles, psychologists are or become reasonably familiar with the judicial or administrative rules governing their roles.

2.02 Providing Services in Emergencies

In emergencies, when psychologists provide services to individuals for whom other mental health services are not available and for which psychologists have not obtained the necessary training, psychologists may provide such services in order to ensure that services are not denied. The services are discontinued as soon as the emergency has ended or appropriate services are available.

2.03 Maintaining Competence

Psychologists undertake ongoing efforts to develop and maintain their competence.

2.04 Bases for Scientific and Professional Judgments

Psychologists' work is based upon established scientific and professional knowledge of the discipline. (See also Standards 2.01e, Boundaries of Competence, and 10.01b, Informed Consent to Therapy.)

2.05 Delegation of Work to Others

Psychologists who delegate work to employees, supervisees, or research or teaching assistants or who use the services of others, such as interpreters, take reasonable steps to (1) avoid delegating such work to persons who have a multiple relationship with those being served that would likely lead to exploitation or loss of objectivity; (2) authorize only those responsibilities that such persons can be expected to perform competently on the basis of their education, training, or experience, either independently or with the level of supervision being provided; and (3) see that such persons perform these services competently. (See also Standards 2.02, Providing Services in Emergencies; 3.05, Multiple Relationships; 4.01, Maintaining Confidentiality; 9.01, Bases for Assessments; 9.02, Use of Assessments; 9.03, Informed Consent in Assessments; and 9.07, Assessment by Unqualified Persons.)

2.06 Personal Problems and Conflicts

(a) Psychologists refrain from initiating an activity when they know or should know that there is a substantial likelihood that their personal problems will prevent them from performing their work-related activities in a competent manner. (b) When psychologists become aware of personal problems that may interfere with their performing work-related duties adequately, they take appropriate measures, such as obtaining professional consultation or assistance, and determine whether they should limit, suspend, or terminate their work-related duties. (See also Standard 10.10, Terminating Therapy.)

3. Human Relations

3.01 Unfair Discrimination

In their work-related activities, psychologists do not engage in unfair discrimination based on age, gender, gender identity, race, ethnicity, culture, national origin, religion, sexual orientation, disability, socioeconomic status, or any basis proscribed by law.

3.02 Sexual Harassment

Psychologists do not engage in sexual harassment. Sexual harassment is sexual solicitation, physical advances, or verbal or nonverbal conduct that is sexual in nature, that occurs in connection with the psychologist's activities or roles as a psychologist, and that either (1) is unwelcome, is offensive, or creates a hostile workplace or educational environment, and the psychologist knows or is told this or (2) is sufficiently severe or intense to be abusive to a reasonable person in the context. Sexual harassment can consist of a single intense or severe act or of multiple persistent or pervasive acts. (See also Standard 1.08, Unfair Discrimination against Complainants and Respondents.)

3.03 Other Harassment

Psychologists do not knowingly engage in behaviour that is harassing or demeaning to persons with whom they interact in their work based on factors such as those persons' age, gender, gender identity, race, ethnicity, culture, national origin, religion, sexual orientation, disability, language, or socioeconomic status.

3.04 Avoiding Harm

Psychologists take reasonable steps to avoid harming their clients/patients, students, supervisees, research participants, organizational clients, and others with whom they work, and to minimize harm where it is foreseeable and unavoidable.

3.05 Multiple Relationships

(a) A multiple relationship occurs when a psychologist is in a professional role with a person and (1) at the same time is in another role with the same person, (2) at the same time is in a relationship with a person closely associated with or related to the person with whom the psychologist has the professional relationship, or (3) promises to enter into another relationship in the future with the person or a person closely associated with or related to the person. A psychologist refrains from entering into a multiple relationship if the multiple relationship could reasonably be expected to impair the psychologist's objectivity, competence, or effectiveness in performing his or her functions as a psychologist, or otherwise risks exploitation or harm to the person with whom the professional relationship exists. Multiple relationships that would not reasonably be expected to cause impairment or risk exploitation or harm are not unethical. (b) If a psychologist finds that, due to unforeseen factors, a potentially harmful multiple relationship has arisen, the psychologist takes reasonable steps to resolve it with due regard for the best interests of the affected person and maximal compliance with the *Ethics Code.* (c) When psychologists are required by law, institutional policy, or extraordinary circumstances to serve in more than one role in judicial or administrative proceedings, at the outset they clarify role expectations and the extent of confidentiality and thereafter as changes occur. (See also Standards 3.04, Avoiding Harm, and 3.07, Third-Party Requests for Services.)

3.06 Conflict of Interest

Psychologists refrain from taking on a professional role when personal, scientific, professional, legal, financial, or other interests or relationships could reasonably be expected to (1) impair their objectivity, competence, or effectiveness in performing their functions as psychologists or (2) expose the person or organization with whom the professional relationship exists to harm or exploitation.

3.07 Third-Party Requests for Services

When psychologists agree to provide services to a person or entity at the request of a third party, psychologists attempt to clarify at the outset of the service the nature of the relationship with all individuals or organizations involved. This clarification includes the role of the psychologist (e.g., therapist, consultant, diagnostician, or expert witness), an identification of who is the client, the probable uses of the services provided or the information obtained, and the fact that there may be limits to confidentiality. (See also Standards 3.05, Multiple Relationships, and 4.02, Discussing the Limits of Confidentiality.)

3.08 Exploitative Relationships

Psychologists do not exploit persons over whom they have supervisory, evaluative, or other authority such as clients/patients, students, supervisees, research participants, and employees. (See also Standards 3.05, Multiple Relationships; 6.04, Fees and Financial Arrangements; 6.05, Barter with Clients/Patients; 7.07, Sexual Relationships with Students and Supervisees; 10.05, Sexual Intimacies with Current Therapy Clients/Patients; 10.06, Sexual Intimacies with Relatives or Significant Others of Current Therapy Clients/Patients; 10.07, Therapy with Former Sexual Partners; and 10.08, Sexual Intimacies with Former Therapy Clients/Patients.)

3.09 Cooperation with Other Professionals

When indicated and professionally appropriate, psychologists cooperate with other professionals in order to serve their clients/patients effectively and appropriately. (See also Standard 4.05, Disclosures.)

3.10 Informed Consent

(a) When psychologists conduct research or provide assessment, therapy, counselling, or consulting services in person or via electronic transmission or other forms of communication, they obtain the informed consent of the individual or individuals using language that is reasonably understandable to that person or persons except when conducting such activities without consent is mandated by law or governmental regulation or as otherwise provided in this *Ethics Code*. (See also Standards 8.02, Informed Consent to Research; 9.03, Informed Consent in Assessments; and 10.01, Informed Consent to Therapy.) (b) For persons who are legally incapable of giving informed consent, psychologists nevertheless (1) provide an appropriate explanation, (2) seek the individual's assent, (3) consider such persons' preferences and best interests, and (4) obtain appropriate permission from a legally authorized person, if such substitute consent is permitted or required by law. When consent by a legally authorized person is not permitted or required by law, psychologists take reasonable steps to protect the individual's rights and welfare. (c) When psychological services are court ordered or otherwise mandated, psychologists inform the individual of the nature of the anticipated services, including whether the services are court ordered or mandated and any limits of confidentiality, before proceeding. (d) Psychologists appropriately document written or oral consent, permission, and assent. (See also Standards 8.02, Informed Consent to Research; 9.03, Informed Consent in Assessments; and 10.01, Informed Consent to Therapy.)

3.11 Psychological Services Delivered to or through Organizations

(a) Psychologists delivering services to or through organizations provide information beforehand to clients and when appropriate those directly affected by the services about (1) the nature and objectives of the services, (2) the intended recipients, (3) which of the individuals are clients, (4) the relationship the psychologist will have with each person and the organization, (5) the probable uses of services provided and information obtained, (6) who will have access to the information, and (7) limits of confidentiality. As soon as feasible, they provide information about the results and conclusions of such services to appropriate persons. (b) If psychologists will be precluded by law or by organizational roles from providing such information to particular individuals or groups, they so inform those individuals or groups at the outset of the service.

3.12 Interruption of Psychological Services

Unless otherwise covered by contract, psychologists make reasonable efforts to plan for facilitating services in the event that psychological services are interrupted by factors such as the psychologist's illness, death, unavailability, relocation, or retirement or by the client's/patient's relocation or financial limitations. (See also Standard 6.02c, Maintenance, Dissemination, and Disposal of Confidential Records of Professional and Scientific Work.)

4. Privacy and Confidentiality

4.01 Maintaining Confidentiality

Psychologists have a primary obligation and take reasonable precautions to protect confidential information obtained through or stored in any medium, recognizing that the extent and limits of confidentiality may be regulated by law or established by institutional rules or professional or scientific relationship. (See also Standard 2.05, Delegation of Work to Others.)

4.02 Discussing the Limits of Confidentiality

(a) Psychologists discuss with persons (including, to the extent feasible, persons who are legally incapable of giving informed consent and their legal representatives) and organizations with whom they establish a scientific or professional relationship (1) the relevant limits of confidentiality and (2) the foreseeable uses of the information generated through their psychological activities. (See also Standard 3.10, Informed Consent.) (b) Unless it is not feasible or is contraindicated, the discussion of confidentiality occurs at the outset of the relationship and thereafter as new circumstances may warrant. (c) Psychologists who offer services, products, or information via electronic transmission inform clients/patients of the risks to privacy and limits of confidentiality.

4.03 Recording

Before recording the voices or images of individuals to whom they provide services, psychologists obtain permission from all such persons or their legal representatives. (See also Standards 8.03, Informed Consent for Recording Voices and Images in Research; 8.05, Dispensing with Informed Consent for Research; and 8.07, Deception in Research.)

4.04 Minimizing Intrusions on Privacy

(a) Psychologists include in written and oral reports and consultations, only information germane to the purpose for which the communication is made. (b) Psychologists discuss confidential information obtained in their work only for appropriate scientific or professional purposes and only with persons clearly concerned with such matters.

4.05 Disclosures

(a) Psychologists may disclose confidential information with the appropriate consent of the organizational client, the individual client/patient, or another legally authorized person on behalf of the client/patient unless prohibited by law. (b) Psychologists disclose confidential information without the consent of the individual only as mandated by law, or where permitted by law for a valid purpose such as to (1) provide needed professional services; (2) obtain appropriate professional consultations; (3) protect the client/patient, psychologist, or others from harm; or (4) obtain payment for services from a client/patient, in which instance disclosure is limited to the minimum that is necessary to achieve the purpose. (See also Standard 6.04e, Fees and Financial Arrangements.)

4.06 Consultations

When consulting with colleagues, (1) psychologists do not disclose confidential information that reasonably could lead to the identification of a client/patient, research participant, or other person or organization with whom they have a confidential relationship unless they have obtained the prior consent of the person or organization or the disclosure cannot be avoided, and (2) they disclose information only to the extent necessary to achieve the purposes of the consultation. (See also Standard 4.01, Maintaining Confidentiality.)

4.07 Use of Confidential Information for Didactic or Other Purposes

Psychologists do not disclose in their writings, lectures, or other public media, confidential, personally identifiable information concerning their clients/patients, students, research participants, organizational clients, or other recipients of their services that they obtained during the course of their work, unless (1) they take reasonable steps to disguise the person or organization, (2) the person or organization has consented in writing, or (3) there is legal authorization for doing so.

5. Advertising and Other Public Statements

5.01 Avoidance of False or Deceptive Statements

(a) Public statements include but are not limited to paid or unpaid advertising, product endorsements, grant applications, licensing applications, other credentialing applications, brochures, printed matter, directory listings, personal resumes or curricula vitae, or comments for use in media such as print or electronic transmission, statements in legal proceedings, lectures and public oral presentations, and published materials. Psychologists do not knowingly make public statements that are false, deceptive, or fraudulent concerning their research, practice, or other work activities or those of persons or organizations with which they are affiliated. (b) Psychologists do not make false, deceptive, or fraudulent statements concerning (1) their training, experience, or competence; (2) their academic degrees; (3) their credentials; (4) their institutional or association affiliations; (5) their services; (6) the scientific or clinical basis for, or results or degree of success of, their services; (7) their fees; or (8) their publications or research findings. (c) Psychologists claim degrees as credentials for their health services only if those degrees (1) were earned from a regionally accredited educational institution or (2) were the basis for psychology licensure by the state in which they practise.

5.02 Statements by Others

(a) Psychologists who engage others to create or place public statements that promote their professional practice, products, or activities retain professional responsibility for such statements. (b) Psychologists do not compensate employees of press, radio, television, or other communication media in return for publicity in a news item. (See also Standard 1.01, Misuse of Psychologists' Work.) (c) A paid advertisement relating to psychologists' activities must be identified or clearly recognizable as such.

5.03 Descriptions of Workshops and Non-Degree-Granting Educational Programs

To the degree to which they exercise control, psychologists responsible for announcements, catalogues, brochures, or advertisements describing workshops, seminars, or other non-degree-granting educational programs ensure that they accurately describe the audience for which the program is intended, the educational objectives, the presenters, and the fees involved.

5.04 Media Presentations

When psychologists provide public advice or comment via print, Internet, or other electronic transmission, they take precautions to ensure that statements (1) are based on their professional knowledge, training, or experience in accord with appropriate psychological literature and practice; (2) are otherwise consistent with this *Ethics Code;* and (3) do not indicate that a professional relationship has been established with the recipient. (See also Standard 2.04, Bases for Scientific and Professional Judgments.)

5.05 Testimonials

Psychologists do not solicit testimonials from current therapy clients/patients or other persons who because of their particular circumstances are vulnerable to undue influence.

5.06 In-Person Solicitation

Psychologists do not engage, directly or through agents, in uninvited in-person solicitation of business from actual or potential therapy clients/patients or other persons who because of their particular circumstances are vulnerable to undue influence. However, this prohibition does not preclude (1) attempting to implement appropriate collateral contacts for the purpose of benefiting an already engaged therapy client/patient or (2) providing disaster or community outreach services.

6. Record Keeping and Fees

6.01 Documentation of Professional and Scientific Work and Maintenance of Records

Psychologists create, and to the extent the records are under their control, maintain, disseminate, store, retain, and dispose of records and data relating to their professional and scientific work in order to (1) facilitate provision of services later by them or by other professionals, (2) allow for replication of research design and analyses, (3) meet institutional requirements, (4) ensure accuracy of billing and payments, and (5) ensure compliance with law. (See also Standard 4.01, Maintaining Confidentiality.)

6.02 Maintenance, Dissemination, and Disposal of Confidential Records of Professional and Scientific Work

(a) Psychologists maintain confidentiality in creating, storing, accessing, transferring, and disposing of records under their control, whether these are written, automated, or in any other medium. (See also Standards 4.01, Maintaining Confidentiality, and 6.01, Documentation of Professional and Scientific Work and Maintenance of Records.) (b) If confidential information concerning recipients of psychological services is entered into databases or systems of records available to persons whose access has not been consented to by the recipient, psychologists use coding or other techniques to avoid the inclusion of personal identifiers. (c) Psychologists make plans in advance to facilitate the appropriate transfer and to protect the confidentiality of records and data in the event of psychologists' withdrawal from positions or practice. (See also Standards 3.12, Interruption of Psychological Services, and 10.09, Interruption of Therapy.)

6.03 Withholding Records for Nonpayment

Psychologists may not withhold records under their control that are requested and needed for a client's/patient's emergency treatment solely because payment has not been received.

6.04 Fees and Financial Arrangements

(a) As early as is feasible in a professional or scientific relationship, psychologists and recipients of psychological services reach an agreement specifying compensation and billing arrangements. (b) Psychologists' fee practices are consistent with law. (c) Psychologists do not misrepresent their fees. (d) If limitations to services can be anticipated because of limitations in financing, this is discussed with the recipient of services as early as is feasible. (See also Standards 10.09, Interruption of Therapy, and 10.10, Terminating Therapy.) (e) If the recipient of services does not pay for services as agreed, and if psychologists intend to use collection agencies or legal measures to collect the fees, psychologists first inform the person that such measures will be taken and provide that person an opportunity to make prompt payment. (See also Standards 4.05, Disclosures; 6.03, Withholding Records for Nonpayment; and 10.01, Informed Consent to Therapy.)

6.05 Barter with Clients/Patients

Barter is the acceptance of goods, services, or other nonmonetary remuneration from clients/patients in return for psychological services. Psychologists may barter only if (1) it is not clinically contraindicated, and (2) the resulting arrangement is not exploitative. (See also Standards 3.05, Multiple Relationships, and 6.04, Fees and Financial Arrangements.)

6.06 Accuracy in Reports to Payers and Funding Sources

In their reports to payers for services or sources of research funding, psychologists take reasonable steps to ensure the accurate reporting of the nature of the service provided or research conducted, the fees, charges, or payments, and where applicable, the identity of the provider, the findings, and the diagnosis. (See also Standards 4.01, Maintaining Confidentiality; 4.04, Minimizing Intrusions on Privacy; and 4.05, Disclosures.)

6.07 Referrals and Fees

When psychologists pay, receive payment from, or divide fees with another professional, other than in an employer–employee relationship, the payment to each is based on the services provided (clinical, consultative, administrative, or other) and is not based on the referral itself. (See also Standard 3.09, Cooperation with Other Professionals.)

7. Education and Training

7.01 Design of Education and Training Programs

Psychologists responsible for education and training programs take reasonable steps to ensure that the programs are designed to provide the appropriate knowledge and proper experiences, and to meet the requirements for licensure, certification, or other goals for which claims are made by the program. (See also Standard 5.03, Descriptions of Workshops and Non-Degree-Granting Educational Programs.)

7.02 Descriptions of Education and Training Programs

Psychologists responsible for education and training programs take reasonable steps to ensure that there is a current and accurate description of the program content (including participation in required course- or program-related counselling, psychotherapy, experiential groups, consulting projects, or community service), training goals and objectives, stipends and benefits, and requirements that must be met for satisfactory completion of the program. This information must be made readily available to all interested parties.

7.03 Accuracy in Teaching

(a) Psychologists take reasonable steps to ensure that course syllabi are accurate regarding the subject matter to be covered, bases for evaluating progress, and the nature of course experiences. This standard does not preclude an instructor from modifying course content or requirements when the instructor considers it pedagogically necessary or desirable, so long as students are made aware of these modifications in a manner that enables them to fulfill course requirements. (See also Standard 5.01, Avoidance of False or Deceptive Statements.) (b) When engaged in teaching or training, psychologists present psychological information accurately. (See also Standard 2.03, Maintaining Competence.)

7.04 Student Disclosure of Personal Information

Psychologists do not require students or supervisees to disclose personal information in course- or program-related activities, either orally or in writing, regarding sexual history, history of abuse and neglect, psychological treatment, and relationships with parents, peers, and spouses or significant others except if (1) the program or training facility has clearly identified this requirement in its admissions and program materials or (2) the information is necessary to evaluate or obtain assistance for students whose personal problems could reasonably be judged to be preventing them from performing their training- or professionally related activities in a competent manner or to be posing a threat to the students or others.

7.05 Mandatory Individual or Group Therapy

(a) When individual or group therapy is a program or course requirement, psychologists responsible for that program allow students in undergraduate and graduate programs the option of selecting such therapy from practitioners unaffiliated with the program. (See also Standard 7.02, Descriptions of Education and Training Programs.) (b) Faculty who are or are likely to be responsible for evaluating students' academic performance do not themselves provide that therapy. (See also Standard 3.05, Multiple Relationships.)

7.06 Assessing Student and Supervisee Performance

(a) In academic and supervisory relationships, psychologists establish a timely and specific process for providing feedback to students and supervisees. Information regarding the process is provided to the student at the beginning of supervision. (b) Psychologists evaluate students and supervisees on the basis of their actual performance on relevant and established program requirements.

7.07 Sexual Relationships with Students and Supervisees

Psychologists do not engage in sexual relationships with students or supervisees who are in their department, agency, or training centre or over whom psychologists have or are likely to have evaluative authority. (See also Standard 3.05, Multiple Relationships.)

8. Research and Publication

8.01 Institutional Approval

When institutional approval is required, psychologists provide accurate information about their research proposals and obtain approval prior to conducting the research. They conduct the research in accordance with the approved research protocol.

8.02 Informed Consent to Research

(a) When obtaining informed consent as required in Standard 3.10, Informed Consent, psychologists inform participants about (1) the purpose of the research, expected duration, and procedures; (2) their right to decline to participate and to withdraw from the research once participation has begun; (3) the foreseeable consequences of declining or withdrawing; (4) reasonably foreseeable factors that may be expected to influence their willingness to participate such as potential risks, discomfort, or adverse effects; (5) any prospective research benefits; (6) limits of confidentiality; (7) incentives for participation; and (8) whom to contact for questions about the research and research participants' rights. They provide opportunity for the prospective participants to ask questions and receive answers. (See also Standards 8.03, Informed Consent for Recording Voices and Images in Research; 8.05, Dispensing with Informed Consent for Research; and 8.07, Deception in Research.) (b) Psychologists conducting intervention research involving the use of experimental treatments clarify to participants at the outset of the research (1) the experimental nature of the treatment; (2) the services that will or will not be available to the control group(s) if appropriate; (3) the means by which assignment to treatment and control groups will be made; (4) available treatment alternatives if an individual does not wish to participate in the research or wishes to withdraw once a study has begun; and (5) compensation for or monetary costs of participating including, if appropriate, whether reimbursement from the participant or a third-party payer will be sought. (See also Standard 8.02a, Informed Consent to Research.)

8.03 Informed Consent for Recording Voices and Images in Research

Psychologists obtain informed consent from research participants prior to recording their voices or images for data collection unless (1) the research consists solely of naturalistic observations in public places, and it is not anticipated that the recording will be used in a manner that could cause personal identification or harm, or (2) the research design includes deception, and consent for the use of the recording is obtained during debriefing. (See also Standard 8.07, Deception in Research.)

8.04 Client/Patient, Student, and Subordinate Research Participants

(a) When psychologists conduct research with clients/patients, students, or subordinates as participants, psychologists take steps to protect the prospective participants from adverse consequences of declining or withdrawing from participation. (b) When research participation is a course requirement or an opportunity for extra credit, the prospective participant is given the choice of equitable alternative activities.

8.05 Dispensing with Informed Consent for Research

Psychologists may dispense with informed consent only (1) where research would not reasonably be assumed to create distress or harm and involves (a) the study of normal educational practices, curricula, or classroom management methods conducted in educational settings; (b) only anonymous questionnaires, naturalistic observations, or archival research for which disclosure of responses would not place participants at risk of criminal or civil liability or damage their financial standing, employability, or reputation, and confidentiality is protected; or (c) the study of factors related to job or organization effectiveness conducted in organizational settings for which there is no risk to participants' employability, and confidentiality is protected or (2) where otherwise permitted by law or federal or institutional regulations.

8.06 Offering Inducements for Research Participation

(a) Psychologists make reasonable efforts to avoid offering excessive or inappropriate financial or other inducements for research participation when such inducements are likely to coerce participation. (b) When offering professional services as an inducement for research participation, psychologists clarify the nature of the services, as well as the risks, obligations, and limitations. (See also Standard 6.05, Barter with Clients/Patients.)

8.07 Deception in Research

(a) Psychologists do not conduct a study involving deception unless they have determined that the use of deceptive techniques is justified by the study's significant prospective scientific, educational, or applied value and that effective nondeceptive alternative procedures are not feasible. (b) Psychologists do not deceive prospective participants about research that is reasonably expected to cause physical pain or severe emotional distress. (c) Psychologists explain any deception that is an integral feature of the design and conduct of an experiment to participants as early as is feasible, preferably at the conclusion of their participation, but no later than at the conclusion of the data collection, and permit participants to withdraw their data. (See also Standard 8.08, Debriefing.)

8.08 Debriefing

(a) Psychologists provide a prompt opportunity for participants to obtain appropriate information about the nature, results, and conclusions of the research, and they take reasonable steps to correct any misconceptions that participants may have of which the psychologists are aware. (b) If scientific or humane values justify delaying or withholding this information, psychologists take reasonable measures to reduce the risk of harm. (c) When psychologists become aware that research procedures have harmed a participant, they take reasonable steps to minimize the harm.

8.09 Humane Care and Use of Animals in Research

(a) Psychologists acquire, care for, use, and dispose of animals in compliance with current federal, state, and local laws and regulations, and with professional standards. (b) Psychologists trained in research methods and experienced in the care of laboratory animals supervise all procedures involving animals and are responsible for ensuring appropriate consideration of their comfort, health, and humane treatment. (c) Psychologists ensure that all individuals under their supervision who are using animals have received instruction in research methods and in the care, maintenance, and handling of the species being used, to the extent appropriate to their role. (See also Standard 2.05, Delegation of Work to Others.) (d) Psychologists make reasonable efforts to minimize the discomfort, infection, illness, and pain of animal subjects. (e) Psychologists use a procedure subjecting animals to pain, stress, or privation only when an alternative procedure is unavailable and the goal is justified by its prospective scientific, educational, or applied value. (f) Psychologists perform surgical procedures under appropriate anesthesia and follow techniques to avoid infection and minimize pain during and after surgery. (g) When it is appropriate that an animal's life be terminated, psychologists proceed rapidly, with an effort to minimize pain and in accordance with accepted procedures.

8.10 Reporting Research Results

(a) Psychologists do not fabricate data. (See also Standard 5.01a, Avoidance of False or Deceptive Statements.) (b) If psychologists discover significant errors in their published data, they take reasonable steps to correct such errors in a correction, retraction, erratum, or other appropriate publication means.

8.11 Plagiarism

Psychologists do not present portions of another's work or data as their own, even if the other work or data source is cited occasionally.

8.12 Publication Credit

(a) Psychologists take responsibility and credit, including authorship credit, only for work they have actually performed or to which they have substantially contributed. (See also Standard 8.12b, Publication Credit.) (b) Principal authorship and other publication credits accurately reflect the relative scientific or professional contributions of the individuals involved, regardless of their relative status. Mere possession of an institutional position, such as department chair, does not justify authorship credit. Minor contributions to the research or to the writing for publications are acknowledged appropriately, such as in footnotes or in an introductory statement. (c) Except under exceptional circumstances, a student is listed as principal author on any multiple-authored article that is substantially based on the student's doctoral dissertation. Faculty advisers discuss publication credit with students as early as feasible and throughout the research and publication process as appropriate. (See also Standard 8.12b, Publication Credit.)

8.13 Duplicate Publication of Data

Psychologists do not publish, as original data, data that have been previously published. This does not preclude republishing data when they are accompanied by proper acknowledgment.

8.14 Sharing Research Data for Verification

(a) After research results are published, psychologists do not withhold the data on which their conclusions are based from other competent professionals who seek to verify the substantive claims through reanalysis and who intend to use such data only for that purpose, provided that the confidentiality of the participants can be protected and unless legal rights concerning proprietary data preclude their release. This does not preclude psychologists from requiring that such individuals or groups be responsible for costs associated with the provision of such information. (b) Psychologists who request data from other psychologists to verify the substantive claims through reanalysis may use shared data only for the declared purpose. Requesting psychologists obtain prior written agreement for all other uses of the data.

8.15 Reviewers

Psychologists who review material submitted for presentation, publication, grant, or research proposal review respect the confidentiality of and the proprietary rights in such information of those who submitted it.

9. Assessment

9.01 Bases for Assessments

(a) Psychologists base the opinions contained in their recommendations, reports, and diagnostic or evaluative statements, including forensic testimony, on information and techniques sufficient to substantiate their findings. (See also Standard 2.04, Bases for Scientific and Professional Judgments.) (b) Except as noted in 9.01c, psychologists provide opinions of the psychological characteristics of individuals only after they have conducted an examination of the individuals adequate to support their statements or conclusions. When, despite reasonable efforts, such an examination is not practical, psychologists document the efforts they made and the result of those efforts, clarify the probable impact of their limited information on the reliability and validity of their opinions, and appropriately limit the nature and extent of their conclusions or recommendations. (See also Standards 2.01, Boundaries of Competence, and 9.06, Interpreting Assessment Results.) (c) When psychologists conduct a record review or provide consultation or supervision and an individual examination is not warranted or necessary for the opinion, psychologists explain this and the sources of information on which they based their conclusions and recommendations.

9.02 Use of Assessments

(a) Psychologists administer, adapt, score, interpret, or use assessment techniques, interviews, tests, or instruments in a manner and for purposes that are appropriate in light of the research on or evidence of the usefulness and proper application of the techniques. (b) Psychologists use assessment instruments whose validity and reliability have been established for use with members of the population tested. When such validity or reliability has not been established, psychologists describe the strengths and limitations of test results and interpretation. (c) Psychologists use assessment methods that are appropriate to an individual's language preference and competence, unless the use of an alternative language is relevant to the assessment issues.

9.03 Informed Consent in Assessments

(a) Psychologists obtain informed consent for assessments, evaluations, or diagnostic services, as described in Standard 3.10, Informed Consent, except when (1) testing is mandated by law or governmental regulations; (2) informed consent is implied because testing is conducted as a routine educational, institutional, or organizational activity (e.g., when participants voluntarily agree to assessment when applying for a job); or (3) one purpose of the testing is to evaluate decisional capacity. Informed consent includes an explanation of the nature and purpose of the assessment, fees, involvement of third parties, and limits of confidentiality and sufficient opportunity for the client/patient to ask questions and receive answers. (b) Psychologists inform persons with questionable capacity to consent or for whom testing is mandated by law or governmental regulations about the nature and purpose of the proposed assessment services, using language that is reasonably understandable to the person being assessed. (c) Psychologists using the services of an interpreter obtain informed consent from the client/patient to use that interpreter, ensure that confidentiality of test results and test security are maintained, and include in their recommendations, reports, and diagnostic or evaluative statements, including forensic testimony, discussion of any limitations on the data obtained. (See also Standards 2.05, Delegation of Work to Others; 4.01, Maintaining Confidentiality; 9.01, Bases for Assessments; 9.06, Interpreting Assessment Results; and 9.07, Assessment by Unqualified Persons.)

9.04 Release of Test Data

(a) The term *test data* refers to raw and scaled scores, client/patient responses to test questions or stimuli, and psychologists' notes and recordings concerning client/patient statements and behaviour during an examination. Those portions of test materials that include client/patient responses are included in the definition of *test data*. Pursuant to a client/patient release, psychologists provide test data to the client/patient or other persons identified in the release. Psychologists may refrain from releasing test data to protect a client/patient or others from substantial harm or misuse or misrepresentation of the data or the test, recognizing that in many instances release of confidential information under these circumstances is regulated by law. (See also Standard 9.11, Maintaining Test Security.) (b) In the absence of a client/patient release, psychologists provide test data only as required by law or court order.

9.05 Test Construction

Psychologists who develop tests and other assessment techniques use appropriate psychometric procedures and current scientific or professional knowledge for test design, standardization, validation, reduction or elimination of bias, and recommendations for use.

9.06 Interpreting Assessment Results

When interpreting assessment results, including automated interpretations, psychologists take into account the purpose of the assessment as well as the various test factors, test-taking abilities, and other characteristics of the person being assessed, such as situational, personal, linguistic, and cultural differences, that might affect psychologists' judgments or reduce the accuracy of their interpretations. They indicate any significant limitations of their interpretations. (See also Standards 2.01b and c, Boundaries of Competence, and 3.01, Unfair Discrimination.)

9.07 Assessment by Unqualified Persons

Psychologists do not promote the use of psychological assessment techniques by unqualified persons, except when such use is conducted for training purposes with appropriate supervision. (See also Standard 2.05, Delegation of Work to Others.)

9.08 Obsolete Tests and Outdated Test Results

(a) Psychologists do not base their assessment or intervention decisions or recommendations on data or test results that are outdated for the current purpose. (b) Psychologists do not base such decisions or recommendations on tests and measures that are obsolete and not useful for the current purpose.

9.09 Test Scoring and Interpretation Services

(a) Psychologists who offer assessment or scoring services to other professionals accurately describe the purpose, norms, validity, reliability, and applications of the procedures and any special qualifications applicable to their use. (b) Psychologists select scoring and interpretation services (including automated services) on the basis of evidence of the validity of the program and procedures as well as on other appropriate considerations. (See also Standard 2.01b and c, Boundaries of Competence.) (c) Psychologists retain responsibility for the appropriate application, interpretation, and use of assessment instruments, whether they score and interpret such tests themselves or use automated or other services.

9.10 Explaining Assessment Results

Regardless of whether the scoring and interpretation are done by psychologists, by employees or assistants, or by automated or other outside services, psychologists take reasonable steps to ensure that explanations of results are given to the individual or designated representative unless the nature of the relationship precludes provision of an explanation of results (such as in some organizational consulting, pre-employment or security screenings, and forensic evaluations), and this fact has been clearly explained to the person being assessed in advance.

9.11 Maintaining Test Security

The term *test materials* refers to manuals, instruments, protocols, and test questions or stimuli and does not include *test data* as defined in Standard 9.04, Release of Test Data. Psychologists make reasonable efforts to maintain the integrity and security of test materials and other assessment techniques consistent with law and contractual obligations, and in a manner that permits adherence to this *Ethics Code*.

10. Therapy

10.01 Informed Consent to Therapy

(a) When obtaining informed consent to therapy as required in Standard 3.10, Informed Consent, psychologists inform clients/patients as early as is feasible in the therapeutic relationship about the nature and anticipated course of therapy, fees, involvement of third parties, and limits of confidentiality and provide sufficient opportunity for the client/patient to ask questions and receive answers. (See also Standards 4.02, Discussing the Limits of Confidentiality, and 6.04, Fees and Financial Arrangements.) (b) When obtaining informed consent for treatment for which generally recognized techniques and procedures have not been established, psychologists inform their clients/patients of the developing nature of the treatment, the potential risks involved, alternative treatments that may be available, and the voluntary nature of their participation. (See also Standards 2.01e, Boundaries of Competence, and 3.10, Informed Consent.) (c) When the therapist is a trainee and the legal responsibility for the treatment provided resides with the supervisor, the client/patient, as part of the informed consent procedure, is informed that the therapist is in training and is being supervised and is given the name of the supervisor.

10.02 Therapy Involving Couples or Families

(a) When psychologists agree to provide services to several persons who have a relationship (such as spouses, significant others, or parents and children), they take reasonable steps to clarify at the outset (1) which of the individuals are clients/patients and (2) the relationship the psychologist will have with each person. This clarification includes the psychologist's role and the probable uses of the services provided or the information obtained. (See also Standard 4.02, Discussing the Limits of Confidentiality.) (b) If it becomes apparent that psychologists may be called on to perform potentially conflicting roles (such as family therapist and then witness for one party in divorce proceedings), psychologists take reasonable steps to clarify and modify, or withdraw from, roles appropriately. (See also Standard 3.05c, Multiple Relationships.)

10.03 Group Therapy

When psychologists provide services to several persons in a group setting, they describe at the outset the roles and responsibilities of all parties and the limits of confidentiality.

10.04 Providing Therapy to Those Served by Others

In deciding whether to offer or provide services to those already receiving mental health services elsewhere, psychologists carefully consider the treatment issues and the potential client's/patient's welfare. Psychologists discuss these issues with the client/patient or another legally authorized person on behalf of the client/patient in order to minimize the risk of confusion and conflict, consult with the other service providers when appropriate, and proceed with caution and sensitivity to the therapeutic issues.

10.05 Sexual Intimacies with Current Therapy Clients/Patients

Psychologists do not engage in sexual intimacies with current therapy clients/patients.

10.06 Sexual Intimacies with Relatives or Significant Others of Current Therapy Clients/Patients

Psychologists do not engage in sexual intimacies with individuals they know to be close relatives, guardians, or significant others of current clients/patients. Psychologists do not terminate therapy to circumvent this standard.

10.07 Therapy with Former Sexual Partners

Psychologists do not accept as therapy clients/patients persons with whom they have engaged in sexual intimacies.

10.08 Sexual Intimacies with Former Therapy Clients/Patients

(a) Psychologists do not engage in sexual intimacies with former clients/patients for at least two years after cessation or termination of therapy. (b) Psychologists do not engage in sexual intimacies with former clients/patients even after a two-year interval except in the most unusual circumstances. Psychologists who engage in such activity after the two years following cessation or termination of therapy and of having no sexual contact with the former client/patient bear the burden of demonstrating that there has been no exploitation, in light of all relevant factors, including (1) the amount of time that has passed since therapy terminated; (2) the nature, duration, and intensity of the therapy; (3) the circumstances of termination; (4) the client's/patient's personal history; (5) the client's/patient's current mental status; (6) the likelihood of adverse impact on the client/patient; and (7) any statements or actions made by the therapist during the course of therapy suggesting or inviting the possibility of a posttermination sexual or romantic relationship with the client/patient. (See also Standard 3.05, Multiple Relationships.)

10.09 Interruption of Therapy

When entering into employment or contractual relationships, psychologists make reasonable efforts to provide for orderly and appropriate resolution of responsibility for client/patient care in the event that the employment or contractual relationship ends, with paramount consideration given to the welfare of the client/patient. (See also Standard 3.12, Interruption of Psychological Services.)

10.10 Terminating Therapy

(a) Psychologists terminate therapy when it becomes reasonably clear that the client/patient no longer needs the service, is not likely to benefit, or is being harmed by continued service. (b) Psychologists may terminate therapy when threatened or otherwise endangered by the client/patient or another person with whom the client/patient has a relationship. (c) Except where precluded by the actions of clients/patients or third-party payors, prior to termination psychologists provide pretermination counselling and suggest alternative service providers as appropriate.

This version of the APA *Ethics Code* was adopted by the American Psychological Association's Council of Representatives during its meeting, August 21, 2002, and is effective beginning June 1, 2003. Inquiries concerning the substance or interpretation of the APA *Ethics Code* should be addressed to the Director, Office of Ethics, American Psychological Association, 750 First Street, NE, Washington, DC 20002-4242. The *Ethics Code* and information regarding the *Code* can be found on the APA website, http://www.apa.org/ethics. The standards in this *Ethics Code* will be used to adjudicate complaints brought concerning alleged conduct occurring on or after the effective date. Complaints regarding conduct occurring prior to the effective date will be adjudicated on the basis of the version of the *Ethics Code* that was in effect at the time the conduct occurred. The APA has previously published its *Ethics Code* as follows: American Psychological Association. (1953). *Ethical standards of psychologists*. Washington, DC: Author. American Psychological Association. (1959). Ethical standards of psychologists. *American Psychologist, 14,* 279–282. American Psychological Association. (1963). Ethical standards of psychologists. *American Psychologist, 18,* 56–60. American Psychological Association. (1968). Ethical standards of psychologists. *American*

Psychologist, 23, 357–361. American Psychological Association. (1977, March). Ethical standards of psychologists. *APA Monitor,* 22–23. American Psychological Association. (1979). *Ethical standards of psychologists.* Washington, DC: Author. American Psychological Association. (1981). Ethical principles of psychologists. *American Psychologist, 36,* 633–638. American Psychological Association. (1990). Ethical principles of psychologists (Amended June 2, 1989). *American Psychologist, 45,* 390–395. American Psychological Association. (1992). Ethical principles of psychologists and code of conduct. *American Psychologist, 47,* 1597–1611. Request copies of the APA's *Ethical Principles of Psychologists and Code of Conduct* from the APA Order Department, 750 First Street, NE, Washington, DC 20002-4242, or phone (202) 336-5510.

Appendix D:
Canadian Code of Ethics for Psychologists

Every discipline that has relatively autonomous control over its entry requirements, training, development of knowledge, standards, methods, and practices does so only within the context of a contract with the society in which it functions. This social contract is based on attitudes of mutual respect and trust, with society granting support for the autonomy of a discipline in exchange for a commitment by the discipline to do everything it can to assure that its members act ethically in conducting the affairs of the discipline within society; in particular, a commitment to try to assure that each member will place the welfare of the society and individual members of that society above the welfare of the discipline and its own members. By virtue of this social contract, psychologists have a higher duty of care to members of society than the general duty of care that all members of society have to each other.

The Canadian Psychological Association recognizes its responsibility to help assure ethical behaviour and attitudes on the part of psychologists. Attempts to assure ethical behaviour and attitudes include articulating ethical principles, values, and standards; promoting those principles, values, and standards through education, peer modelling, and consultation; developing and implementing methods to help psychologists monitor the ethics of their behaviour and attitudes; adjudicating complaints of unethical behaviour; and taking corrective action when warranted.

This *Code* articulates ethical principles, values, and standards to guide all members of the Canadian Psychological Association, whether scientists, practitioners, or scientist practitioners, or whether acting in a research, direct service, teaching, student, trainee, administrative, management, employer, employee, supervisory, consultative, peer review, editorial, expert witness, social policy, or any other role related to the discipline of psychology.

STRUCTURE AND DERIVATION OF *CODE*

Structure. Four ethical principles, to be considered and balanced in ethical decision making, are presented. Each principle is followed by a statement of those values that are included in and give definition to the principle. Each values statement is followed by a list of ethical standards that illustrate the application of the specific principle and values to the activities of psychologists. The standards range from minimal behavioural expectations (e.g., Standards

I.28, II.28, III.33, IV.27) to more idealized, but achievable, attitudinal and behavioural expectations (e.g., Standards I.12, II.12, III.10, IV.6).

Derivation. The four principles represent those ethical principles used most consistently by Canadian psychologists to resolve hypothetical ethical dilemmas sent to them by the CPA Committee on Ethics during the initial development of the *Code*. In addition to the responses provided by Canadian psychologists, the values statements and ethical standards have been derived from interdisciplinary and international ethics codes, provincial and specialty codes of conduct, and ethics literature.

WHEN PRINCIPLES CONFLICT

- **Principle I: Respect for the Dignity of Persons.** This principle, with its emphasis on moral rights, generally should be given the highest weight, except in circumstances in which there is a clear and imminent danger to the physical safety of any person.
- **Principle II: Responsible Caring.** This principle generally should be given the second-highest weight. Responsible caring requires competence and should be carried out only in ways that respect the dignity of persons.
- **Principle III: Integrity in Relationships.** This principle generally should be given the third-highest weight. Psychologists are expected to demonstrate the highest integrity in all of their relationships. However, in rare circumstances, values such as openness and straightforwardness might need to be subordinated to the values contained in the Principles of Respect for the Dignity of Persons and Responsible Caring.
- **Principle IV: Responsibility to Society.** This principle generally should be given the lowest weight of the four principles when it conflicts with one or more of them. Although it is necessary and important to consider responsibility to society in every ethical decision, adherence to this principle must be subject to and guided by Respect for the Dignity of Persons, Responsible Caring, and Integrity in Relationships. When a person's welfare appears to conflict with benefits to society, it is often possible to find ways of working for the benefit of society that do not violate respect and responsible caring for the person. However, if this is not possible, the dignity and well-being of a person should not be sacrificed to a vision of the greater good of society, and greater weight must be given to respect and responsible caring for the person.

Even with the above ordering of the principles, psychologists will be faced with ethical dilemmas that are difficult to resolve. In these circumstances, psychologists are expected to engage in an ethical decision-making process that is explicit enough to bear public scrutiny. In some cases, resolution might be a matter of personal conscience. However, decisions of personal conscience are also expected to be the result of a decision-making process that is based on a reasonably coherent set of ethical principles and that can bear public scrutiny. If the psychologist can demonstrate that every reasonable effort was made to apply the ethical principles of this *Code* and resolution of the conflict has had to depend on the personal conscience of the psychologist, such a psychologist would be deemed to have followed this *Code*.

THE ETHICAL DECISION-MAKING PROCESS

The ethical decision-making process might occur very rapidly, leading to an easy resolution of an ethical issue. This is particularly true of issues for which clear-cut guidelines or standards exist and for which there is no conflict between principles. On the other hand, some ethical issues (particularly those in which ethical principles conflict) are not easily resolved, might be emotionally distressful, and might require time-consuming deliberation.

The following basic steps typify approaches to ethical decision making:

1. Identification of the individuals and groups potentially affected by the decision.
2. Identification of ethically relevant issues and practices, including the interests, rights, and any relevant characteristics of the individuals and groups involved and of the system or circumstances in which the ethical problem arose.
3. Consideration of how personal biases, stresses, or self-interest might influence the development of or choice between courses of action.
4. Development of alternative courses of action.
5. Analysis of likely short-term, ongoing, and long-term risks and benefits of each course of action on the individual(s)/group(s) involved or likely to be affected (e.g., client, client's family or employees, employing institution, students, research participants, colleagues, the discipline, society, self).
6. Choice of course of action after conscientious application of existing principles, values, and standards.
7. Action, with a commitment to assume responsibility for the consequences of the action.
8. Evaluation of the results of the course of action.
9. Assumption of responsibility for consequences of action, including correction of negative consequences, if any, or re-engaging in the decision-making process if the ethical issue is not resolved.
10. Appropriate action, as warranted and feasible, to prevent future occurrences of the dilemma (e.g., communication and problem solving with colleagues; changes in procedures and practices).

Psychologists engaged in time-consuming deliberation are encouraged and expected to consult with parties affected by the ethical problem, when appropriate, and with colleagues and/or advisory bodies when such persons can add knowledge or objectivity to the decision-making process. Although the decision for action remains with the individual psychologist, the seeking and consideration of such assistance reflects an ethical approach to ethical decision making.

USES OF THE *CODE*

This *Code* is intended to guide psychologists in their everyday conduct, thinking, and planning, and in the resolution of ethical dilemmas; that is, it advocates the practice of both proactive and reactive ethics.

The *Code* also is intended to serve as an umbrella document for the development of codes of conduct or other more specific codes. For example, the *Code* could be used as an ethical framework for the identification of behaviours that would be considered enforceable in a jurisdiction, the violation of which would constitute misconduct; or, jurisdictions could identify those standards in the *Code* that would be considered of a more serious nature and, therefore, reportable and subject to possible discipline. In addition, the principles and values could be used to help specialty areas develop standards that are specific to those areas. Some work in this direction has already occurred within CPA (e.g., *Guidelines for the Use of Animals in Research and Instruction in Psychology, Guidelines for Non-Discriminatory Practice, Guidelines for Psychologists in Addressing Recovered Memories*). The principles and values incorporated into this *Code,* insofar as they come to be reflected in other documents guiding the behaviour of psychologists, will reduce inconsistency and conflict between documents.

A third use of the *Code* is to assist in the adjudication of complaints against psychologists. A body charged with this responsibility is required to investigate allegations, judge whether unacceptable behaviour has occurred, and determine what corrective action should be taken. In judging whether unacceptable conduct has occurred, many jurisdictions refer to a code of conduct. Some complaints, however, are about conduct that is not addressed directly in a code of conduct. The *Code* provides an ethical framework for determining whether the complaint is of enough concern, either at the level of the individual psychologist or at the level of the profession as a whole, to warrant corrective action (e.g., discipline of the individual psychologist, general educational activities for members, or incorporation into the code of conduct). In determining corrective action for an individual psychologist, one of the judgments the adjudicating body needs to make is whether an individual conscientiously engaged in an ethical decision-making process and acted in good faith, or whether there was a negligent or willful disregard of ethical principles. The articulation of the ethical decision-making process contained in this *Code* provides guidance for making such judgments.

RESPONSIBILITY OF THE INDIVIDUAL PSYCHOLOGIST

The discipline's contract with society commits the discipline and its members to act as a moral community that develops its ethical awareness and sensitivity, educates new members in the ethics of the discipline, manages its affairs and its members in an ethical manner, is as self-correcting as possible, and is accountable both internally and externally.

However, responsibility for ethical action depends foremost on the integrity of each individual psychologist; that is, on each psychologist's commitment to behave as ethically as possible in every situation. Acceptance to membership in the Canadian Psychological Association, a scientific and professional association of psychologists, commits members:

1. To adhere to the Association's *Code* in all current activities as a psychologist.
2. To apply conscientiously the ethical principles and values of the *Code* to new and emerging areas of activity.
3. To assess and discuss ethical issues and practices with colleagues on a regular basis.
4. To bring to the attention of the Association ethical issues that require clarification or the development of new guidelines or standards.
5. To bring concerns about possible unethical actions by a psychologist directly to the psychologist when the action appears to be primarily a lack of sensitivity, knowledge, or experience, and attempt to reach an agreement on the issue and, if needed, on the appropriate action to be taken.

6. To bring concerns about possible unethical actions of a more serious nature (e.g., actions that have caused or could cause serious harm, or actions that are considered misconduct in the jurisdiction) to the person(s) or body(ies) best suited to investigating the situation and to stopping or offsetting the harm.
7. To consider seriously others' concerns about one's own possibly unethical actions and attempt to reach an agreement on the issue and, if needed, take appropriate action.
8. In bringing or in responding to concerns about possible unethical actions, not to be vexatious or malicious.
9. To cooperate with duly constituted committees of the Association that are concerned with ethics and ethical conduct.

RELATIONSHIP OF *CODE* TO PERSONAL BEHAVIOUR

This *Code* is intended to guide and regulate only those activities a psychologist engages in by virtue of being a psychologist. There is no intention to guide or regulate a psychologist's activities outside of this context. Personal behaviour becomes a concern of the discipline only if it is of such a nature that it undermines public trust in the discipline as a whole or if it raises questions about the psychologist's ability to carry out appropriately his/her responsibilities as a psychologist.

RELATIONSHIP OF *CODE* TO PROVINCIAL REGULATORY BODIES

In exercising its responsibility to articulate ethical principles, values, and standards for those who wish to become and remain members in good standing, the Canadian Psychological Association recognizes the multiple memberships that some psychologists have (both regulatory and voluntary). The *Code* has attempted to encompass and incorporate those ethical principles most prevalent in the discipline as a whole, thereby minimizing the possibility of variance with provincial/territorial regulations and guidelines. Psychologists are expected to respect the requirements of their provincial/territorial regulatory bodies. Such requirements might define particular behaviours that constitute misconduct, are reportable to the regulatory body, and/or are subject to discipline.

DEFINITION OF TERMS

For the purposes of this *Code:*

a. **"Psychologist"** means any person who is a Fellow, Member, Student Affiliate or Foreign Affiliate of the Canadian Psychological Association, or a member of any psychology voluntary association or regulatory body adopting this *Code*. (Readers are reminded that provincial/territorial jurisdictions might restrict the legal use of the term psychologist in their jurisdiction and that such restrictions are to be honoured.)
b. **"Client"** means an individual, family, or group (including an organization or community) receiving service from a psychologist.
c. Clients, research participants, students, and any other persons with whom psychologists come in contact in the course of their work, are **"independent"** if they can

independently contract or give informed consent. Such persons are **"partially dependent"** if the decision to contract or give informed consent is shared between two or more parties (e.g., parents and school boards, workers and Workers' Compensation Boards, adult members of a family). Such persons are considered to be **"fully dependent"** if they have little or no choice about whether or not to receive service or participate in an activity (e.g., patients who have been involuntarily committed to a psychiatric facility, or very young children involved in a research project).

d. **"Others"** means any persons with whom psychologists come in contact in the course of their work. This may include, but is not limited to clients seeking help with individual, family, organizational, industrial, or community issues; research participants; employees; students; trainees; supervisees; colleagues; employers; third-party payers; and, members of the general public.

e. **"Legal or civil rights"** means those rights protected under laws and statutes recognized by the province or territory in which the psychologist is working.

f. **"Moral rights"** means fundamental and inalienable human rights that might or might not be fully protected by existing laws and statutes. Of particular significance to psychologists, for example, are rights to distributive justice; fairness and due process; and developmentally appropriate privacy, self-determination, and personal liberty. Protection of some aspects of these rights might involve practices that are not contained or controlled within current laws and statutes. Moral rights are not limited to those mentioned in this definition.

g. **"Unjust discrimination"** or **"unjustly discriminatory"** means activities that are prejudicial or promote prejudice to persons because of their culture, nationality, ethnicity, colour, race, religion, sex, gender, marital status, sexual orientation, physical or mental abilities, age, socioeconomic status, or any other preference or personal characteristic, condition, or status.

h. **"Sexual harassment"** includes either or both of the following: (i) The use of power or authority in an attempt to coerce another person to engage in or tolerate sexual activity. Such uses include explicit or implicit threats of reprisal for noncompliance, or promises of reward for compliance. (ii) Engaging in deliberate and/or repeated unsolicited sexually oriented comments, anecdotes, gestures, or touching, if such behaviours are offensive and unwelcome; create an offensive, hostile, or intimidating working, learning, or service environment; or can be expected to be harmful to the recipient.[1]

i. The **"discipline of psychology"** refers to the scientific and applied methods and knowledge of psychology, and to the structures and procedures used by its members for conducting their work in relationship to society, to members of the public, to students or trainees, and to each other.

REVIEW SCHEDULE

To maintain the relevance and responsiveness of this *Code,* it will be reviewed regularly by the CPA Board of Directors, and revised as needed. You are invited to forward comments and suggestions, at any time, to the CPA office. In addition to psychologists, this invitation is extended to all readers, including members of the public and other disciplines.

[1]Adapted from: Canadian Psychological Association. (1985). *Guidelines for the elimination of sexual harassment.* Ottawa: Author.

PRINCIPLE I: RESPECT FOR THE DIGNITY OF PERSONS

Values Statement

In the course of their work as scientists, practitioners, or scientist-practitioners, psychologists come into contact with many different individuals and groups, including: research participants; clients seeking help with individual, family, organizational, industrial, or community issues; students; trainees; supervisees; employees; business partners; business competitors; colleagues; employers; third party payers; and the general public.

In these contacts, psychologists accept as fundamental the principle of respect for the dignity of persons; that is, the belief that each person should be treated primarily as a person or an end in him/herself, not as an object or a means to an end. In so doing, psychologists acknowledge that all persons have a right to have their innate worth as human beings appreciated and that this worth is not dependent upon their culture, nationality, ethnicity, colour, race, religion, sex, gender, marital status, sexual orientation, physical or mental abilities, age, socioeconomic status, or any other preference or personal characteristic, condition, or status.

Although psychologists have a responsibility to respect the dignity of all persons with whom they come in contact in their role as psychologists, the nature of their contract with society demands that their greatest responsibility be to those persons in the most vulnerable position. Normally, persons directly receiving or involved in the psychologist's activities are in such a position (e.g., research participants, clients, students). This responsibility is almost always greater than their responsibility to those indirectly involved (e.g., employers, third-party payers, the general public).

Adherence to the concept of moral rights is an essential component of respect for the dignity of persons. Rights to privacy, self-determination, personal liberty, and natural justice are of particular importance to psychologists, and they have a responsibility to protect and promote these rights in all of their activities. As such, psychologists have a responsibility to develop and follow procedures for informed consent, confidentiality, fair treatment, and due process that are consistent with those rights.

As individual rights exist within the context of the rights of others and of responsible caring (see Principle II), there might be circumstances in which the possibility of serious detrimental consequences to themselves or others, a diminished capacity to be autonomous, or a court order, would disallow some aspects of the rights to privacy, self-determination, and personal liberty. Indeed, such circumstances might be serious enough to create a duty to warn or protect others (see Standards I.45 and II.39). However, psychologists still have a responsibility to respect the rights of the person(s) involved to the greatest extent possible under the circumstances, and to do what is necessary and reasonable to reduce the need for future disallowances.

Psychologists recognize that, although all persons possess moral rights, the manner in which such rights are promoted, protected, and exercised varies across communities and cultures. For instance, definitions of what is considered private vary, as does the role of families and other community members in personal decision making. In their work, psychologists acknowledge and respect such differences, while guarding against clear violations of moral rights.

In addition, psychologists recognize that as individual, family, group, or community vulnerabilities increase, or as the power of persons to control their environment or their lives decreases, psychologists have an increasing responsibility to seek ethical advice and to establish safeguards to protect the rights of the persons involved. For this reason, psychologists consider it their responsibility to increase safeguards to protect and promote the rights of persons involved in their activities proportionate to the degree of dependency and the lack of voluntary initiation. For example, this would mean that there would be more safeguards to protect and promote the rights of fully dependent persons than partially dependent persons, and more safeguards for partially dependent than independent persons.

Respect for the dignity of persons also includes the concept of distributive justice. With respect to psychologists, this concept implies that all persons are entitled to benefit equally from the contributions of psychology and to equal quality in the processes, procedures, and services being conducted by psychologists, regardless of the person's characteristics, condition, or status. Although individual psychologists might specialize and direct their activities to particular populations, or might decline to engage in activities based on the limits of their competence or acknowledgment of problems in some relationships, psychologists must not exclude persons on a capricious or unjustly discriminatory basis.

By virtue of the social contract that the discipline has with society, psychologists have a higher duty of care to members of society than the general duty of care all members of society have to each other. However, psychologists are entitled to protect themselves from serious violations of their own moral rights (e.g., privacy, personal liberty) in carrying out their work as psychologists.

Ethical Standards

In adhering to the Principle of Respect for the Dignity of Persons, psychologists would:

General respect

I.1 Demonstrate appropriate respect for the knowledge, insight, experience, and areas of expertise of others.

I.2 Not engage publicly (e.g., in public statements, presentations, research reports, or with clients) in degrading comments about others, including demeaning jokes based on such characteristics as culture, nationality, ethnicity, colour, race, religion, sex, gender, or sexual orientation.

I.3 Strive to use language that conveys respect for the dignity of persons as much as possible in all written or oral communication.

I.4 Abstain from all forms of harassment, including sexual harassment.

General rights

I.5 Avoid or refuse to participate in practices disrespectful of the legal, civil, or moral rights of others.

I.6 Refuse to advise, train, or supply information to anyone who, in the psychologist's judgment, will use the knowledge or skills to infringe on human rights.

I.7 Make every reasonable effort to ensure that psychological knowledge is not misused, intentionally or unintentionally, to infringe on human rights.

I.8 Respect the right of research participants, clients, employees, supervisees, students, trainees, and others to safeguard their own dignity.

Non-discrimination

I.9 Not practice, condone, facilitate, or collaborate with any form of unjust discrimination.

I.10 Act to correct practices that are unjustly discriminatory.

I.11 Seek to design research, teaching, practice, and business activities in such a way that they contribute to the fair distribution of benefits to individuals and groups, and that they do not unfairly exclude those who are vulnerable or might be disadvantaged.

Fair treatment/due process

I.12 Work and act in a spirit of fair treatment to others.

I.13 Help to establish and abide by due process or other natural justice procedures for employment, evaluation, adjudication, editorial, and peer review activities.

I.14 Compensate others fairly for the use of their time, energy, and knowledge, unless such compensation is refused in advance.

I.15 Establish fees that are fair in light of the time, energy, and knowledge of the psychologist and any associates or employees, and in light of the market value of the product or service. (Also see Standard IV.12.)

Informed consent

I.16 Seek as full and active participation as possible from others in decisions that affect them, respecting and integrating as much as possible their opinions and wishes.

I.17 Recognize that informed consent is the result of a process of reaching an agreement to work collaboratively, rather than of simply having a consent form signed.

I.18 Respect the expressed wishes of persons to involve others (e.g., family members, community members) in their decision making regarding informed consent. This would include respect for written and clearly expressed unwritten advance directives.

I.19 Obtain informed consent from all independent and partially dependent persons for any psychological services provided to them except in circumstances of urgent need (e.g., disaster or other crisis). In urgent circumstances, psychologists would proceed with the assent of such persons, but fully informed consent would be obtained as soon as possible. (Also see Standard I.29.)

I.20 Obtain informed consent for all research activities that involve obtrusive measures, invasion of privacy, more than minimal risk of harm, or any attempt to change the behaviour of research participants.

I.21 Establish and use signed consent forms that specify the dimensions of informed consent or that acknowledge that such dimensions have been explained and are understood, if such forms are required by law or if such forms are desired by the psychologist, the person(s) giving consent, or the organization for whom the psychologist works.

I.22 Accept and document oral consent, in situations in which signed consent forms are not acceptable culturally or in which there are other good reasons for not using them.

I.23 Provide, in obtaining informed consent, as much information as reasonable or prudent persons would want to know before making a decision or consenting to the activity. The psychologist would relay this information in language that the persons understand (including providing translation into another language, if necessary) and would take whatever reasonable steps are needed to ensure that the information was, in fact, understood.

I.24 Ensure, in the process of obtaining informed consent, that at least the following points are understood: purpose and nature of the activity; mutual responsibilities; confidentiality protections and limitations; likely benefits and risks; alternatives; the likely consequences of non-action; the option to refuse or withdraw at any time, without prejudice; over what period of time the consent applies; and how to rescind consent if desired. (Also see Standards III.23–30.)

I.25 Provide new information in a timely manner, whenever such information becomes available and is significant enough that it reasonably could be seen as relevant to the original or ongoing informed consent.

I.26 Clarify the nature of multiple relationships to all concerned parties before obtaining consent, if providing services to or conducting research at the request or for the use of third parties. This would include, but not be limited to: the purpose of the service or research; the reasonably anticipated use that will be made of information collected; and, the limits on confidentiality. Third parties may include schools, courts, government agencies, insurance companies, police, and special funding bodies.

Freedom of consent

I.27 Take all reasonable steps to ensure that consent is not given under conditions of coercion, undue pressure, or undue reward. (Also see Standard III.32.)

I.28 Not proceed with any research activity, if consent is given under any condition of coercion, undue pressure, or undue reward. (Also see Standard III.32.)

I.29 Take all reasonable steps to confirm or re-establish freedom of consent, if consent for service is given under conditions of duress or conditions of extreme need.

I.30 Respect the right of persons to discontinue participation or service at any time, and be responsive to non-verbal indications of a desire to discontinue if a person has difficulty with verbally communicating such a desire (e.g., young children, verbally disabled persons) or, due to culture, is unlikely to communicate such a desire orally.

Protections for vulnerable persons

I.31 Seek an independent and adequate ethical review of human rights issues and protections for any research involving members of vulnerable groups, including persons of diminished capacity to give informed consent, before making a decision to proceed.

I.32 Not use persons of diminished capacity to give informed consent in research studies, if the research involved may be carried out equally well with persons who have a fuller capacity to give informed consent.

I.33 Seek to use methods that maximize the understanding and ability to consent of persons of diminished capacity to give informed consent, and that reduce the need for a substitute decision maker.

I.34 Carry out informed consent processes with those persons who are legally responsible or appointed to give informed consent on behalf of persons not competent to consent on their own behalf, seeking to ensure respect for any previously expressed preferences of persons not competent to consent.

I.35 Seek willing and adequately informed participation from any person of diminished capacity to give informed consent, and proceed without this assent only if the service or research activity is considered to be of direct benefit to that person.

I.36 Be particularly cautious in establishing the freedom of consent of any person who is in a dependent relationship to the psychologist (e.g., student, employee). This may include, but is not limited to, offering that person an alternative activity to fulfill their educational or employment goals, or offering a range of research studies or experience opportunities from which the person can select, none of which is so onerous as to be coercive.

Privacy

I.37 Seek and collect only information that is germane to the purpose(s) for which consent has been obtained.

I.38 Take care not to infringe, in research, teaching, or service activities, on the personally, developmentally, or culturally defined private space of individuals or groups, unless clear permission is granted to do so.

I.39 Record only that private information necessary for the provision of continuous, coordinated service, or for the goals of the particular research study being conducted, or that is required or justified by law. (Also see Standards IV.17 and IV.18.)

I.40 Respect the right of research participants, employees, supervisees, students, and trainees to reasonable personal privacy.

I.41 Collect, store, handle, and transfer all private information, whether written or unwritten (e.g., communication during service provision, written records, e-mail or fax communication, computer files, videotapes), in a way that attends to the needs for privacy and security. This would include having adequate plans for records in circumstances of one's own serious illness, termination of employment, or death.

I.42 Take all reasonable steps to ensure that records over which they have control remain personally identifiable only as long as necessary in the interests of those to whom they refer and/or to the research project for which they were collected, or as required or justified by law (e.g., the possible need to defend oneself against future allegations), and render anonymous or destroy any records under their control that no longer need to be personally identifiable. (Also see Standards IV.17 and IV.18.)

Confidentiality

I.43 Be careful not to relay information about colleagues, colleagues' clients, research participants, employees, supervisees, students, trainees, and members of organizations, gained in the process of their activities as psychologists, that the psychologist has reason to believe is considered confidential by those persons, except as required or justified by law. (Also see Standards IV.17 and IV.18.)

I.44 Clarify what measures will be taken to protect confidentiality, and what responsibilities family, group, and community members have for the protection of each other's confidentiality, when engaged in services to or research with individuals, families, groups, or communities.

I.45 Share confidential information with others only with the informed consent of those involved, or in a manner that the persons involved cannot be identified, except as required or justified by law, or in circumstances of actual or possible serious physical harm or death. (Also see Standards II.39, IV.17, and IV.18.)

I.46 Encourage others, in a manner consistent with this *Code,* to respect the dignity of persons and to expect respect for their own dignity.

I.47 Assume overall responsibility for the scientific and professional activities of their assistants, employees, students, supervisees, and trainees with regard to Respect for the Dignity of Persons, all of whom, however, incur similar obligations.

PRINCIPLE II: RESPONSIBLE CARING

Values Statement

A basic ethical expectation of any discipline is that its activities will benefit members of society or, at least, do no harm. Therefore, psychologists demonstrate an active concern for the welfare of any individual, family, group, or community with whom they relate in their role as psychologists. This concern includes both those directly involved and those indirectly involved in their activities. However, as with Principle I, psychologists' greatest responsibility is to protect the welfare of those in the most vulnerable position. Normally, persons directly involved in their activities (e.g., research participants, clients, students) are in such a position. Psychologists' responsibility to those indirectly involved (e.g., employers, third-party payers, the general public) normally is secondary.

As persons usually consider their own welfare in their personal decision making, obtaining informed consent (see Principle I) is one of the best methods for ensuring that their welfare will be protected. However, it is only when such consent is combined with the responsible caring of the psychologist that there is considerable ethical protection of the welfare of the person(s) involved.

Responsible caring leads psychologists to take care to discern the potential harm and benefits involved, to predict the likelihood of their occurrence, to proceed only if the potential benefits outweigh the potential harms, to develop and use methods that will minimize harms and maximize benefits, and to take responsibility for correcting clearly harmful effects that have occurred as a direct result of their research, teaching, practice, or business activities.

In order to carry out these steps, psychologists recognize the need for competence and self-knowledge. They consider incompetent action to be unethical per se, as it is unlikely to be of benefit and likely to be harmful. They engage only in those activities in which they have competence or for which they are receiving supervision, and they perform their activities as competently as possible. They acquire, contribute to, and use the existing knowledge most relevant to the best interests of those concerned. They also engage in self-reflection regarding how their own values, attitudes, experiences, and social context (e.g., culture, ethnicity, colour, religion, sex, gender, sexual orientation, physical and mental abilities, age, and socioeconomic status) influence their actions, interpretations, choices, and recommendations. This is done with the intent of increasing the probability that their activities will benefit and not harm the individuals, families, groups, and communities to whom they relate in their role as psychologists. Psychologists define harm and benefit in terms of both physical and psychological dimensions. They are concerned about such factors as: social, family, and community relationships; personal and cultural identity; feelings of self-worth, fear, humiliation, interpersonal trust, and cynicism; self-knowledge and general knowledge; and such factors as physical safety, comfort, pain, and injury. They are concerned about immediate, short-term, and long-term effects.

Responsible caring recognizes and respects (e.g., through obtaining informed consent) the ability of individuals, families, groups, and communities to make decisions for themselves and to care for themselves and each other. It does not replace or undermine such ability, nor does it substitute one person's opinion about what is in the best interests of another person for that other person's competent decision making. However, psychologists recognize that, as vulnerabilities increase or as power to control one's own life decreases, psychologists have an increasing responsibility to protect the well-being of the individual, family, group, or community involved. For this reason, as in Principle I, psychologists consider it their responsibility to increase safeguards proportionate to the degree of dependency and the lack of voluntary initiation on the part of the persons involved. However, for Principle II, the safeguards are for the well-being of persons rather than for the rights of persons.

Psychologists' treatment and use of animals in their research and teaching activities are also a component of responsible caring. Although animals do not have the same moral rights as persons (e.g., privacy), they do have the right to be treated humanely and not to be exposed to unnecessary discomfort, pain, or disruption.

By virtue of the social contract that the discipline has with society, psychologists have a higher duty of care to members of society than the general duty of care all members of society have to each other. However, psychologists are entitled to protect their own basic well-being (e.g., physical safety, family relationships) in their work as psychologists.

Ethical Standards

In adhering to the Principle of Responsible Caring, psychologists would:

General caring

II.1 Protect and promote the welfare of clients, research participants, employees, supervisees, students, trainees, colleagues, and others.

II.2 Avoid doing harm to clients, research participants, employees, supervisees, students, trainees, colleagues, and others.

II.3 Accept responsibility for the consequences of their actions.

II.4 Refuse to advise, train, or supply information to anyone who, in the psychologist's judgment, will use the knowledge or skills to harm others.

II.5 Make every reasonable effort to ensure that psychological knowledge is not misused, intentionally or unintentionally, to harm others.

Competence and self-knowledge

II.6 Offer or carry out (without supervision) only those activities for which they have established their competence to carry them out to the benefit of others.

II.7 Not delegate activities to persons not competent to carry them out to the benefit of others.

II.8 Take immediate steps to obtain consultation or to refer a client to a colleague or other appropriate professional, whichever is more likely to result in providing the client with competent service, if it becomes apparent that a client's problems are beyond their competence.

II.9 Keep themselves up to date with a broad range of relevant knowledge, research methods, and techniques, and their impact on persons and society, through the reading of relevant literature, peer consultation, and continuing education activities, in order that their service or research activities and conclusions will benefit and not harm others.

II.10 Evaluate how their own experiences, attitudes, culture, beliefs, values, social context, individual differences, specific training, and stresses influence their interactions with others, and integrate this awareness into all efforts to benefit and not harm others.

II.11 Seek appropriate help and/or discontinue scientific or professional activity for an appropriate period of time, if a physical or psychological condition reduces their ability to benefit and not harm others.

II.12 Engage in self-care activities that help to avoid conditions (e.g., burnout, addictions) that could result in impaired judgment and interfere with their ability to benefit and not harm others.

Risk/benefit analysis

II.13 Assess the individuals, families, groups, and communities involved in their activities adequately enough to ensure that they will be able to discern what will benefit and not harm the persons involved.

II.14 Be sufficiently sensitive to and knowledgeable about individual, group, community, and cultural differences and vulnerabilities to discern what will benefit and not harm persons involved in their activities.

II.15 Carry out pilot studies to determine the effects of all new procedures and techniques that might carry more than minimal risk, before considering their use on a broader scale.

II.16 Seek an independent and adequate ethical review of the balance of risks and potential benefits of all research and new interventions that involve procedures of unknown consequence, or where pain, discomfort, or harm are possible, before making a decision to proceed.

II.17 Not carry out any scientific or professional activity unless the probable benefit is proportionately greater than the risk involved.

Maximize benefit

II.18 Provide services that are coordinated over time and with other service providers, in order to avoid duplication or working at cross purposes.

II.19 Create and maintain records relating to their activities that are sufficient to support continuity and appropriate coordination of their activities with the activities of others.

II.20 Make themselves aware of the knowledge and skills of other disciplines (e.g., law, medicine, business administration) and advise the use of such knowledge and skills, where relevant to the benefit of others.

II.21 Strive to provide and/or obtain the best possible service for those needing and seeking psychological service. This may include, but is not limited to selecting interventions that are relevant to the needs and characteristics of the client and that have reasonable theoretical or empirically supported efficacy in light of those needs and characteristics; consulting with, or including in service delivery, persons relevant to the culture or belief systems of those served; advocating on behalf of the client; and recommending professionals other than psychologists when appropriate.

II.22 Monitor and evaluate the effect of their activities, record their findings, and communicate new knowledge to relevant others.

II.23 Debrief research participants in such a way that the participants' knowledge is enhanced and the participants have a sense of contribution to knowledge. (Also see Standards III.26 and III.27.)

II.24 Perform their teaching duties on the basis of careful preparation, so that their instruction is current and scholarly.

II.25 Facilitate the professional and scientific development of their employees, supervisees, students, and trainees by ensuring that these persons understand the values and ethical prescriptions of the discipline, and by providing or arranging for adequate working conditions, timely evaluations, and constructive consultation and experience opportunities.

II.26 Encourage and assist students in publication of worthy student papers.

Minimize harm

II.27 Be acutely aware of the power relationship in therapy and, therefore, not encourage or engage in sexual intimacy with therapy clients, neither during therapy, nor for that period of time following therapy during which the power relationship reasonably could be expected to influence the client's personal decision making. (Also see Standard III.31.)

II.28 Not encourage or engage in sexual intimacy with students or trainees with whom the psychologist has an evaluative or other relationship of direct authority. (Also see Standard III.31.)

II.29 Be careful not to engage in activities in a way that could place incidentally involved persons at risk.

II.30 Be acutely aware of the need for discretion in the recording and communication of information, in order that the information not be misinterpreted or misused to the detriment of others. This includes, but is not limited to not recording information that could lead to misinterpretation and misuse; avoiding conjecture; clearly labelling opinion; and communicating information in language that can be understood clearly by the recipient of the information.

II.31 Give reasonable assistance to secure needed psychological services or activities, if personally unable to meet requests for needed psychological services or activities.

II.32 Provide a client, if appropriate and if desired by the client, with reasonable assistance to find a way to receive needed services in the event that third-party payments are exhausted and the client cannot afford the fees involved.

II.33 Maintain appropriate contact, support, and responsibility for caring until a colleague or other professional begins service, if referring a client to a colleague or other professional.

II.34 Give reasonable notice and be reasonably assured that discontinuation will cause no harm to the client, before discontinuing services.

II.35 Screen appropriate research participants and select those least likely to be harmed, if more than minimal risk of harm to some research participants is possible.

II.36 Act to minimize the impact of their research activities on research participants' personalities, or on their physical or mental integrity.

Offset/correct harm

II.37 Terminate an activity when it is clear that the activity carries more than minimal risk of harm and is found to be more harmful than beneficial, or when the activity is no longer needed.

II.38 Refuse to help individuals, families, groups, or communities to carry out or submit to activities that, according to current knowledge, or legal or professional guidelines, would cause serious physical or psychological harm to themselves or others.

II.39 Do everything reasonably possible to stop or offset the consequences of actions by others when these actions are likely to cause serious physical harm or death. This may include reporting to appropriate authorities (e.g., the police), an intended victim, or a family member or other support person who can intervene, and would be done even when a confidential relationship is involved. (Also see Standard I.45.)

II.40 Act to stop or offset the consequences of seriously harmful activities being carried out by another psychologist or member of another discipline, when there is objective information about the activities and the harm, and when these activities have come to their attention outside of a confidential client relationship between themselves and the psychologist or member of another discipline. This may include reporting to the appropriate regulatory body, authority, or committee for action, depending on the psychologist's judgment about the person(s) or body(ies) best suited to stop or offset the harm, and depending upon regulatory requirements and definitions of misconduct.

II.41 Act also to stop or offset the consequences of harmful activities carried out by another psychologist or member of another discipline, when the harm is not serious or the activities appear to be primarily a lack of sensitivity, knowledge, or experience, and when the activities have come to their attention outside of a confidential client relationship between themselves and the psychologist or member of another discipline. This may include talking informally with the psychologist or member of the other discipline, obtaining objective information and, if possible and relevant, the assurance that the harm will discontinue and be corrected. If in a vulnerable position (e.g., employee, trainee) with respect to the other psychologist or member of the other discipline, it may include asking persons in less vulnerable positions to participate in the meeting(s).

II.42 Be open to the concerns of others about perceptions of harm that they as a psychologist might be causing, stop activities that are causing harm, and not punish or seek punishment for those who raise such concerns in good faith.

II.43 Not place an individual, group, family, or community needing service at a serious disadvantage by offering them no service in order to fulfill the conditions of a research design, when a standard service is available.

II.44 Debrief research participants in such a way that any harm caused can be discerned, and act to correct any resultant harm. (Also see Standards III.26 and III.27.)

Care of animals

II.45 Not use animals in their research unless there is a reasonable expectation that the research will increase understanding of the structures and processes underlying behaviour, or increase understanding of the particular animal species used in the study, or result eventually in benefits to the health and welfare of humans or other animals.

II.46 Use a procedure subjecting animals to pain, stress, or privation only if an alternative procedure is unavailable and the goal is justified by its prospective scientific, educational, or applied value.

II.47 Make every effort to minimize the discomfort, illness, and pain of animals. This would include performing surgical procedures only under appropriate anesthesia, using techniques to avoid infection and minimize pain during and after surgery and, if disposing of experimental animals is carried out at the termination of the study, doing so in a humane way.

II.48 Use animals in classroom demonstrations only if the instructional objectives cannot be achieved through the use of videotapes, films, or other methods, and if the type of demonstration is warranted by the anticipated instructional gain.

Extended responsibility

II.49 Encourage others, in a manner consistent with this *Code,* to care responsibly.

II.50 Assume overall responsibility for the scientific and professional activities of their assistants, employees, supervisees, students, and trainees with regard to the Principle of Responsible Caring, all of whom, however, incur similar obligations.

PRINCIPLE III: INTEGRITY IN RELATIONSHIPS

Values Statement

The relationships formed by psychologists in the course of their work embody explicit and implicit mutual expectations of integrity that are vital to the advancement of scientific knowledge and to the maintenance of public confidence in the discipline of psychology. These expectations include accuracy and honesty; straightforwardness and openness; the maximization of objectivity and minimization of bias; and avoidance of conflicts of interest. Psychologists have a responsibility to meet these expectations and to encourage reciprocity.

In addition to accuracy, honesty, and the obvious prohibitions of fraud or misrepresentation, meeting expectations of integrity is enhanced by self-knowledge and the use of critical analysis. Although it can be argued that science is value-free and impartial, scientists are not. Personal values and self-interest can affect the questions psychologists ask, how they ask those questions, what assumptions they make, their selection of methods, what they observe and what they fail to observe, and how they interpret their data.

Psychologists are not expected to be value-free or totally without self-interest in conducting their activities. However, they are expected to understand how their backgrounds, personal needs, and values interact with their activities, to be open and honest about the influence of such factors, and to be as objective and unbiased as possible under the circumstances.

The values of openness and straightforwardness exist within the context of Respect for the Dignity of Persons (Principle I) and Responsible Caring (Principle II). As such, there will be circumstances in which openness and straightforwardness will need to be tempered. Fully open and straightforward disclosure might not be needed or desired by others and, in some circumstances, might be a risk to their dignity or well-being, or considered culturally inappropriate. In such circumstances, however, psychologists have a responsibility to ensure that their decision not to be fully open or straightforward is justified by higher-order values and does not invalidate any informed consent procedures.

Of special concern to psychologists is the provision of incomplete disclosure when obtaining informed consent for research participation, or temporarily leading research participants to believe that a research project has a purpose other than its actual purpose. These actions sometimes occur in research where full disclosure would be likely to influence the responses of the research participants and thus invalidate the results. Although research that uses such techniques can lead to knowledge that is beneficial, such benefits must be weighed against the research participant's right to self-determination and the importance of public and individual trust in psychology. Psychologists have a serious obligation to avoid as much as possible the use of such research procedures. They also have a serious obligation to consider the need for, the possible consequences of, and their responsibility to correct any resulting mistrust or other harmful effects from their use.

As public trust in the discipline of psychology includes trusting that psychologists will act in the best interests of members of the public, situations that present real or potential conflicts of interest are of concern to psychologists. Conflict-of-interest situations are those that can lead to distorted judgment and can motivate psychologists to act in ways that meet their own personal, political, financial, or business interests at the expense of the best interests of members of the public. Although avoidance of all conflicts of interest and potential exploitation of others is not possible, some are of such a high risk to protecting the interests of members of the public and to maintaining the trust of the public, that they are considered never acceptable (see Standard III.31). The risk level of other conflicts of interest (e.g., dual or multiple relationships) might be partially dependent on cultural factors and the specific type of professional relationship (e.g., long-term psychotherapy vs. community development activities). It is the responsibility of psychologists to avoid dual or multiple relationships and other conflicts of interest when appropriate and possible. When such situations cannot be avoided or are inappropriate to avoid, psychologists have a responsibility to declare that they have a conflict of interest, to seek advice, and to establish safeguards to ensure that the best interests of members of the public are protected.

Integrity in relationships implies that psychologists, as a matter of honesty, have a responsibility to maintain competence in any specialty area for which they declare competence, whether or not they are currently practising in that area. It also requires that psychologists, in as much as they present themselves as members and representatives of a specific discipline, have a responsibility to actively rely on and be guided by that discipline and its guidelines and requirements.

Ethical Standards

In adhering to the Principle of Integrity in Relationships, psychologists would:

Accuracy/honesty

III.1　Not knowingly participate in, condone, or be associated with dishonesty, fraud, or misrepresentation.

III.2　Accurately represent their own and their colleagues' credentials, qualifications, education, experience, competence, and affiliations, in all spoken, written, or printed communications, being careful not to use descriptions or information that could be misinterpreted (e.g., citing membership in a voluntary association of psychologists as a testament of competence).

III.3　Carefully protect their own and their colleagues' credentials from being misrepresented by others, and act quickly to correct any such misrepresentation.

III.4　Maintain competence in their declared area(s) of psychological competence, as well as in their current area(s) of activity. (Also see Standard II.9.)

III.5　Accurately represent their own and their colleagues' activities, functions, contributions, and likely or actual outcomes of their activities (including research results) in all spoken, written, or printed communication. This includes, but is not limited to advertisements of services or products; course and workshop descriptions; academic grading requirements; and research reports.

III.6 Ensure that their own and their colleagues' activities, functions, contributions, and likely or actual outcomes of their activities (including research results) are not misrepresented by others, and act quickly to correct any such misrepresentation.

III.7 Take credit only for the work and ideas that they have actually done or generated, and give credit for work done or ideas contributed by others (including students), in proportion to their contribution.

III.8 Acknowledge the limitations of their own and their colleagues' knowledge, methods, findings, interventions, and views.

III.9 Not suppress disconfirming evidence of their own and their colleagues' findings and views, acknowledging alternative hypotheses and explanations.

Objectivity/lack of bias

III.10 Evaluate how their personal experiences, attitudes, values, social context, individual differences, stresses, and specific training influence their activities and thinking, integrating this awareness into all attempts to be objective and unbiased in their research, service, and other activities.

III.11 Take care to communicate as completely and objectively as possible, and to clearly differentiate facts, opinions, theories, hypotheses, and ideas, when communicating knowledge, findings, and views.

III.12 Present instructional information accurately, avoiding bias in the selection and presentation of information, and publicly acknowledge any personal values or bias that influence the selection and presentation of information.

III.13 Act quickly to clarify any distortion by a sponsor, client, agency (e.g., news media), or other persons, of the findings of their research.

Straightforwardness/openness

III.14 Be clear and straightforward about all information needed to establish informed consent or any other valid written or unwritten agreement (for example: fees, including any limitations imposed by third-party payers; relevant business policies and practices; mutual concerns; mutual responsibilities; ethical responsibilities of psychologists; purpose and nature of the relationship, including research participation; alternatives; likely experiences; possible conflicts; possible outcomes; and expectations for processing, using, and sharing any information generated).

III.15 Provide suitable information about the results of assessments, evaluations, or research findings to the persons involved, if appropriate and if asked. This information would be communicated in understandable language.

III.16 Fully explain reasons for their actions to persons who have been affected by their actions, if appropriate and if asked.

III.17 Honour all promises and commitments included in any written or verbal agreement, unless serious and unexpected circumstances (e.g., illness) intervene. If such circumstances occur, then the psychologist would make a full and honest explanation to other parties involved.

III.18 Make clear whether they are acting as private citizens, as members of specific organizations or groups, or as representatives of the discipline of psychology, when making statements or when involved in public activities.

III.19 Carry out, present, and discuss research in a way that is consistent with a commitment to honest, open inquiry, and to clear communication of any research aims, sponsorship, social context, personal values, or financial interests that might affect or appear to affect the research.

III.20 Submit their research, in some accurate form and within the limits of confidentiality, to persons with expertise in the research area, for their comments and evaluations, prior to publication or the preparation of any final report.

III.21 Encourage and not interfere with the free and open exchange of psychological knowledge and theory between themselves, their students, colleagues, and the public.

III.22 Make no attempt to conceal the status of a trainee and, if a trainee is providing direct client service, ensure that the client is informed of that fact.

Avoidance of incomplete disclosure

III.23 Not engage in incomplete disclosure, or in temporarily leading research participants to believe that a research project or some aspect of it has a different purpose, if there are alternative procedures available or if the negative effects cannot be predicted or offset.

III.24 Not engage in incomplete disclosure, or in temporarily leading research participants to believe that a research project or some aspect of it has a different purpose, if it would interfere with the person's understanding of facts that clearly might influence a decision to give adequately informed consent (e.g., withholding information about the level of risk, discomfort, or inconvenience).

III.25 Use the minimum necessary incomplete disclosure or temporary leading of research participants to believe that a research project or some aspect of it has a different purpose, when such research procedures are used.

III.26 Debrief research participants as soon as possible after the participants' involvement, if there has been incomplete disclosure or temporary leading of research participants to believe that a research project or some aspect of it has a different purpose.

III.27 Provide research participants, during such debriefing, with a clarification of the nature of the study, seek to remove any misconceptions that might have arisen, and seek to re-establish any trust that might have been lost, assuring the participants that the research procedures were neither arbitrary nor capricious, but necessary for scientifically valid findings. (Also see Standards II.23 and II.44.)

III.28 Act to re-establish with research participants any trust that might have been lost due to the use of incomplete disclosure or temporarily leading research participants to believe that the research project or some aspect of it had a different purpose.

III.29 Give a research participant the option of removing his or her data, if the research participant expresses concern during the debriefing about the incomplete disclosure or the temporary leading of the research participant to believe that the research project or some aspect of it had a different purpose, and if removal of the data will not compromise the validity of the research design and hence diminish the ethical value of the participation of the other research participants.

III.30 Seek an independent and adequate ethical review of the risks to public or individual trust and of safeguards to protect such trust for any research that plans to provide incomplete disclosure or temporarily lead research participants to believe that the research project or some aspect of it has a different purpose, before making a decision to proceed.

Avoidance of conflict of interest

III.31 Not exploit any relationship established as a psychologist to further personal, political, or business interests at the expense of the best interests of their clients, research participants, students, employers, or others. This includes, but is not limited to: soliciting clients of one's employing agency for private practice; taking advantage of trust or dependency to encourage or engage in sexual intimacies (e.g., with clients not included in Standard II.27, with clients' partners or relatives, with students or trainees not included in Standard II.28, or with research participants); taking advantage of trust or dependency to frighten clients into receiving services; misappropriating students' ideas, research or work; using the resources of one's employing institution for purposes not agreed to; giving or receiving kickbacks or bonuses for referrals; seeking or accepting loans or investments from clients; and, prejudicing others against a colleague for reasons of personal gain.

III.32 Not offer rewards sufficient to motivate an individual or group to participate in an activity that has possible or known risks to themselves or others. (Also see Standards I.27, I.28, II.2, and II.49.)

III.33 Avoid dual or multiple relationships (e.g., with clients, research participants, employees, supervisees, students, or trainees) and other situations that might present a conflict of interest or that might reduce their ability to be objective and unbiased in their determinations of what might be in the best interests of others.

III.34 Manage dual or multiple relationships that are unavoidable due to cultural norms or other circumstances in such a manner that bias, lack of objectivity, and risk of exploitation are minimized. This might include obtaining ongoing supervision or consultation for the duration of the dual or multiple relationship, or involving a third party in obtaining consent (e.g., approaching a client or employee about becoming a research participant).

III.35 Inform all parties, if a real or potential conflict of interest arises, of the need to resolve the situation in a manner that is consistent with Respect for the Dignity of Persons (Principle I) and Responsible Caring (Principle II), and take all reasonable steps to resolve the issue in such a manner.

Reliance on the discipline

III.36 Familiarize themselves with their discipline's rules and regulations, and abide by them, unless abiding by them would be seriously detrimental to the rights or welfare of others as demonstrated in the Principles of Respect for the Dignity of Persons or Responsible Caring. (See Standards IV.17 and IV.18 for guidelines regarding the resolution of such conflicts.)

III.37 Familiarize themselves with and demonstrate a commitment to maintaining the standards of their discipline.

III.38 Seek consultation from colleagues and/or appropriate groups and committees, and give due regard to their advice in arriving at a responsible decision, if faced with difficult situations.

Extended responsibility

III.39 Encourage others, in a manner consistent with this *Code,* to relate with integrity.

III.40 Assume overall responsibility for the scientific and professional activities of their assistants, employees, supervisees, students, and trainees with regard to the Principle of Integrity in Relationships, all of whom, however, incur similar obligations.

PRINCIPLE IV: RESPONSIBILITY TO SOCIETY

Values Statement

Psychology functions as a discipline within the context of human society.[2] Psychologists, both in their work and as private citizens, have responsibilities to the societies in which they live and work, such as the neighbourhood or city, and to the welfare of all human beings in those societies.

Two of the legitimate expectations of psychology as a science and a profession are that it will increase knowledge and that it will conduct its affairs in such ways that it will promote the welfare of all human beings.

Freedom of inquiry and debate (including scientific and academic freedom) is a foundation of psychological education, science, and practice. In the context of society, the above expectations imply that psychologists will exercise this freedom through the use of activities and methods that are consistent with ethical requirements.

The above expectations also imply that psychologists will do whatever they can to ensure that psychological knowledge, when used in the development of social structures and policies, will be used for beneficial purposes, and that the discipline's own structures and policies will support those beneficial purposes. Within the context of this document, social structures and policies that have beneficial purposes are defined as those that more readily support and reflect respect for the dignity of persons, responsible caring, integrity in relationships, and responsibility to society. If psychological knowledge or structures are used against these purposes, psychologists have an ethical responsibility to try to draw attention to and correct the misuse. Although this is a collective responsibility, those psychologists having direct involvement in the structures of the discipline, in social development, or in the theoretical or research database

[2]Society is used here in the broad sense of a group of persons living as members of one or more human communities, rather than in the limited sense of state or government.

that is being used (e.g., through research, expert testimony, or policy advice) have the greatest responsibility to act. Other psychologists must decide for themselves the most appropriate and beneficial use of their time and talents to help meet this collective responsibility.

In carrying out their work, psychologists acknowledge that many social structures have evolved slowly over time in response to human need and are valued by the societies that have developed them. In such circumstances, psychologists convey respect for such social structures and avoid unwarranted or unnecessary disruption. Suggestions for and action toward changes or enhancement of such structures are carried out through processes that seek to achieve a consensus within those societies and/or through democratic means.

On the other hand, if structures or policies seriously ignore or oppose the principles of respect for the dignity of persons, responsible caring, integrity in relationships, or responsibility to society, psychologists involved have a responsibility to speak out in a manner consistent with the principles of this *Code,* and advocate for appropriate change to occur as quickly as possible.

In order to be responsible and accountable to society, and to contribute constructively to its ongoing development, psychologists need to be willing to work in partnership with others, be self-reflective, and be open to external suggestions and criticisms about the place of the discipline of psychology in society. They need to engage in even-tempered observation and interpretation of the effects of societal structures and policies, and their process of change, developing the ability of psychologists to increase the beneficial use of psychological knowledge and structures, and avoid their misuse. The discipline needs to be willing to set high standards for its members, to do what it can to assure that such standards are met, and to support its members in their attempts to maintain the standards. Once again, individual psychologists must decide for themselves the most appropriate and beneficial use of their time and talents in helping to meet these collective responsibilities.

Ethical Standards

In adhering to the Principle of Responsibility to Society, psychologists would:

Development of knowledge

IV.1   Contribute to the discipline of psychology and of society's understanding of itself and human beings generally, through free inquiry and the acquisition, transmission, and expression of knowledge and ideas, unless such activities conflict with other basic ethical requirements.

IV.2   Not interfere with, or condone interference with, free inquiry and the acquisition, transmission, and expression of knowledge and ideas that do not conflict with other basic ethical requirements.

IV.3   Keep informed of progress in their area(s) of psychological activity, take this progress into account in their work, and try to make their own contributions to this progress.

Beneficial activities

IV.4   Participate in and contribute to continuing education and the professional and scientific growth of self and colleagues.

IV.5 Assist in the development of those who enter the discipline of psychology by helping them to acquire a full understanding of their ethical responsibilities, and the needed competencies of their chosen area(s), including an understanding of critical analysis and of the variations, uses, and possible misuses of the scientific paradigm.

IV.6 Participate in the process of critical self-evaluation of the discipline's place in society, and in the development and implementation of structures and procedures that help the discipline to contribute to beneficial societal functioning and changes.

IV.7 Provide and/or contribute to a work environment that supports the respectful expression of ethical concern or dissent, and the constructive resolution of such concern or dissent.

IV.8 Engage in regular monitoring, assessment, and reporting (e.g., through peer review, and in program reviews, case management reviews, and reports of one's own research) of their ethical practices and safeguards.

IV.9 Help develop, promote, and participate in accountability processes and procedures related to their work.

IV.10 Uphold the discipline's responsibility to society by promoting and maintaining the highest standards of the discipline.

IV.11 Protect the skills, knowledge, and interpretations of psychology from being misused, used incompetently, or made useless (e.g., loss of security of assessment techniques) by others.

IV.12 Contribute to the general welfare of society (e.g., improving accessibility of services, regardless of ability to pay) and/or to the general welfare of their discipline, by offering a portion of their time to work for which they receive little or no financial return.

IV.13 Uphold the discipline's responsibility to society by bringing incompetent or unethical behaviour, including misuses of psychological knowledge and techniques, to the attention of appropriate authorities, committees, or regulatory bodies, in a manner consistent with the ethical principles of this *Code,* if informal resolution or correction of the situation is not appropriate or possible.

IV.14 Enter only into agreements or contracts that allow them to act in accordance with the ethical principles and standards of this *Code.*

Respect for society

IV.15 Acquire an adequate knowledge of the culture, social structure, and customs of a community before beginning any major work there.

IV.16 Convey respect for and abide by prevailing community mores, social customs, and cultural expectations in their scientific and professional activities, provided that this does not contravene any of the ethical principles of this *Code.*

IV.17 Familiarize themselves with the laws and regulations of the societies in which they work, especially those that are related to their activities as psychologists, and abide by them. If those laws or regulations seriously conflict with the ethical principles contained herein, psychologists would do whatever they could to uphold the ethical principles. If upholding the ethical principles could result in serious personal consequences (e.g., jail or physical harm), decision for final action would be considered a matter of personal conscience.

IV.18 Consult with colleagues, if faced with an apparent conflict between abiding by a law or regulation and following an ethical principle, unless in an emergency, and seek consensus as to the most ethical course of action and the most responsible, knowledgeable, effective, and respectful way to carry it out.

Development of society

IV.19 Act to change those aspects of the discipline of psychology that detract from beneficial societal changes, where appropriate and possible.

IV.20 Be sensitive to the needs, current issues, and problems of society, when determining research questions to be asked, services to be developed, content to be taught, information to be collected, or appropriate interpretation of results or findings.

IV.21 Be especially careful to keep well informed of social issues through relevant reading, peer consultation, and continuing education, if their work is related to societal issues.

IV.22 Speak out, in a manner consistent with the four principles of this *Code,* if they possess expert knowledge that bears on important societal issues being studied or discussed.

IV.23 Provide thorough discussion of the limits of their data with respect to social policy, if their work touches on social policy and structure.

IV.24 Consult, if feasible and appropriate, with groups, organizations, or communities being studied, in order to increase the accuracy of interpretation of results and to minimize risk of misinterpretation or misuse.

IV.25 Make themselves aware of the current social and political climate and of previous and possible future societal misuses of psychological knowledge, and exercise due discretion in communicating psychological information (e.g., research results, theoretical knowledge), in order to discourage any further misuse.

IV.26 Exercise particular care when reporting the results of any work regarding vulnerable groups, ensuring that results are not likely to be misinterpreted or misused in the development of social policy, attitudes, and practices (e.g., encouraging manipulation of vulnerable persons or reinforcing discrimination against any specific population).

IV.27 Not contribute to or engage in research or any other activity that contravenes international humanitarian law, such as the development of methods intended for use in the torture of persons, the development of prohibited weapons, or destruction of the environment.

IV.28 Provide the public with any psychological knowledge relevant to the public's informed participation in the shaping of social policies and structures, if they possess expert knowledge that bears on the social policies and structures.

IV.29 Speak out and/or act, in a manner consistent with the four principles of this *Code,* if the policies, practices, laws, or regulations of the social structure within which they work seriously ignore or contradict any of the principles of this *Code.*

Extended responsibility

IV.30 Encourage others, in a manner consistent with this *Code,* to exercise responsibility to society.

IV.31 Assume overall responsibility for the scientific and professional activities of their assistants, employees, supervisees, students, and trainees with regard to the Principle of Responsibility to Society, all of whom, however, incur similar obligations.

Index

Aboriginals
  foster care and, 132, 133, 134
  high-needs children of, 132
  social justice and, 129, 130–31
  youth of, in jails, 134–35
abortion, 53, 56
abuse
  of children, 24–28
  physical, defined, 25
  teenage prostitution and, 94
  treatment, compliance, and, 115
  of women and children, 149–51
accountability, 145–54
accuracy and honesty, 275–76
addiction. *See also* alcohol
  to gambling, 147
  guardianship and, 116–17
  informed consent and, 110–11
  to narcotics, 147
  treatment centres, alcohol use, and,
    146–48
addicts helping addicts, 147
adoption
  addictions and, 116–17
  changes in policy for, 132–34
  cultural issues and, 54–57
  foster parents and, 132–34
  high-risk and high-needs children and,
    132–34
advertising and public statements, 242–43
Alberta College of Social Workers
  Code of Ethics of, 51
alcohol. *See also* addiction
  employee use of, 146–48
  professional obligations and, 167–69
Alcoholics Anonymous, 146, 148
American Counseling Association, 2
  Code of Ethics of (*see Code of Ethics* [ACA])
American Psychological Association
  code of conduct (*see Ethics Code* [APA])
  dissociative identity disorder and, 74
animals, use of, in research, 248, 273
Aristotle, 36, 37, 187
assessment, 249–52
Australian Association of Social Workers, 2

BC Addictions Recovery and Wellness Centre,
    146–48
behaviour
  abusive, 24–28
  corporal punishment and, 54
  disorders of, 4–8
  personal, 261
  right and wrong, 24, 53, 189
beneficence and nonmaleficence, 233
benefit, maximizing, 271
"best interest," 23
bias, 77–78
billing, 223
bioethics principles, 32, 33
bipolar disorder, 113
birth control, 56
boundaries
  of competence, 236
  ethical guidelines to, 164
  humour and, 183
  power, professional relationships, and, 163–71
  reducing burnout and, 182–83
  setting and maintaining, 163–64, 167
Building on Values, 153
burnout
  reducing, boundaries and, 182–83
  self-care and, 179–83
  strategies for assessing and preventing, 181
  strategies to address, 181–82
  strategies to reduce, 182
burnout self-assessment, 180

Canadian Association of Social Workers
  Code of Ethics (CASW) of (*see Code of Ethics*
    [CASW])
  Guidelines for Ethical Practice and (*see Guidelines*
    for Ethical Practice)
Canadian Charter of Rights and Freedoms, 57
Canadian Psychological Association, 257
  ethical code of (*see Code* [CPA])
capacity, 205–6
charity organizations, 126
children. *See also* youth
  abused, transition houses for, 149–50
  abuse of (*see* abuse)